Ali, Pelé, Lillee and Me

Also by Brian Viner

Tales of the Country

Ali, Pelé, Lillee and Me

A Personal Odyssey Through the Sporting Seventies

BRIAN VINER

SIMON &
SCHUSTER

London · New York · Sydney · Toronto

A CBS COMPANY

First published in Great Britain by Simon & Schuster UK Ltd, 2006
A CBS COMPANY

1 3 5 7 9 10 8 6 4 2

Simon & Schuster UK Ltd
Africa House
64–78 Kingsway
London WC2B 6AH

www.simonsays.co.uk

Simon & Schuster Australia
Sydney

A CIP catalogue record for this book is available
from the British Library.

ISBN 0-7432-8570-0
EAN 9780743285704

Typeset in Horley by M Rules
Printed and bound in Great Britain by
Mackays of Chatham plc

For Eleanor, Joseph and Jacob
Always keep your eyes on the ball

Contents

Prologue

For lovers of sport, there has never been a better decade to be alive, and in front of the telly, than the 1970s. This book will attempt to prove as much, not by diminishing other eras, but by bigging up – if I might express myself in the argot of the early twenty-first century – the decade of the Rumble in the Jungle between Muhammad Ali and George Foreman, the Thrilla in Manila between Ali and Joe Frazier, the Duel in the Sun between Jack Nicklaus and Tom Watson, the Duel very much out of the Sun between Bobby Fischer and Boris Spassky, and Kevin Keegan falling off his bike on *Superstars*.

It was the decade in which Red Rum won three Grand Nationals and Björn Borg won the first four of five consecutive men's finals at Wimbledon. Also at Wimbledon, a British woman did something that now seems as improbable and incongruous as a fish riding a bicycle: she won a singles title. And better still, Virginia Wade's victory came in the summer of the Queen's Silver Jubilee.

At the 1976 Olympic Games, 14-year-old Nadia Comaneci of Romania scored seven perfect 10s; before her, no other Olympic gymnast had scored even one. A year earlier, Dennis Lillee and Jeff Thomson joined forces in the Australian cricket team and together became the formidable Lilian Thomson, mother of all fast-bowling partnerships. In rugby union, to this day, there has been no finer try than the one scored by Gareth Edwards, for the Barbarians against the mighty All Blacks, at Cardiff Arms Park in 1973. Nor, for as long as football has been played, wherever it has been played, has there been a finer team than the 1970 Brazilians.

As for the FA Cup, it scaled heights of excitement in the 1970s that it has never approached since. Ray Crawford of Colchester United, Ronnie Radford of Hereford United and Jim Montgomery of Sunderland were the supreme FA Cup heroes in the supreme decade of FA Cup heroics. Even in more mundane departments, it was a golden age. It was, for example, the absolute heyday of typographical errors in newspapers, of which my favourite is this: 'A brilliant save by Mulhearn kept out a rocket of a shit from Greenhoff.' We can only hope that Mulhearn was wearing goalkeeping gloves. It was the heyday, too, of broadcasting bloopers, and Harry Carpenter's, following the BBC's transmission of the 1977 Boat Race, was a classic that would endure the test of time. 'Ah, isn't that nice,' he said, 'the wife of the Cambridge President is kissing the cox of the Oxford crew.'

I could go on, and in the forthcoming pages, I will. However, I am prepared to concede that I am hopelessly biased. Most of us are inclined to romanticise our youth and I am no exception. I turned nine in October 1970 and nineteen in October 1980. The intervening years were my formative years as a sports nut, which explains my nostalgic zeal. No period in our lives later unleashes the juices of nostalgia like that impressionable decade between nine, the last year of single figures, and nineteen, the last year of teenage, when we gradually shed the innocence of childhood. My daughter, born in 1993, will doubtless hark back to the Busted and McFly years as affectionately as her mother, born in 1962, harks back to the David Cassidy and Bay City Rollers years. We get through a lot of harking in our house.

Like all those whose interest in sport burgeoned around the turn of the 1970s, I benefited greatly from the introduction into Britain of colour television. Suddenly, the Aga Khan's racing colours really were in colour. And the Dutch not only played their glorious 'Total Football' in the nation's living rooms, they played it in vivid orange. That had never happened before, and it would never be a novelty again. This book makes some attempt at evoking those years, not only through sport as it was performed at the highest level, but also as it was performed at the lowest level. Principally by me. There are lots of sporting memoirs by people who were good at sport, or even great at sport, but not many by people who, relatively speaking, weren't all that much cop at sport. This book unashamedly seeks to redress that balance.

It is a story which occasionally lurches clumsily forward in time. How else could I share with you the details of how I masqueraded as a professional golfer at the Open Championship in the heady summer of 1984? It also links my modern incarnation, as a sports writer with the *Independent*, with my past. It has been my privilege to meet, interview and generally knock about with some of the people whose antics in the sporting arena so thrilled me as a boy. But sometimes this has felt more like a punishment than a privilege. They say that, on the whole, you should never meet your heroes. I don't know who 'they' are, but they're clearly a pretty perceptive bunch.

1

Alan Hudson's Bowels

Mark Salthouse is not a name with which I ever expected to start a book. It will surprise him, too, wherever and whatever he is now. He might be a computer programmer, or a bus driver, or a surgeon. He might be destitute. He might be a millionaire.

We were on friendly terms without being friends, exactly. We played in the same dinner time game of football – which formed a bond between us in the sense that we both knew what it was like to incur the purple wrath of T. B. Johnson, the English teacher whose study window was occasionally rattled by a rising volley – but I was friendlier with his best mate, Dave Kime. Kimey. Salthouse could never be Salty because there had been a lad in our year called Steve Salt who, despite having left school after his O levels to join the merchant navy, had retained the irrevocable right to be known as Salty. So Salthouse was just Salthouse. And to him, I was Viner.

That was how it worked at old-fashioned grammar schools for boys in the north of England in the late 1970s. At any rate, that was how it worked at King George V School, Southport.

You had three or four best friends whose first names you used and everyone else was identifiable only by a surname or a nickname. Even the school had a nickname: KGV.

Sometimes, nicknames were born of pragmatism. In my class at KGV there were three boys called Rimmer, which would have been horribly confusing except that Gary Rimmer was nicknamed Bean, for reasons I forget, while Malcolm Rimmer was Skinny and Andy Rimmer was Mugsy. They weren't related; Rimmer is just a very common west Lancashire name. Jimmy Rimmer – who played in goal for Manchester United, Arsenal, Aston Villa and, once, on a summer tour to the USA, for England – came from Southport too. One year he opened Southport Flower Show and let kids take penalties against him. Mine hit a woman carrying a begonia. But at least I could always say that I had taken a penalty against Jimmy Rimmer, whose birthplace, in the *Rothmans Football Yearbook*, was listed in unequivocal black and white. His goalkeeping understudy at Villa, Nigel Spink, was born in Chelmsford, which meant nothing to me. But I derived huge proprietorial pleasure from the information that Jimmy Rimmer – ht 5 11, wt 11 12 – was born in Southport.

Jimmy Rimmer hadn't gone to KGV. He'd gone to the adjacent secondary modern, the curiously named Meols Cop, although more curious by far was the quaint ritual of Meols Cop teachers addressing pupils, and pupils addressing each other, by their Christian names. So it was rumoured at KGV, anyway.

My children are amazed when I tell them now that there were boys I saw every day for seven years, except at weekends and during school holidays, and that I knew which part of town they lived in and which football teams they supported, without ever learning their first names. In all honesty, I'm not absolutely certain that Salthouse was a Mark. I do recall that he was a tall Manchester City fan with a lugubrious wit. Most of the Man City fans I have known down the years have had a lugubrious wit. Whether because lugubriously witty types are instinctively drawn to City, or because supporting City imbues them with witty lugubriousness, I'm not sure. Probably the latter.

Anyway, one morning in the spring of 1978, Salthouse found me outside the school library. He had been looking for me. 'Hey, Viner,' he said. 'Guess who I've just seen, mowing the grass?'

Years and years later, in homage to my wife's grandma, Nellie, this rhetorical challenge would have drawn the immediate response 'Jackie Charlton'. One day when Nellie was well into her nineties, her daughter Jose, my wife's aunt, who lived with her in the South Yorkshire village where they had both spent all their lives, came home from her regular Wednesday shopping expedition to Barnsley, and said to Nellie: 'Guess who I've just seen in a Range Rover, in t' multistorey car park.'

'Jackie Charlton?' ventured Nellie, gamely, from the armchair in the corner where she spent most of her waking hours.

'No, our Thelma!' snapped Jose, massively irritated that her mother had taken her literally and actually had hazarded a guess, fatally blunting the impact of her news.

To her credit, Nellie did her best to redeem herself by responding with due amazement to the revelation that the sighting in the multistorey car park in Barnsley had been of our Thelma, but the wind had already flown from Jose's sails. Happily, my wife, Jane, was present to hear this exchange, which is why, from that day forth, guess-who questions in our house have always elicited one answer. Guess who phoned this morning! Jackie Charlton? Guess who's getting married! Jackie Charlton? You'll never guess who was sitting opposite me on the train! Jackie Charlton? Guess who got top marks in her geography test! Jackie Charlton?

I once related this story in a newspaper column, and was hugely gratified to receive a letter from a man who said he'd been so tickled by the tale of Nellie's brave stab at answering Jose's question that he had started the same tradition in his workplace. Thus, although Nellie is long gone now, her indomitable spirit lives on every time someone in an office in St Albans says, 'Guess who I saw flirting with Gemma from accounts?' and someone else says 'Jackie Charlton?'

But all that came much later. Asked by Salthouse who I thought he had seen mowing the school grass all I could manage was a feeble 'Who?'

'George Wood,' Salthouse said.

'The Everton goalkeeper George Wood?' I said.

'Yes,' he said.

'Yeah, right,' I said.

'I knew you wouldn't believe me,' he said. 'If it's not him, it's his identical twin brother. Go and look.'

I looked through the window. There was a tall, flaxen-haired man pushing a lawnmower across the grass outside a classroom. He did indeed look like George Wood – ht 6 3, wt 14 0, birthplace Douglas – and as Salthouse was well aware, hardly anyone was better qualified than I was to recognise Everton's handsome Scottish goalie, whose name I ritually chanted every other Saturday at Goodison Park, and at most away games too. 'We all agree, Shilton is better than Clemence!' was the preliminary cry from Goodison's Gwladys Street End, addressing the question – the answer to which eluded even England manager Ron Greenwood – of whether Peter Shilton of Nottingham Forest was a better goalkeeper than Liverpool's Ray Clemence. And then the heartfelt follow-up: 'We all agree, Georgie is better than Shilton!'

Georgie Wood was my favourite Everton player, which was saying something, because I would readily have had the babies of Bob Latchford and Duncan McKenzie. Not that I was homosexually inclined, at least no more than most adolescent boys at a single-sex school. If I had been struggling with my sexual identity, though, KGV might not have been a bad place to find my bearings. A fellow-pupil a few years ahead of me, with a coterie of flamboyantly effeminate friends, was Marc Almond, later to rival Boy George as the most outré gay pop star of the 1980s. I'm rather proud now to share an alma mater with Marc Almond, but in 1978 I suppose it was a blessing of sorts that he hadn't yet become KGV's most famous old boy. We were already taunted for being 'poofs' by the hard knocks of Meols Cop: most famous old boy, Jimmy Rimmer, who was definitely not known for wearing eyeliner and singing plaintively about tainted love.

I took particular interest in the fortunes of Georgie Wood – and, to a lesser extent, those of Jimmy Rimmer – because I was a goalie myself. I played in goal most dinner times, with blazers or rucksacks as goalposts and T. B. Johnson's study window as backstop.

We didn't have a school football team – at KGV, as at most northern grammar schools, rugby was deemed far more likely to equip boys for the rigours and responsibilities of manhood – but even if we had I wouldn't have played for it. For one thing, sports enthusiast though I was, svelte I was not. Far too many Curly Wurlys and cans of strawberry Cresta, which, of course, are all we consumed in the seventies, had given me a figure that was more Jimmy Osmond than Jimmy Rimmer. And for another thing, I could only dive one way. I was able to launch myself to my left, which was not a pretty spectacle but quite often resulted in a save of sorts, whereas to my right I could only manage a kind of ineffectual crumple, as if someone had whacked me in the right knee.

The same limitation would later hamper my wicketkeeping career, although I was lucky enough at university to keep wicket to a guy called Richard Wells-Furby whose bowling was quick but wildly erratic, and inclined to stray down a right-handed batsman's leg-side, sometimes by the best part of a kilometre. While everyone else was urging Wells-Furby to bowl straighter, I used to sail repeatedly but cheerfully to my left, happy to be given an opportunity to demonstrate the one bit of agility in my repertoire.

But in 1978 I wasn't yet a wicketkeeper; only a goalkeeper, like George Wood. I stared hard at the man pushing the mower. Salthouse was right; it was Georgie Wood. And yet how could it be? Why the fuck would Scotland's, Scotland's, Number One! Scotland's! Number One! be tending our school lawn? It made no kind of sense.

By now there was a growing group of boys looking through the window, wrestling with the same conundrum. Some of them were ardent Evertonians, like me. Our school was about twenty miles from Goodison and Anfield, and about forty miles from Old Trafford and Maine Road, so of those boys who liked football, the vast majority supported Everton, Liverpool, Manchester United or Manchester City. Meanwhile, the crumbling edifice that was the home of Southport FC, Haig Avenue, stood scarcely 500 yards across our school field, silently reproaching us for our glory-hunting affiliations.

Most of us had an affection for humble Southport, and had cut our teeth as football supporters on the draughty Haig Avenue terraces. For a while, the most dashing Southport players – titans such as big Jim Fryatt, Eric Redrobe and Andy Provan – had seemed at least as heroic to me as the Everton stars, whom I'd never seen in the flesh. I exulted in the fact that Fryatt had scored the fastest League goal ever recorded, four seconds after kick-off, albeit for Bradford Park Avenue rather than Southport, against Tranmere Rovers on 25 April 1964. And the first football song I can remember trilling was 'Andy . . . Andy Provan . . . Andy Provan on the wi-ing . . .' in honour of the little Scottish trickster who later ended up on a different kind of wing, as a psychiatric nurse in Torquay.

But even though we retained a soft spot for Southport, who were to be ejected from the Football League at the end of that 1977–8 season and at the time of writing have yet to return (while astoundingly, the team that replaced them, Wigan Athletic, climbed to second place in the Premiership in October 2005), our main allegiance was for the big First Division clubs.

Consequently, there was a strange kind of kudos enjoyed by those who supported only Southport, the most notable of whom was a lad higher up the school called Collinson. Needless to say, I never knew what his first name was, or even if he had one. Collinson was one of the more notorious stalwarts of Haig Avenue's Scarisbrick New Road or 'Brick' End, and was well known for being 'rock', the abbreviated form of rock-hard. I was never really sure whether that was because he'd actually been seen beating up hordes of opposition fans, or just because he wore awe-inspiring trousers known as parallels that had room for most of the Lower Fifth up each leg and flapped madly even when it wasn't windy. All the hardest boys wore 'parries', and the flappier the better. Collinson also wore amber scarves tied round both wrists, even on school days. That was another sign that he was rock. Suffice to say that not even the Meols Cop boys ever called him a poof.

I wonder where Collinson is now? And Georgie Wood, for that matter. I hope the latter is living contentedly and in comfort. The former, too, of course. Although Collinson must be pushing fifty now, it's not too late for him to turn up at my door with amber scarves round both wrists and a dangerous glint in his eye. But I hope especially that Georgie Wood's life is in good shape. He deserves eternal happiness if only for a miraculous save I once saw him make, a save which made that famous Gordon Banks stop from Pelé look prosaic.

Georgie Wood's miracle save was an acrobatic tip-over from a snap shot just inside the penalty area by Alan Hudson, when Hudson played for Arsenal. Hudson was one of those footballers in whom the 1970s seemed to specialise. Stan Bowles, Rodney Marsh, Tony Currie, Frank Worthington and Everton's own Duncan McKenzie were others; men blessed with outrageous skills, whose fiendish trickery was a source of wonder whether or not you supported the team they played for. And yet they all promised more than they ever quite delivered.

Most of them had a self-destructive streak, too, and you feared for them once their abilities began to wane. Even at the top of their game Marsh and Bowles both managed to torpedo their own international careers, the latter by walking out of the England camp a couple of days before a match against Scotland, preferring to watch greyhound racing at White City. Marsh did not go to the dogs quite as literally, but became an outcast by giving cheek to Alf Ramsey. Mind you, at least it was humorous cheek. Ramsey told him before a match that if he performed lackadaisically again, he would pull him off at half-time. 'That's nice,' retorted Marsh. 'At Man City we just get a cup of tea and an orange.'

McKenzie was not always a managerial favourite either, but it was clear that he would be OK once his football career ended. As the Goodison faithful knew, he had not only passed ten O levels, but could, according to the impeccable source that was *Shoot!* magazine, throw a golf ball the length of a football pitch. Maybe my memory is nutmegging me and he could throw a golf ball merely the width of a football pitch, but either way it was an enviable skill. I also learnt from *Shoot!* that McKenzie could jump over a Mini. It didn't say when or how he first discovered that he could jump over a Mini, or why it might ever prove necessary, or indeed whether he ever jumped over anything else, but in those years, when Everton laboured so diligently yet forlornly in Liverpool's long shadow, at least it was something Kenny Dalglish couldn't do. Like golf ball-throwing, Mini-jumping was hardly a career option, but McKenzie was plainly equipped to deal with life after football. For most of those other so-called mavericks, however, the future was always likely to be less certain.

In May 2002 I had lunch with Alan Hudson. Arsenal were shortly to play Chelsea in the FA Cup final, and I wanted someone for my interview slot in the *Independent* who had played for both clubs, even though it was Stoke City where he had spent his halcyon years, between 1973 and 1977.

I went to collect him from his home just off the King's Road, the area where he had grown up. His address sounded rather glamorous, so I was shocked to find that he lived in a heartbreakingly shabby council flat, with photographs of him in his pomp carefully cut from magazines and Blu-tacked to the wall. There was a picture of him making his England debut, against West Germany in 1975. And I noticed another picture taken at the opening of his nightclub in Stoke-on-Trent. George Best, perhaps the ultimate in self-destructive footballers, was the guest of honour that night. If ever an enterprise was destined to go belly-up, Alan Hudson's Stoke nightclub, opened by Georgie Best, was surely it.

The council estate where Hudson lived had been built in the early 1970s when both it and he were spruced up and looking in their prime. Neither had aged well. Yet Hudson bore the ravages not only of age, and plenty of what he endearingly called 'socialising', but also of a road accident in 1997 which had nearly killed him. After colliding with a car while crossing the Mile End Road in the East End of London after 'a few glasses of wine', he had spent eighty-nine days in hospital slipping in and out of consciousness, and came within fifteen minutes of having both legs amputated. The accident happened just after 9 p.m. 'Earliest I'd ever gone home,' he told me. 'Which just shows, never go home early.'

He chuckled, and I was pleased to see that the cheeky Bugs Bunny grin and distinctive jawline were still in place. Much else was not. There were bumps and hollows on his forehead, a legacy of the surgery to remove a brain clot. His pelvis had been shattered, and his sphincter ripped apart.

Our lunch took place almost five years after the accident, but still the quarter-mile walk from his flat to the restaurant was painfully slow going. Largely this was on account of Hudson's pronounced limp, but we were further slowed down by well-wishers. ''Allo, Alan, love,' said the woman in the dry-cleaner's. ''Allo, love,' he replied. 'All right, Alan old son,' said the guy behind the flower stall. 'All right, mate,' said Hudson. I was powerfully reminded of those films set along the King's Road in the 1960s, all mini-skirts, glottal stops and commu-nity spirit. It would have come as no surprise if the guy behind the flower stall had been Arthur Mullard, and the woman in the dry-cleaner's had been Peggy Mount, and if both had said 'cor lumme!' as a young Terence Stamp and Julie Christie roared by in an E-type Jag.

Eventually we got to the restaurant, and over a plate of antipasti Hudson told me about a device planted inside him which he activated with a sort of television remote control unit whenever he needed the loo. As my appetite for Parma ham and marinated artichokes receded, he kindly let me prod it, then whipped out his remote. 'I just press this and it opens my bowels,' he said. 'Otherwise I'd need a colostomy bag.'

It is safe to say that prodding Alan Hudson's abdomen, to feel how he opened his bowels, was not a situation I had ever anticipated being in. There have been many occasions during my time in sports journalism when I have tried to imagine just how improbable a particular encounter would have seemed when I was seventeen: playing tennis with John McEnroe, receiving a golf lesson from Seve Ballesteros, being sworn at by an enraged Ian Botham, sitting in the directors' box at Goodison Park with a rug over my knees, these were all experiences that I could hardly have foreseen. But prodding Alan Hudson's abdomen, in an Italian restaurant on the King's Road, most definitely took the biscotti.

Moreover, it was hard to reconcile the damaged man before me with my memory of the impish midfield player whose impishness included the infamous Goal That Never Was, for Chelsea against Ipswich Town. At Stamford Bridge on 26 September 1970, with the score at 0-0, a shot by Hudson hit the stanchion at the back of the side-netting and bounced straight back into play. All the players trotted back to await a goal-kick, but the referee, Mr Roy Capey from Crewe, hoodwinked by an optical illusion, thought Hudson's shot had gone in. He duly pointed to the centre-spot, undeterred by the Ipswich players, who were going nuts.

Their manager, one Robert William Robson, would be on the receiving end of another, more consequential travesty nearly sixteen years later as manager of England, when Diego Maradona deployed the infamous 'Hand of God' to score Argentina's opening goal in the 1986 World Cup quarterfinal, and was as unrepentant as Hudson had been. Not that Hudson had cheated like Maradona, but he could have told the ref that the goal wasn't legitimate. The Ipswich players implored him to explain that his shot had actually flown just wide. Even his own team mate, David Webb, advised him to come clean. 'Tell him, Hud,' he said. But Hud didn't tell. He said, 'David, we're on thirty pounds a point. I can't afford to tell him.' So the goal stood, Chelsea won 2-1, and Mr Capey went home to Crewe.

Keen football fans always know where referees come from, incidentally. It is one of the game's quirkier conventions, that referees drag their home town around with them as if it's part of their name. Say Clive Thomas to a football fan of a certain age, and he will immediately think 'Treorchy'. That's unless he's an Everton fan, who has never forgiven Thomas for disallowing Bryan Hamilton's perfectly good 'winning' goal in the 1977 FA Cup semi-final against Liverpool. He will immediately think not 'Treorchy' but 'bastard'.

Most referees' names, though, are rendered almost double-barrelled by this odd depth of knowledge on the part of fans. Other referees from the 1970s included Jack Taylor-Wolverhampton, Keith Hackett-Sheffield, Roger Milford-Bristol and George Courtenay-Spennymoor. Among more recent whistle-blowers, Andy D'Urso became synonymous with Billericay, Graham Poll with Tring. I suppose it is considered useful for the fans to know where a ref comes from, in order to banish any suspicions of regional bias. Mr Capey from Crewe can't possibly have had a soft spot for Chelsea.

Whatever, Hudson pocketed £60 for the two points secured, which helped to alleviate his financial worries. By 2002, however, they were back with a vengeance. His weekly income amounted to just £180; the fee he got for his column in the Stoke *Evening Sentinel*. As we had sat down for lunch he had asked me whether, in return for his anecdotes, I could give him any money. This was uncomfortable territory. Although some newspapers did cough up for interviews, the *Independent* was emphatically not among them. With modern sports stars this was rarely a problem – you wouldn't expect Nick Faldo to hold his hand out for a few quid – but with old-timers who had fallen on hard times it was different. Sometimes, as in Hudson's case, anecdotes were just about all they had left to flog.

Feeling awkward, I'd told him I was happy to stand him a plate of antipasti, some spaghetti carbonara and a bottle of Pinot Grigio, but regrettably could offer nothing more. He shrugged and grinned, as though it was nothing less than he'd expected. I asked him the obvious question. He had earned £200 a week in the late 1970s, a handsome sum in those days but nothing to make Croesus envious. Neither of us had yet heard of Roman Abramovich, but still there were players at his old club up the road, blokes with a fraction of his talent, who were earning upwards of £30,000 a week. Was he resentful of modern footballers' wages?

He smiled. 'When you look at Hasselbaink, Gudjohnsen, Henry, Bergkamp, Vieira . . . if there's big money going round then I say give 'em it. They're world-class players. But the likes of Dennis Wise, Jody Morris, and several others I can think of? They're millionaires too, but I can't see them as even good players. I don't feel nothing, though. I think it's madness, but you'd go off your 'ead if you worried about it.'

Back in the 1970s, of course, nobody would have entertained the crazy notion that contemporary top-class footballers might ever look back on their careers and feel hard done by. Not only were they treated like gods, their names chanted every week by tens of thousands of people, they seemed bloody well remunerated, too. Several of the Everton and Liverpool players lived in huge detached houses overlooking Royal Birkdale golf course. The idea that they might ever be considered unfortunate to have played in the wrong era, plying their trade at a time when the pecuniary rewards in football were relatively modest, would have been laughable, had anyone actually had it. Certainly, nobody looking at a photograph of George Best opening Alan Hudson's nightclub in Stoke would have thought 'Poor sod, it's bound to fail, and by 2002 Hudson'll be living on his uppers in some council flat somewhere.' These were talented, glamorous, gilded young men.

And to me, none was more talented, glamorous or gilded than George Wood, which was why it was so surreal to see him emptying grass clippings from his mower just outside the room where Mr Clark was talking about coefficients to an A-level maths class. After a while, egged on by thirty boys at several windows, I went out to talk to him.

'Erm, I'm a big Everton fan, and I, we, was, were, erm, just wondering what you were doing here?'

He smiled shyly and told me that he was a good friend of a man called Tom Pope, a neighbour of his in nearby Parbold, who had won the contract to look after our school grounds. The Everton players weren't training that day so he'd agreed to come to lend Tom a hand. There was nothing more surreal about it than that.

With the brassy naivety of youth, I asked him if he fancied a game of football that dinner time. In the north of England, circa 1978, lunch was always dinner.

'I'm sorry but I can't,' he said. 'The manager wouldn't want me to, just in case I pick up an injury. But I'll come and watch, if that's OK?'

OK? O-bloody-K? Georgie Wood was going to watch our game of footie, with me in goal? He was going to stand behind me, watching me dive this way and that – or this way and this, given the constraints of my diving ability – just as I had stood behind him, watching him deal with shots from Alan Hudson or Kenny Dalglish. It was the greatest day of my school life. No, bugger that; it was the greatest day of my life.

He was as good as his word, too. Shortly before afternoon registration, when Dave Kime – Kimey – bore down on me and thumped a shot mercifully to my left, which I tipped spectacularly over the Adidas bag that was my left-hand post, Georgie Wood was behind me, applauding. A few days later, at Goodison Park, I returned the compliment with more fervour than ever.

I had been a Toffees fan since 1969–70, the season I celebrated my eighth birthday. There was no tradition in my family of supporting Everton, even though my dad had been born and raised in Liverpool. He was born in 1916, and would therefore have been an impressionable twelve when Dixie Dean's sixty goals helped Everton to win the 1927–28 First Division title. So it was surprising, in a way, that he hadn't embraced the faith. Instead, his all-encompassing sporting passion was for horse racing. For a few years, fairly disastrously, he was a bookmaker. He had a shop in Moorfields in Liverpool city centre, and was a living contradiction of the old adage that the bookie always wins. But that's a story for a later chapter.

The reason I supported Everton was that my friends Jem and Chris Sykes did. They lived a few doors from me at 66 Lynton Road, a road of between-the-wars semis backing on to the Liverpool-to-Southport railway line. I lived at number 58. Jem was a few months older than me; Chris a couple of years older than him. Their dad, like mine, was uninterested in football, although he did have the immeasurable consolation of being called Jabez Sykes, a fabulously Dickensian name for 1970s Southport. Whatever, it wasn't their dad but another neighbour, John Williams from number 54, who turned us all

into Evertonians, simply by telling Chris that he reminded
him of the Goodison midfield maestro Alan Ball. So Chris
became an Everton fan overnight and Jem followed his big
brother's lead, with me not far behind. By such capricious
boyhood impulses are entire lifetimes influenced. If Chris
Sykes had reminded John Williams of Denis Law of
Manchester United, or Roger Hunt of Liverpool, or for that
matter Peter Glaze of *Crackerjack* or even Dougal of *The
Magic Roundabout*, I might have a very different tale to tell.

But the Toffees it was, and by a stroke of luck the dawning
of my devotion coincided with Everton's finest season ever in
the top division. In the spring of 1970 Harry Catterick's team
clinched the title with 66 points, nine clear of runners-up
Leeds United. In these days of 3 points for a win, those 66
points would have been 95, the same lordly dominance
achieved in the 2004–5 season by Jose Mourinho's Chelsea.
Moreover, in the course of the 1969–70 season Everton
defeated all other twenty-one clubs at least once. I had chosen
well.

Just to compound my growing obsession with football, the
domestic season was followed by the World Cup in Mexico,
and the flowering of the greatest team there had ever been
before, or has ever been since. There are those who press the
claims of the 1953 Hungarians to be considered the best ever,
and those who reckon that even Puskas and co. would have
struggled to hold the 1998 French side with Zinedine Zidane
at its hub. The England team that won the 1966 World Cup
has its advocates too (guess who wore the number 5 shirt, by
the way, and it wasn't our Thelma), as does the England XI of
the late 1940s: Matthews, Mortensen, Lawton, Mannion and
Finney were the moderately useful strike force which
drubbed the World Cup holders Italy 4-0 in Turin on 16 May
1948. And the Holland side, coached by Rinus Michels and

spearheaded by Johan Cruyff, was so good it gave its name to an entire philosophy: Total Football.

A reasonable case might also be made for various club sides to be proclaimed the best of all time, among them the silky aristocrats of Real Madrid, who won the European Cup five years in succession from 1956 to 1960, and the fabulous AC Milan of Rijkaard, Gullit and Van Basten. But none of those teams had Pelé at number 10, not to mention Jaïrzinho, Rivellino, Tostão, Gérson and Carlos Alberto.

I had them, in miniature. The Subbuteo version of the Brazil team was one of my most cherished possessions, and each player had a number carefully felt-tipped on the back of his shirt, which is how I knew that it was Clodoaldo, the hard-tackling number 5, whose head was attached to his body with a kind of balaclava helmet made out of Sellotape, following an off-the-ball clash with the bottom of somebody's shoe. Subbuteo players were more injury-prone than Darren Anderton and Jamie Redknapp combined. Most of them ended their careers if not in a Hoover bag then with an undignified blob of dried glue between their legs. A university friend, Chris Barry, later told me that he had once been forced to make a substitution of questionable legality, after the family labrador walked across the pitch and broke his goalkeeper, by bringing on a metal Grenadier Guard.

I didn't have a pitch of my own. The custom in Lynton Road was that the Sykes boys came to my house to play Battling Tops and I went to theirs to play Subbuteo. They had all the accessories, too, the most exciting of which were the floodlights, little plastic pylons with tiny, battery-powered bulbs. These weren't as authentic as they might have been, not least because you had to move an entire floodlight every time you took a corner. But then Subbuteo enthusiasts took a relaxed view of authenticity. The specialist corner-kickers used to kick the ball at the equivalent of around 470 mph, and were about eight times the size of the other players, which apart from looking a bit weird was tactically unsound. Imagine if, in the 2006 World Cup qualifying campaign, Sven-Göran Eriksson had played Peter Crouch on the wing, aiming crosses towards the head of Shaun Wright-Phillips. Actually, it's precisely the sort of thing Sven might have cooked up, but my point is that strange things happened on the Subbuteo pitch, including the fixtures themselves.

For some curious reason Jem and Chris had a team wearing Portsmouth colours, so Brazil against Portsmouth was a regular fixture at number 66. I was reminded of this a few years ago when I walked into our living room to find my son Joseph, then aged eight, absorbed in a football match being televised by Sky. At the top of the screen both teams were abbreviated; it was a Nationwide League match between Norwich City and Reading, represented as NOR v. REA. 'What's the match?' I asked Joseph. Like his father a generation earlier, his interest in football had really started to burgeon in that season of his eighth birthday, but he still had plenty to learn. He looked up at me solemnly. 'It's Norway v. Real Madrid,' he said.

In January 2000 the manufacturers of Subbuteo, Hasbro, announced that they were going to halt production of the venerable game. The decision was later rescinded but for a week or so you could hardly open a newspaper or listen to the radio without hearing middle-aged men reminiscing about plastic perimeter fencing. Unashamedly I joined this nostalgia-fest, relating not only my own Subbuteo memories in my column but also those of two friends from KGV days, Chris Taylor and Jonny Cook.

I knew Chris and Jonny had been Subbuteo obsessives, and phoned them to impart the unhappy news that the game was facing the final whistle. They were both duly saddened, and movingly recalled the European glamour that swept the game following the 1974 World Cup. 'I had a sheet of little black hexagons to stick on to the ball to make it look continental,' Jonny recalled. 'And then they produced a comprehensive list of kits, so that your teams could double up. I was delighted when I bought Sheffield United, then found they could be Athletico Bilbao as well. And I might be wrong, but I think Manchester City in their away kit doubled up as Eintracht Frankfurt.'

He was dead right, in fact. Indeed, the zest for Subbuteo exotica was catchily summed up by the band Half Man Half Biscuit, who in 1986 recorded a song called 'All I Want for Christmas Is a Dukla Prague Away Kit'.

> And he'd managed to get hold of a Dukla Prague away
>   kit,
> 'Cause his uncle owned a sports shop and he'd kept it
>   to one side
> And after only five minutes you'd be down to ten men
> 'Cause he'd sent off your right back for taking the base
>   from under his left winger . . .

These were possibly not lyrics to make Cole Porter sit up in his grave applauding, but Subbuteo sentimentalists welcomed them. And nobody was more sentimental than those of us whose boyhoods coincided with Subbuteo's 1970s heyday. Around the time that Jonny Cook got his sheet of little black hexagons, Chris Taylor bought a set of jazzy new continental goals, which were designed without the familiar stanchion so that balls, in Chris's evocative words, could 'ripple down the netting'. I asked Chris if he still had his Subbuteo set, perhaps packed away safely in his parents' attic. 'I have a horrible feeling that I eventually traded it with Gary Szabo for his

Scalextric,' he said, forlornly. If he did, it was truly a school-boy error. Like Alan Hudson and Stan Bowles, Scalextric always promised more than it delivered. But that, too, is a story for a later chapter.

The burst of Subbuteo nostalgia following the Hasbro announcement eventually led to the publication, in 2004, of a splendid book called *Flick To Kick: An Illustrated History of Subbuteo*, written by Daniel Tatarsky. In it, Tatarsky explains why the game is called Subbuteo. Peter Adolph, who invented it, was a dedicated birdwatcher, and *Falco subbuteo* was the Latin name of his favourite bird, the hobby, a kind of falcon. That, I think you will agree, is a piece of information that should come in extremely useful next time you need to fill an awkward silence at a dinner party.

Tatarsky's book also includes examples of the ways in which Subbuteo and real football have collided. This doesn't stretch, alas, to the tremendously witty abuse that was dished out to the diminutive Burnley player Brian Flynn whenever he came to Goodison Park – 'Fuck off back to your Subbuteo pitch, Flynn!' – but it does include a story about Bill Shankly, frequently recounted by the great Liverpool manager's favourite centre-forward, Ian St John.

According to St John, whenever Liverpool played Manchester United in the late 1960s, Shankly liked to moti-vate his players before the game by gathering them around a Subbuteo pitch, on which there were figures representing all the United players. Starting with the Alex Stepney figure in goal, he would growl 'He can't play!' and put the inch-high Stepney in his pocket. He would then go through the team damning this one and that with 'He can't play!', until eight of the eleven players were in his pocket. The three that were left were Bobby Charlton, Denis Law and George Best. Not even Shankly had the gall to suggest that they were useless. But he would always conclude by thundering, 'If eleven of you cannae beat three of them, you shouldnae be wearing the jersey of Liverpool Football Club.'

It's a good story, one of many that St John tells about Shankly. Among the more enjoyable assignments I have had as a sports writer, even an Everton-supporting sports writer, unfolded at St John's house in the Wirral footballer belt one afternoon in the spring of 2000. As I sat listening to his yarns I was at first plied with coffee by the fragrant Mrs St John; then, after nigh on three hours, as afternoon turned to dusk, out came the Glenfiddich.

I didn't risk puncturing the whisky-fuelled bonhomie by telling St John that I was of the Blue rather than the Red persuasion. Besides, if I had, he might have been less inclined to stick the boot into the then-Liverpool manager Gérard Houllier for what St John perceived as certain character flaws. 'I don't even want to meet the man,' said St John, giving me what in the world of newspapers is known as good copy. Houllier is gone as Liverpool manager now, so St John's dim opinion of him doesn't really matter any more. In any case, in his 2005 autobiography, St John went even further, slagging off Houllier royally. But back in 2000 there was an interesting postscript to our interview. Houllier, being a worldly, intelligent sort of chap, was a keen reader of the *Independent*. He read St John's comments and went ballistic. I even heard that St John was told he wouldn't be welcome at Anfield unless he retracted what he'd said, which was like telling St Peter that he wouldn't be welcome through the gates of heaven.

Fellow Evertonians will be wondering at this point why I'm banging on about Liverpool. The painful truth is that no sports book focusing on the 1970s can possibly avoid Liverpool, whose dominance was such that it seemed unlikely ever to end. From Aston Villa in the 1890s to Manchester

United in the 1990s, no English football team has ever ruled a decade like Liverpool did the seventies. They won the League Championship four times, the European Cup twice, the UEFA Cup twice, and the FA Cup once. And in the 1980s, frankly, it got worse: six championships, two European Cups, two FA Cups and four League Cups.

But the seeds of Liverpool's success even in the 1980s were sown in the 1960s by Shankly, with whom no British football manager, with the possible exception of Brian Clough, can stand anecdotal comparison. Over a couple of hefty whiskies St John recalled that Shankly's concern for his players' welfare even extended to sex. Or rather, no sex. 'At first he told us to wear boxing gloves in bed on Friday nights, then later he would tell us to send the wife to her mother.' The Saint wiped away a tear of mirth. 'Oh, bloody hell. He was a big boxing fan, too, and he read once that Joe Louis trained on steaks. So that was it. On Fridays, we'd have steak. Saturday lunch, steak. Saturday night on the way back from the match, steak. When you left Liverpool you went vegetarian.'

I don't suppose St John really went vegetarian when he left Liverpool. It was 1971, a time when only hippies were vegetarian. His star had started to wane at Anfield just as my interest in football, less than twenty miles up the A565, was taking shape. It was only later that I discovered quite what an idol he had been to the Kop. Alan Bleasdale, the brilliant television writer and a devoted Liverpool fan, told me once that he had gone out with a girl for the simple reason that she looked like Ian St John. Just imagine his quandary if she'd reminded him of Tommy Smith.

Four months before my afternoon with Ian St John I had interviewed Smith, too. His face still looked like a relief map of the Lake District, although in many other respects he was a different man to the one who scored Liverpool's second goal in the 1977 European Cup final – since then he'd had a pair of new knees, a new elbow and a new hip installed, and was waiting for a new shoulder. He was riddled with rheumatoid arthritis just about everywhere else and to combat the pain was taking nine tablets a day, one of them to settle the stomach after swallowing the other eight. Remembering the way he'd once tackled Duncan McKenzie in a Merseyside derby at Goodison Park, leaving McKenzie quite incapable of jumping over even Dinky-toy Minis for several weeks afterwards, I suppose I might have drawn some cruel satisfaction from Smith's state of health. It was clearly a legacy of the uncompromising way he played football. But even in the 1970s, even when he was clattering into Everton players, I'd had a grudging respect for him.

Smith had been declared formally disabled in 1990, and had recently been involved in a well-publicised battle with the Department of Social Security after a DSS inspector had watched him take a penalty – against his old mate Alex Stepney, whose inch-high alter ego had been rubbished by Bill Shankly years earlier – in an exhibition shoot-out before the 1996 FA Cup final. The inspector ruled that if he could take a penalty then he must be able-bodied, and was therefore not entitled to further disability benefit. Smith protested that he had been so full of painkillers he'd practically been rattling, but the inspector stuck to his guns. The inspector, of course, turned out to be an Evertonian. So, as with St John, I didn't tell Smith I was an Everton fan, although in this case less to preserve the mood than to preserve myself.

After all, Smith had been known as the Iron Man of Anfield, and several years of rust hadn't made him any less iron. He told me that Shankly had encouraged him to exploit his hard man reputation to the full.

'He used to say to me, "Smithy, if you can win the game in

the corridor, win it in the corridor."' And Smith soon learnt which opposing players he could intimidate. 'Denis Law, Besty, they didn't give a shit. But there were one or two . . . Leighton James, you could scare the living daylights out of him. I used to say in the corridor, "What are you doing here, this is no place for you?" In fact the joke was that I used to hand them a hospital menu before we went out on the park. Me and Jimmy Case had some laughs. Remember that little winger at Man United, Gordon Hill? He was terrified. I used to shout to Jimmy, "Send him down the line and I'll kick him over the fucking stand." But Jimmy is deaf in his right ear. So he'd cock his left ear and shout, "What was that?" and I'd have to repeat it. And Jimmy would shout, "No, no, I'm going to kick him over the fucking stand meself." You could see the fear in their eyes, and it put them right off their game.'

At Anfield, Smith added, Shankly used to pop his head round the away team's dressing-room door half an hour before every game. 'He'd say "Just coming to wish you all the best, boys." He'd have his head round the door for thirty seconds, then he'd come back and say, "Right, the left-half has got his elbow strapped up, so it wouldn't be out of the way just to give him a tap there, the right-back's got his left ankle strapped . . ."'

We both roared with laughter at this story, which I'm sure had been polished in a thousand after-dinner speeches. Moments later, however, Smith was furiously lambasting modern players for trying to win penalties by diving. It had been imported into the game from abroad, he asserted, along with spitting. And it was disgusting, absolutely fucking disgusting. A courageous interviewer might have pointed out the inconsistency, hypocrisy even, of making a joke out of verbal and physical intimidation, yet a crime out of diving and spitting. I, on the other hand, concurred wholeheartedly.

Alan Hudson's Bowels

There was one other thing that Smith told me which I was unable to quote, because his former team-mate Emlyn Hughes, whom he loathed with a slightly frightening intensity, would have sued for libel. Hughes is dead now, so he can't sue, but because he is dead I don't suppose Smith will ever repeat something he said to me that, for an interviewer with a tape recorder, was dynamite. Unfortunately, it was dynamite I couldn't detonate; all I could do was let the fuse burn for a second and then fizzle out. What Smith told me was this: before a fixture against Arsenal at Highbury in the early 1970s, with Liverpool's final league position already assured, Hughes went round his team-mates one by one inviting them to accept a bribe to throw the game.

I have no way of knowing whether that's true or not. It seems hard to believe of a man who radiated such passion for the game. But even if it isn't true, it appears that the 1970s were perhaps not the innocent days of yore they are often made out to be.

2

Jaïrzinho's Feet

Whether or not there was skulduggery such as match-fixing going on, to read Hunter Davies's seminal book *The Glory Game*, first published in 1972, is to revisit a conspicuously guileless age. Among the many joys of *The Glory Game* – which is a chronicle of the season Hunter spent behind the scenes at Tottenham Hotspur – is the questionnaire he conducted with Spurs players in which he asked them whether they kept abreast of current affairs.

Now 1972, just to refresh your memory, was the year of Northern Ireland's Bloody Sunday massacre, and the year in which an IRA bomb killed seven at Aldershot barracks. At the Munich Olympics, eleven Israeli athletes were murdered by Black September terrorists. It was also the last full year of the Vietnam War, the year in which the long conflict yielded its most enduringly horrifying image, the photograph of 9-year-old Kim Phuc running away, naked and distraught, from an American napalm attack. It was in 1972, too, that Idi Amin expelled 50,000 Asians from Uganda, while US President Richard Nixon made ground-breakingly historic visits to both

Moscow and Peking. And there were dirty political shenani-
gans on both sides of the Atlantic. In America, there occurred
the Watergate break-in that would ultimately bring Nixon
down. In Britain, Home Secretary Reginald Maudling
resigned in the wake of the Paulson corruption scandal. Oh,
and Chi-Chi, London Zoo's famous panda, died. News-wise,
those were twelve fairly eventful months. Yet almost all the
Spurs players professed no interest whatever in anything other
than football.

'I'm not that way minded,' said Cyril Knowles. Nice one,
Cyril. But nor was Martin Chivers, who said, 'I only read the
sports pages. I've never read a book in my life. I haven't the
time. I'm just not interested.' And Joe Kinnear, later to
manage Wimbledon FC in the Premier League, said, 'Outside
football, I don't know anything. The world could be coming to
an end and I wouldn't know, unless it was on the sports pages.'

The same is undoubtedly true of many top footballers now,
but the difference, paradoxically, is that they're far too media-
savvy to admit it. Certainly, for a journalist to be given such
access now as Hunter was then is beyond the furthest frontiers
of the imagination; these days, when you try to get a one-to-
one interview with a Premiership footballer, you have to send
the club's press liaison man several e-mails, then several faxes,
then a crate of beer, then your sister in her underwear, and
even if the player finally gives his gracious consent you're
made to feel grateful if you are granted an audience lasting
more than fifteen minutes.

In October 2004 I was generously permitted by West
Bromwich Albion FC to interview striker Robert Earnshaw
(on that occasion without having to send my sister in her
underwear, I ought to point out). I was told to get myself to
the training-ground, which abuts a lonely stretch of the A34
near Walsall, by no later than twelve noon. I was then asked to

wait for over an hour while Earnshaw did some extra training, and in the meantime was informed that the interview would have to be conducted standing up outside the door of the manager's office, and that it would last no longer than twenty minutes. This was Robert Earnshaw, don't forget, not bloody Ronaldinho. Yet I was left in little doubt that I was supposed to feel privileged; after all, the local newspaper boys only got five minutes. And West Brom, I should swiftly add, is one of the better clubs in terms of liaising with the press.

So *The Glory Game* could not possibly be written now; even if a club sanctioned that degree of access, the players' meddling agents never would. Besides, Hunter could knock about with the Spurs players in 1972 at least feeling that they all occupied the same planet. The income of a top footballer was not so different from that of a successful journalist, indeed most of the first team expressed some concern about what they might do when their playing careers were over. 'All I hope is that I'll end up with enough money saved to start a little business,' Pat Jennings told Hunter. I think we can safely say that saving enough money to start a little business is not the sort of ambition that David Beckham, or even Robert Earnshaw, currently nurtures. I can imagine Beckham saying that he hopes to save up enough money to buy a little country, or perhaps a little fleet of Boeing 747s, but not a little business.

Still, not all the Spurs players were worried about their financial futures. Joe Kinnear might not have known about anything outside football but he had still managed to build up a tidy property portfolio, while Mike England owned a successful timber business, and Ralph Coates had 'a few investments'.

The former Burnley man Coates, moreover, was one of the very few who did take a keen interest in current affairs, declaring his favourite television programme to be *News at Ten*. I have to confess that until I reread *The Glory Game* my memories of Ralph Coates pretty much began and ended with his bald head; he is always one of the first players to be picked for the All-time Slapheads XI that is drawn up on the regrettably rare occasions that I get drunk with my Subbuteo-loving mates Jonny and Chris. So it is nice to think of him in 1972 not just spending his evenings combing rogue strands of hair across his shiny pate, Bobby Charlton-style, but also hanging on every word uttered by Andrew Gardner and Reggie Bosanquet on *News at Ten*. In which respect he at least had a soulmate in the big Spurs centre-half England (whose surname provided great amusement to those of us who were ten years old in 1972, on account of his being Welsh). To Hunter's question about current affairs, England said, with what I like to think was a touch of indignation: 'I think I keep well in touch. I know what's happening in Vietnam.'

My own knowledge of what was happening in the Vietnam War was rather sparser than Mike England's, but I knew that it dominated the television news night after night and even now I can remember the likes of Sandy Gall and Leonard Parkin signing off their reports from Saigon, while my parents marvelled at the wonders of television satellite technology.

My first memory of current affairs, though, if that's not a confusingly oxymoronic notion, dates from the early summer of 1968. I was six years old, and my dad was driving us home from a few days in a gloomy hotel in Barnstaple, Devon; I suppose it must have been the half-term holiday and I dimly recall that it piddled with rain for the entire duration of our stay. I also dimly recall meeting a little girl of about my age, who came from Yorkshire and pronounced Barnstaple 'Baaaaarnstaple', which I thought was extraordinarily funny. What I can recall with absolute clarity, however, is that on the journey home we were listening to Cliff Richard singing 'Congratulations' on the car radio, and that Cliff was rudely interrupted by a news flash to say that Senator Robert Kennedy had been assassinated in Los Angeles. The reason why all this is still so vivid is doubtless because of my parents' reaction. My dad immediately pulled into a lay-by and he and my mum listened to the bulletin in horror. I think there may even have been tears. Whatever, sitting quietly on the back seat, I was impressed.

So, although I can't remember where I was when I heard that JFK had been shot, which is supposed to be the daddy of all 'where I was when . . .' moments, I can at least place myself in the back seat of a Vauxhall Viva somewhere on the long journey from Barnstaple to Southport when the news came through that RFK was a goner.

Incidentally, just to take a slight detour from the road home from Barnstaple, in November 2004 I happened to read an obituary of a man called Vaughn Meader, of whom I had never previously heard, but who had enjoyed glittering celebrity in early 1960s America thanks to his uncanny ability to impersonate President Kennedy. Shortly after the Cuban missile crisis, a period when the country was ready for a bit of light relief, a record was released on which Meader poked affectionate fun at John and Jacqueline Kennedy. It was called *The First Family*, and the skits included one in which the President treated the family breakfast as a press conference, and another in which he led his entire motorcade into a petrol station, then left in a tiff because they didn't offer Green Shield stamps. You are probably not vibrating with uncontrollable mirth at these ideas, but it was pretty irreverent stuff at the time, and it certainly found an audience. For more than six weeks, an average of a million people a week bought *The First Family*; it won a Grammy and became the fastest-selling album in US history, leaving Elvis, at a time when he was indisputably alive, for dead.

Happily, JFK took it well. At a Democratic Party dinner he stood up and joked that he had only come because Vaughn Meader was busy. And in December 1962 he gave out 100 copies of the album as Christmas presents. But then, for both Kennedy and Meader, disaster struck. Meader certainly had cause never to forget where he was when he heard the news. On 22 November 1963 he was in Milwaukee, where a taxi driver asked him if he had heard about the President in Dallas. 'No,' said Meader, chuckling in anticipation, 'how does it go?'

The bullets from Lee Harvey Oswald's rifle killed his career as surely as they had killed Kennedy, indeed the notoriously sacrilegious comedian Lenny Bruce worked the assassination into his stand-up routine, opening his act by saying, 'Boy, did Vaughn Meader get fucked!' It was true enough. Meader's livelihood was dealt a fatal blow overnight. Like a man I once knew who claimed to be able to fart the chorus of 'Waltzing Matilda', he was the owner of a talent nobody wanted, and spent much of the rest of his life a broken man.

To get back to the road from Barnstaple, my vivid recollection of hearing the news about Bobby Kennedy was partly why I so enjoyed the brilliant beginning to Colin Shindler's 1998 book, *Manchester United Ruined My Life*. I've never met Shindler, although I have no doubt that, being a Manchester City fan, he is blessed with the same lugubrious wit as my old schoolmate Mark Salthouse. His book, at any rate, contains oodles of wit, much of it lugubrious, and begins with an account of City's 1961 signing of a defender called Bobby Kennedy from Kilmarnock. The fee, incidentally, was then a record for a half-back, a whopping £45,000. How quaint.

Anyway, Kennedy was an uncompromising defender in the

mould of his fellow Scotsman Dave Mackay, and since Mackay had just helped Tottenham Hotspur to win the Double, it was hoped that Kennedy might prove a similar catalyst for City. He didn't. However, he was a useful member of the squad in the 1967–8 season in which Manchester City won the League Championship, a win clinched with an unbelievably dramatic 4-3 victory over Newcastle United at St James's Park.

On Wednesday 5 June 1968, less than a month after City had won the title and as I settled down to my last night in moist Barnstaple, Shindler went to his first May Ball at Cambridge University. He eventually fell into bed at about 6 a.m., but was awoken two hours later by his neighbour Martyn Jones, who burst into the room yelling, 'They've shot him! They've shot Bobby Kennedy!' Even in his somnolent state, Shindler realised that this was horrible news. He sat bolt upright. 'Why the hell would anyone shoot Bobby Kennedy?' he asked. 'We've just won the League.'

I love that marriage of the banal and the momentous, being able to remember exactly where you were and who you were with when events of world-shattering importance took place elsewhere. In November 1993, on the thirtieth anniversary of the first Kennedy assassination, I was working for the *Hampstead & Highgate Express* in north London, and took it upon myself to phone a number of famous or merely very old people to ask if they could remember what they were doing at some of the century's defining moments. I even found one local nonagenarian who could remember the event that supposedly kicked off the First World War. She had been on holiday at Sandbanks, Dorset, in 1914, when the Archduke Francis Ferdinand, regrettably for the whole of Europe but perhaps most especially for him, copped an assassin's bullet in Sarajevo.

And Denis Healey – who didn't live in Hampstead or Highgate, but whose phone number I happened to have in my contacts book, courtesy of my wife who worked for the BBC – remembered being in his bedroom in Keighley, just before he was due to start his final year at Oxford University, when he heard about the outbreak of the Second World War. 'I was working on Kant's transcendental synthetic unity of apperception,' he told me. 'Oh yes, a doddle,' I wanted to reply but didn't. 'It is about the mystery of self-consciousness,' he continued, 'and the most difficult thing in the world to understand. Then I heard my mother rushing up the stairs. "Put your book down, Denis, war's been declared," she said. I remember being more surprised that she had told me to put my book down than that we were at war.'

I can see that one might tend to remember one's whereabouts on occasions like that. Besides, news of the kind that elicits the interest of the whole world tends to be bad. As with the announcement that Robert Kennedy had been shot, I can remember precisely where I was when I heard that Princess Diana had died in a car crash (in bed with a hangover), and that two planes had been flown into the Twin Towers of the World Trade Center (in the car on my way to catch a flight at Stansted Airport, slightly alarmingly). But for me, and doubtless for Colin Shindler, it is sport which illuminates the past more vividly than anything else. Nothing whisks me more often and more powerfully back to a time and place than great sporting occasions.

I wrote a column about this once and was deluged by e-mails from readers sharing their own 'where I was when . . .' memories. One of the best was from a guy called Mark Stickings who remembered where he was when Derek Underwood more or less single-handedly bowled out Australia at the Oval on the last day of the last Test in August

1968, thereby winning the match for England and squaring the series.

'I was 16,' he wrote,

> and listening on a crackly old transistor radio in a youth hostel in Cologne, Germany. When John Inverarity was finally out, a group of Eastern Europeans, who were also listening to a radio, began to hit the table and kick the floor in anger. They were terribly worked up. I went over and asked why they were supporting Australia. Relatives over there, perhaps? 'No.' they said. 'The radio has just reported that Russian troops have invaded our country, Czechoslovakia!'

Mr Stickings did not report whether he had tried to cheer up those bouncing Czechs with the news England had just drawn the Ashes, but I very much hope he did.

For me, although sporting memories whisk me back to a variety of places, the time is usually the 1970s, beginning with the 1970 World Cup final between Brazil and Italy. I was eight years old and I watched it in the plush lounge of some family friends, 'Uncle' Ronnie and 'Auntie' Sybil. Calling your mum and dad's friends 'auntie' and 'uncle' is a social convention that seems to have disappeared since the 1970s. Many things have disappeared since the 1970s, and not all of them need be mourned; white dog shit and the prison drama *Within These Walls*, starring Googie Withers, to choose but two examples. But I think it's a shame that my children don't call my oldest friends 'auntie' or 'uncle'. They don't even call their aunties and uncles 'auntie' or 'uncle', just as I am plain Brian to my own nieces and nephews. I don't want to get all Victor Meldrewish about it, and blame it on a general decline of respect towards older members of society, but it's worth remembering that in 1977 nobody thought there was anything odd about Richard O'Sullivan's character Robin Tripp, in that towering sitcom *Robin's Nest*, referring to his partner Vicky's father, played by Tony Britton, as Mr Nicholls. I'm glad I've got that off my chest.

Uncle Ronnie and Auntie Sybil lived in a handsome bungalow on Hartley Road. We were there because they had a colour telly, one of those big faux-antique cabinet jobs, and we didn't. I had to endure the following World Cup in monochrome, too. We didn't get a colour telly until 1975, and then only so that my dad could distinguish between jockeys' silks in the ITV Seven.

He died the following February, having had only a few months to sit in his favourite armchair savouring the sheer apricot-ness of Lord Howard de Walden's racing colours. It was a sudden heart attack that felled him, on a train, during the Winter Olympics. He was sixty and I was fourteen. The very next day I watched John Curry skating to gold, but couldn't get too enthusiastic about it.

Still, my father's untimely departure for a higher-quality Parker Knoll at least lifted the barrier on his First Division football veto. Since my eleventh birthday I'd been allowed to go to Haig Avenue to watch Southport but not to Goodison Park, which he thought too dangerous for a boy, to watch Everton. I thought about my dad's veto on 19 April 2003, when I stood at the side of the pitch at Goodison, before the derby match against Liverpool, tearfully watching my son Joseph taking penalties against the Everton goalkeeper Richard Wright. It was Joseph's eighth birthday and through various strokes of good fortune he had ended up as one of the mascots. In truth, it was a fulfilment of my own dream rather than his, but then what's the point of having children if you can't live your dreams through them?

An hour before the match we were taken into the Everton dressing room, which Joseph took perfectly in his stride while my heart thumped like a timpani drum. The captain that day, David Weir, signed Joe's autograph-book, then, with a kindly smile, stooped to ask him: 'Who's going to win the game today?'

Joseph looked at him blankly. He had never been addressed by a man from Falkirk before, and had no more idea of what had been said than if it were a man from Friedrichstad or Famagusta.

'Pardon,' he said.

Weir repeated the question. All he wanted was the partisan answer 'Ev-er-ton!' and then he could crack on with arguably more important matters like getting his boots on. Joseph looked at me uncertainly.

'Who's going to win today's game, darling?' I translated.

'Oh,' he said, and frowned. Weir waited patiently for the answer. Joseph thought about it some more. 'I don't know,' he finally concluded. It was an exquisite meeting between the pedantic logic of a child and the cheerful bluster of an adult. How could he possibly know who was going to win? If Weir had asked him which team he *hoped* would win, obviously that was different.

Just as obviously, in fairness to my late father who would no sooner have taken me to a football match when I was eight than sold me into slavery, things have changed since the 1970s. Football hooliganism was rampant then and it wasn't as if he had the slightest interest in going to matches himself. But then he died and my newly widowed mother didn't feel as strongly about it, or perhaps didn't have the strength to argue with me about it, so in 1977 I was able to buy myself a season ticket for Goodison's Gwladys Street terraces. The fortnightly Saturday afternoon journey to Goodison Park from the Ribble Bus

Station in Southport became a ritual for the next three years, and never did the ritual glean a more handsome reward than on 28 October 1978, when Everton beat Liverpool for the first time in seven seasons. I even remember the smell of the occasion: part Bovril, part body odour. It was the day Marcel Proust met Andy King.

But I am getting ahead of myself. The decade had begun with Everton winning the League and Brazil winning the World Cup, and my interest in football mushrooming. Every day after tea (in the north of England, supper was always tea) in that golden footballing summer of 1970 I called for Jem and Chris Sykes, or they called for me, and we crossed Lynton Road and walked along Clovelly Drive to the local recreation ground – Hillside rec – where we played football, sometimes until after sundown.

Mostly, we tried to recreate dramatic goalmouth action we had seen in the World Cup, and the exotic names of the towns and cities where the matches took place – Guadalajara, Pueblo, Toluca, Mexico City – remain almost tearjerkingly evocative for me. So does the England team's World Cup anthem, 'Back Home', which on the rare occasions I hear it now, has precisely the same effect on me as the sound of Vera Lynn singing about bluebirds over the white cliffs of Dover has on folk who endured the Blitz, making me want to stand to attention and look misty-eyed into the middle distance. Similarly evocative, of course, are the names of the men whose headers and back-heels, volleys and saves we tried to replicate, especially the foreign ones: the Italians Riva, Rivera and Boninsegna; the West Germans Müller, Maier and Beckenbauer; and above all the Brazilians, Jaïrzinho, who scored in every round, Rivellino, and the incomparable Pelé.

I never got to be Pelé on the rec – that was Chris's privilege as the oldest of us and the most skilful footballer – but I did sometimes get to be the England goalkeeper Gordon Banks. Regrettably, however, to make his unforgettable point-blank save from Pelé's header in England's famous Group Three match against Brazil, Banks had leapt spectacularly to his . . . right. And, as we have seen, I have only ever been able to dive to my . . . left. So when it came to restaging that particular bit of goalmouth action I had to be Jaïrzinho instead, ghosting past Terry Cooper, which wasn't difficult, since we didn't have a Terry Cooper, before crossing the ball for Pelé (Chris) to head and Banks (Jem) to keep out miraculously. We did that on the rec, with jumpers for goalposts, night after night after night.

I sometimes find myself reflecting that it would have been nice to have grown up on Merseyside a few years earlier, perhaps to have been born in 1945 rather than 1961. That way, I would have reached adolescence just before the Beatles became famous and could reminisce fondly about Saturday nights at the Cavern. But these reveries don't last long before I realise that, for a kid in the process of becoming a football nut, it was the sweetest possible piece of luck to be eight years old in the summer of 1970. Admittedly, that made me too young to have been swept up in the excitement when England won the World Cup (and Everton the FA Cup) in 1966, but even those dogmatic old-timers, who think that football has been in terminal decline since the day Duncan Edwards died, or at least since the day Stanley Matthews retired, have to admit that the definitive World Cup, unmatched both before and since, took place in 1970 in Mexico. And even the similarly dogmatic whippersnappers, for whom 1990 represents football's dim past and 1980 its Jurassic Period, have to concede that 1970, from what they have seen of the archive footage, was the Beautiful Game's most beautiful moment.

Shortly before I started writing this book I decided to look up Jem and Chris Sykes to see whether their memories of long, warm evenings playing footie on the rec, pretending to be Jaïrzinho and Boninsegna and Müller and even Franny Lee, corresponded with mine. We had lost touch completely after I left Southport when I was eighteen, and even in the few years before that our close boyhood friendship had pretty much petered out. But finding them was not too tricky. I knew they still lived in Southport and I was vaguely in touch with another Lynton Road contemporary and rec regular, John Hepworth from number 43. Heppy still lived in Southport, too. So I phoned him, and sure enough, it turned out that his daughter and Jem's daughter played football together, confirmation, if any were needed, that somehow or other we had all shuffled rather a long way into middle age.

The Sykes brothers, Heppy and I duly met in a pub in Southport, and wallowed unashamedly in Lynton Road nostalgia and Theakston's Bitter. They reminded me of their rather forbidding next-door neighbour, the gloriously named Colonel Pepper, who famously died while sitting on the toilet. And I had clean forgotten about a boy we had known called Ian Hunt. 'Don't you remember,' said Chris. 'We used to call him Isaac.'

At this juncture I'd just like to mention the thoroughly admirable Sir Archibald Clark Kerr, Britain's ambassador in Moscow during the Second World War, who memorably wrote to his friend Lord Pembroke: 'My dear Reggie, In these dark days, man tends to look for little shafts of light that spill from heaven . . . So I propose to share with you a tiny flash that has illuminated my sombre life, and tell you that God has given me a new Turkish colleague whose card tells me that he is called Mustapha Kunt. We all feel like that, Reggie, now and then, especially when spring is upon us, but few of us would care to put it on our cards.' I love that.

Anyway, Jem and Chris hadn't changed much in the twenty-odd years since I had last seen them. Jem now called himself Jez, but was otherwise the same warm, witty guy I had known when, as Rolf Harris sang (in a number one hit that coincidentally re-entered the charts during the 1970 World Cup), we were two little boys. Jez was still a devoted Evertonian too, a Goodison Park season-ticket-holder, who had somehow wound up with a former Liverpool star, Mark Lawrenson, as a brother-in-law. Chris, too, was as I remembered him; rollicking good company with an explosive laugh that made the veins on his neck stand out.

Jez, Chris and I got extremely drunk that night, whereas Heppy left us before we lurched off into the night to find a curry house. That in itself was a reminder of times gone by. On those halcyon June evenings in 1970, and on innumerable occasions later, Heppy would leave the rec at a sensible hour, while the Sykes boys and I played on, tirelessly.

Occasionally, my mum or theirs would come to find us, but more often than not we only knew it was time to trudge home when we could no longer see the goal from the (notional) penalty spot. I must say I find it pretty tiresome these days when parents of roughly my age bang on about how much freedom they had as children compared with the freedom their own kids have, and I try not to do it myself, but it is indubitably true. I don't know why. It's not as though paedophiles were only invented in more recent times, indeed we would sometimes see decidedly dubious characters watching us from a distance. Maybe it was naive of us, or our parents, but they were never considered a threat. I don't even recall my folks asking too many questions when I went home and told them that a slightly unkempt, bearded man called Sam had joined our regular kickabouts.

At the time I was a big fan of the Catweazle books, about

an eleventh-century tramp who travels forward through time, and I remember thinking that Sam was a ringer for Catweazle. But that observation didn't seem to trouble my parents, either. More excitingly, Sam claimed to have once played in goal for York City, which was unimaginably glamorous for Hillside rec. I'm sure he was perfectly nice and had no improper intentions, but I wouldn't fancy his chances now of becoming playmate with a bunch of pre-pubescent boys, not without a lynch mob following him home.

On 25 October 1970 I celebrated my ninth birthday. There was no chance of being a mascot at Goodison Park but I did have a party with a magician, 'Dextrous' Dexter. And in recognition of my steadily growing passion, I received *The Boys' Book of Soccer 1971* from my great-aunt Ella and great-uncle John, and a white-leather football from my mum and dad. Footballs in leather casing, known as caseys, were sacred possessions. It was not unknown even for weedy-looking boys with glasses, and possibly ginger hair and freckles as well, to be invited to join kickabouts on the rec just because they had a nice-looking casey.

But I had never owned one before and had never thought I would. Although I was an only child, I was never indulged. Quite the opposite. My parents, much as they loved me, seemed almost perversely determined not to buy me whatever was the fashionable toy. Thus, I was never allowed a Chopper bike, an Action Man with authentic hair, Scalextric, a full Subbuteo set or a Spacehopper. When my friends and I staged a Spacehopper Olympics along Lynton Road one day, I had to sit astride somebody's slightly under-inflated beach ball, which wasn't the same at all. Had I been born thirty-five years later, I would be the kid without the X-Box, the Yu-Gi-O cards or the Beyblades. And yet my mum and dad bought me a casey. And not just any casey but a white casey; it was the difference between any Rolls Royce Corniche and a white Rolls Royce Corniche. For once, I was the envy of Lynton Road.

But not for long. Sometime during the night of 26 October 1970 my white-leather casey was stolen. It remains one of the great unsolved crimes of the twentieth century, not that Southport CID was given the slightest opportunity to solve it. While I pleaded for the police to be called in, and drew up a list of suspects which included the IRA, the Viet Cong and the Nolan brothers from Lynton Drive, my parents pinned all the blame on me for leaving my casey – never a football, always a casey – in the front garden overnight. Needless to say, I was inconsolable. The lovely white leather, with its wonderful smell, was hardly even scuffed. It was the first and last proper casey I ever owned, and I owned it for scarcely thirty-six hours.

The Boys' Book of Soccer 1971, by stark contrast, I have managed to keep for thirty-six years. I have it next to my Apple Mac keyboard right now, and it is a marvellous chronicle of a bygone age. In the chapter about Everton, champions the previous season, there is a reference to 'the fine new Goodison Road stand still under construction'. That's the same stand now held as an example of football stadium decrepitude, at least when compared with the gleaming monoliths of Old Trafford, the Reebok at Bolton and the City of Manchester Stadium, merely to confine things to the northwest of England.

As for the lost white casey, hard though I looked for it even on occasional trips to see relatives on the northern outskirts of London, thinking that it might perchance have been spirited down to a playing field in Cockfosters, I got over the loss eventually. I think it was when my wife gave birth to our first child that I realised there was just no point continuing to fret about it.

In the meantime, at least there were some happy developments in my playing career. One Sunday afternoon on the rec, instead of the usual business of two captains each picking from the bunch of kids congregated there – which invariably left me and a boy called Nigel Evans, both trying to look nonchalant, as the last to be selected – a cabal of older boys decided that we should pick teams according to which network of roads we lived in. Thus were Hillside Hornets and Ryder Rovers created, removing at a stroke the humiliation I felt when Nige Evans got the penultimate nod, and indeed his shame when I was chosen ahead of him. From now on we would both be Hornets.

These Hillside Hornets and Ryder Rovers fixtures went on for about a year, and we even developed a transfer system with sweets as the currency. Our star player was a twinkle-toed, slinky-hipped boy called Duncan McDonald, who must have been fourteen or fifteen when I was ten. To me he was every bit as good as Jaïrzinho and I was devastated when Rovers bought him for 100 sickly little sweets called Mojos, even though we scrupulously shared this unprecedentedly high transfer fee between us. To see Dunc McDonald shimmying over the bumpy surface of the rec towards our two piles of jumpers, rather than towards theirs, I found at least as upsetting as when Wayne Rooney, more than three decades later, returned to Goodison Park in a Manchester United shirt. A hundred Mojos didn't ease the pain in 1972, any more than £27 million did in 2004. Football at any level is a dangerously capricious creature to which to plight one's troth.

But I didn't care. I was besotted with the game. And nothing, not even the World Cup, made my pulse throb quite like the FA Cup final. It didn't matter whether Everton were involved, which was just as well, because between 1968 and 1984 they weren't. I needn't even need to favour one side over the other. And I certainly didn't need to be there in person. I just loved the occasion for its passion and pageantry, all of which was conveyed more than adequately on television, which, as a thrilling bonus, also offered such unmissable treats as *Cup Final It's a Knockout* and *Meet the Players' Wives*.

These days, of course, we have no need to meet the players' wives. We already know quite enough about Victoria Beckham and Coleen McLoughlin. In fact, it might be nice to know a bit less. Unfortunately, footballers' wives are celebrities in their own right now; they've even inspired a bloody TV drama series. But then as L. P. Hartley wrote so perspicaciously in *The Go-Between* – a text I would get to know intimately while studying for my English A level in T. B. Johnson's study, with neither I nor a tight-lipped Mr Johnson making any mention of the fact that I had earlier shared responsibility for the muddy imprint of a football on the window behind him – the past is a foreign country: they do things differently there.

Old L. P. was spot on. And the past in football is not just any foreign country. It's not France or Spain but Uzbekistan or Sierra Leone, in the sense that it is truly, comprehensively foreign. It is played differently, governed differently and certainly covered differently, to wit my earlier example of Hunter Davies getting a season with Tottenham Hotspur and me getting twenty minutes with Robert Earnshaw. Of course, there have been many good things introduced and many bad things abolished, but there is no doubt that some of the magic has evaporated.

If this reads like the sentimental wittering of a middle-aged fool, well, it's my book and I'll witter if I want to. But I'm happy to concede that if there ever was a golden age of English football, determining its start and finish is an entirely subjective business. Of course, it is reasonable to argue that the golden age is now, with so many of the world's greatest players plying their trade here. A similarly strong case can be made for the 1950s, the era of Stanley Matthews, Tom Finney and the Busby Babes. Or indeed for the decades between the wars, the era of Dixie Dean and Herbert Chapman's Arsenal, and all that newsreel footage of men in flat caps whirling rattles.

Maybe English football's golden age was when it was still a truly working-class game. Football had first evolved, oddly enough, as a recreation for the upper classes. The man who published the first known set of rules, in 1862, was an Old Etonian by the splendid name of Charles Thring. But within twenty years or so the game had been commandeered by the working man. Where there were mills, factories and docks, so there were well-supported football clubs, which is why Lancashire became football's heartland from the 1880s until at least the 1950s. More seasons than not, there were as many clubs from the industrial north-west in the top division as from all other regions of England put together. It's all there in L. S. Lowry's painting of thousands of stick men descending on Burnden Park, the home of Bolton Wanderers. The painting, which is now owned by the Professional Footballers' Association, is called 'Going to The Match', and is rather romantic, in a sooty kind of way.

But since old Lowry applied the last bit of paint to his canvas, the game's fan base has changed. I remember the comedian Frank Skinner saying ruefully that he felt some responsibility for the growth of middle-class interest in football. He reckoned that Nick Hornby, by writing *Fever Pitch*, and he and David Baddiel, with their television show *Fantasy Football League*, had helped to create a monster, in the form of the arriviste football fan. Skinner explained that he had grown up watching football among hard-bitten assembly-line operatives and steelworkers, and that was how he preferred it.

'At head level,' he said, 'I think it's brilliant that women and posh people like football, that I can go and see a private doctor in Sloane Square for my ITV medical and he says "Aren't Tottenham doing well?" But at gut level I think, "What the fuck's it got to do with you?" It's partly class prejudice, partly gender prejudice. I know it's wrong. And I like getting a free sandwich at Wembley, but I look at all the corporate johnnies and I can't help thinking, "Where were you in the pissing rain against Bristol City on a Tuesday night?"'

Skinner recalled being on the terraces at The Hawthorns once, watching his beloved West Bromwich Albion, when a man just in front of him launched an extraordinarily loud and foul-mouthed tirade against the Albion players, which offended even the tough-looking characters around him. At one point, another supporter could stand it no longer. 'Hey mate, tone down the language, will you,' he said. 'There are youngsters here.'

The man did briefly stop his tirade against the players, but only to redirect it at his critic. 'Look, pal,' he snapped. 'I work in a miserable fucking factory all fucking week, for shit fucking pay which I take home to my fat ungrateful fucking wife, who spends most of it feeding our horrible fucking kids and the rest of it on her fucking bingo. The only time I get all fucking week to let off fucking steam is fucking watching fucking Albion, so if it gives me pleasure to stand here and fucking swear at those bastards, then I fucking will!' And Skinner, listening to this exchange with interest, thought, 'Yeah, fair enough.' The man's rant at the players then continued unabated until the end of the match.

After that rather exciting, invective-ridden paragraph, let us return to the question of dating English football's golden age. For me, it was unequivocally the 1970s, the first full decade of colour television, the first decade in which the entire nation, not just the 100,000 lucky buggers with tickets, could enjoy, on an invariably sunny Saturday afternoon every May, the kaleidoscopic spectacle of Wembley Stadium packed to the rafters. And there was the added pleasure of planning the viewing schedule days beforehand: poring over the *Radio Times* (which unfathomably was allowed to list only BBC programmes) and then the *TV Times* (which, equally unfathomably, carried only ITV programming) to see when to switch over from BBC to ITV, from BBC1's *Cup Final Multicoloured Swap Shop* to ITV's visit to the team hotels.

There were only three TV channels in those days, and two of them covered the FA Cup final live. Its stature as the blue riband event in the English sporting calendar was unassailable, as was my place on our lounge couch (which oddly enough I would now describe as our living-room sofa: like football itself, I have become irretrievably gentrified). Every final from 1970 to 1980 has an indelible place in my mind's eye, but the perspective is from that couch, with a red-and-cream gramophone on one side of the telly and a pine bookcase on the other, on which stood my parents' alcohol supply, its centrepiece a soda syphon and a half-finished bottle of a custardy substance called Advocaat. All middle-class households in the 1970s had a soda syphon and a half-finished bottle of Advocaat. The funny thing is that I don't remember anyone drinking the Advocaat, ever. I think they sold it in half-empty bottles.

As for the extent of my FA Cup football recall, give me a year in the seventies, any year, and I'll give you the finalists, result, scorers and both teams. Go on, try me. Just pluck a year out of the air; 1979, say. That was Arsenal 3 (Talbot, Stapleton, Sunderland), Manchester United 2 (McQueen, McIlroy); and the other players were Jennings, Rice, Nelson, O'Leary, Young, Brady, Price and Rix for Arsenal; Bailey, Nicholl, Albiston, Buchan, Coppell, Greenhoff, Jordan,

Macari and Thomas for United. And that's without consulting my *Rothmans* (now, alas, renamed the *Sky Sports Football Yearbook*). My wife thinks I should be wearing a quilted anorak, if not a straitjacket, when I come up with these things, but the sad truth is that most football lovers of my generation can pull off the same party piece. Yet ask us to name all twenty-two Arsenal and Manchester United players who started the 2005 FA Cup final and we would struggle. It's bizarre.

Or maybe it's not so bizarre. One is more awestruck by events during one's childhood, hence they stay lodged in the mind. But it's not just that. I'm convinced that my children will not remember the FA Cup finals of their formative years. The occasion has been seriously, probably fatally diminished, not least because it seems to have been annexed by the very richest clubs. What chance now of a team from the second tier of English football overcoming one of the powerhouses, as humble Sunderland did by beating mighty Leeds United in 1973? None. When humble Millwall did somehow manage to reach the Cup final in 2004, they were predictably battered by Manchester United.

I might be wrong about all this. It might be that thirty years from now there will be a wave of football nostalgia just as strong for the so-called noughties as there now is for the seventies. But even if there is, will it embrace FA Cup finals? I very much doubt it. For a series in the *Independent* called 'Heroes and Villains' the novelist and Chelsea fan Roddy Doyle once wrote a moving paean to his hero Charlie Cooke, the tricksy Scottish winger who in the 1970 FA Cup final replay against Leeds – when Roman Abramovich was barely knee-high to a samovar, or would have been if samovars had knees – crafted Peter Osgood's equaliser.

It was a wonderful piece of writing, and there was no need

to be a Chelsea supporter to enjoy it; you just had to be over about thirty-five. After all, no subsequent generation of football fans has had to confront the oddly unsettling spectacle of its favourite players going off to play in the United States when they still had something to offer the game in England, as Roddy Doyle and I did during the brief 1970s heyday of the North American Soccer League. Charlie Cooke, lamented Doyle, 'ended his career playing for American teams called Los Angeles Aztecs, Memphis Rogues and – and this one really upsets me – California Surf. I hate to think of him playing on the beach, watched by the cast of Baywatch. "Yo, Charlie!" "Way to go, Charlie-ie-ie!" Jesus.'

Unlike Doyle, I did not experience the rapture of watching my team winning the FA Cup. Not in those impressionable years, anyway. I'd been only four when Brian Labone lifted the Cup for Everton in 1966, and I was twenty-two when Kevin Ratcliffe lifted it in 1984. But that never really mattered to me. If anything, the mystique of the FA Cup intensified with Everton's failure to win the thing. And the mystique did not apply just to the final. On 5 February 1972, non-league Hereford United beat First Division Newcastle United in a third round replay at Edgar Street, having first held them 2-2 at St James's Park. Before the match, Newcastle's Malcolm Macdonald predicted that he would score ten goals. In the event, he scored just once, in the eighty-fifth minute. But it seemed enough, until Ronnie Radford scored a thirty-five-yard screamer with a minute to go, followed by Ricky George's injury-time winner. It remains the greatest act of giant-killing in FA Cup history, and it marked the commentary-box debut of one John Motson.

He and his fellow commentators pop up in a later chapter, but let me just relate that some twenty-five years later I found myself on the phone to Motson, who was earnestly giving me directions to his house in suburban Hertfordshire. It was faintly surreal hearing the familiar tones in a non-footballing context, although with his celebrated attention to (arguably unnecessary) detail Motty managed to mention every sleeping policeman I would encounter between the motorway and his house. I also have a recollection of him lacing his directions with footie-speak: 'We live in a cul-de-sac, Brian, and when you turn into the road [escalating excitement in his voice] . . . it's there . . . top right-hand corner!' I might be making that bit up, but I'm pretty sure I'm not.

To get back to Hereford United's heroics, they have become more meaningful for me in recent years because in 2002 my family and I settled in the lovely county of Herefordshire. My daughter goes to school in Hereford and several times a week I drive along Edgar Street, gazing at the shabby old stadium and wishing I'd been there on that epic, wintery day in 1972.

But then I have an unhappy knack, both as a fan and as a player, of finding myself in the right place at the wrong time. In this respect I am not alone. To flit briefly back to Motty, his football trivia book *Motson's National Obsession* contains the heartrending story of Richard and Mary Hayter, who left their home on the Isle of Wight on the morning of 24 February 2004 intending to spend some time with their son, the 24-year-old Bournemouth footballer James Hayter, his girlfriend, and the couple's three-day-old baby. They then planned to watch James play in Bournemouth's evening match at home to Wrexham, before heading back across the Solent.

Unfortunately, James wasn't in the starting XI, and when Bournemouth sent on their second substitute twenty-five minutes or so into the second half, and it wasn't James, the Hayters reasoned that he probably wouldn't get on at all. Wanting to be sure of making the 10.30 p.m. ferry, they left the ground in the eightieth minute of the match. Four minutes later, James was sent on and promptly scored a hat trick in 140 seconds, beating a 52-year-old League record. He only touched the ball four times, and three of them were goal-scoring touches. By this time the Hayters were in their car on the way to the ferry terminal, listening to the match commentary on the radio. 'All I can remember is the commentator shouting out James's name over and over again,' Richard later reported. 'I was going mad. I didn't know whether to laugh or cry.'

My own stories of being in the right place at the wrong time, or the wrong place at the right time, are less dramatic than Mr Hayter's. But it does seem to be a recurring theme in my sporting life, and, typically, my three seasons as a Goodison Park season-ticket-holder were not in the irrepressible Howard Kendall years between 1984 and 1987, when the team won two championships, appeared in three consecutive FA Cup finals and won the European Cup-Winner's Cup. By then I was away at St Andrews University in Scotland, followed by a year even further away, at Emory University in Atlanta, Georgia. For reasons too complicated to explain here, I listened to the 1986 Everton v. Liverpool FA Cup final on a tiny transistor radio wired to the tin roof of a hut beside the Buffalo River, Tennessee. No, the years I spent slavishly following Everton home and away had been between 1977 and 1980, when the team was managed by Gordon Lee, a man with the *joie de vivre* of an undertaker with toothache, who steps in a dog turd on the way to report the theft of his wallet.

Mercifully, Lee did not create teams in his own hangdog image. Everton during his tenure were capable of playing exciting football, and at Goodison in the 1977–8 season inflicted 6-0 thrashings on both Coventry City and Chelsea, as well as 5-1 away defeats of Leicester City and Queen's Park Rangers. They finished third that season and fourth the next, which would have been good enough now to qualify for the

Champions' League, yet there were only two tangible achievements for Evertonians to celebrate in those years.

One was Bob Latchford's second goal a few minutes from
the end of the last game of the 1977–8 season, the routing of
Chelsea, which took his tally for the season to thirty. This was
significant for no reason other than that the *Daily Express* had
offered £10,000 for the first man to score thirty league goals,
although there was also a spooky parallel with the sixty League
goals in a season scored by Dixie Dean, an Everton centre
forward even finer than Latchford, because Dean, too, had
reached his milestone, exactly fifty years earlier, with hardly
any time remaining in the final match of the season (albeit
against Arsenal rather than Chelsea).

I suppose it was odd that thousands upon thousands of
Evertonians, not a few of them unemployed, should celebrate
Bob Latchford securing a cheque for ten grand. After all, he
needed the money less than practically everyone else in the
ground. But it was something Liverpool fans couldn't celebrate, that was the point. And six months later, on an
unseasonally warm October afternoon, we got to celebrate
something else that Liverpool couldn't: beating them 1-0 at
Goodison Park.

I doubt whether I will ever feel as euphoric about the result
of a football match as I did that day. Everton's last victory over
Liverpool had been way back in the mists of time, in
November 1971, when the scorer in another 1-0 home win was
19-year-old David Johnson. By the time he signed for
Liverpool nearly six years later, after a period with Ipswich
Town, Johnson was still the last Everton forward to have
scored in a Merseyside derby. It was a desperately long time to
go without bragging rights, and as my friends and I stepped
around the steaming ordure that was a by-product of a
heavier-than-usual mounted police presence outside Goodison

Park that Saturday afternoon, the humiliation seemed likely to continue. The Liverpool line-up was Clemence, Neal, Kennedy (A.), Thompson, Kennedy (R.), Hansen, Dalglish, Case, Heighway, Johnson (bloody turncoat) and Souness, which even the Goodison faithful knew to be stronger than Everton's starting XI of Wood, Todd, Pejic, Kenyon, Wright, Nulty, King, Dobson, Latchford, Walsh and Thomas.

Just consider those twenty-two names, incidentally. On that October day in 1978, every last player on the Goodison pitch came from the British Isles, which now seems impossibly old-fashioned, a part of English football's heritage as firmly consigned to history as baggy shorts and wooden rattles.

However, there was already a whiff of change in the air, as well as the stronger whiff of horseshit. The trickle of foreign players, which in due course would become a flood, had begun that very season, with the exciting arrival at Tottenham of Osvaldo Ardiles and Ricky Villa, and at Ipswich of Arnold Muhren, whose thorough foreign-ness was underlined by his marvellously exotic full name: Arnoldus Johannus Hyacinthus Muhren. The best we could do for exotica at Everton was Micky Pejic, who had a Yugoslav father, and whose long ball upfield it was that Martin Dobson headed down into the path of Andy King, who from just outside the penalty area hit a speculative shot that on another day could have ended up high in the Park End crowd, but on this day of days ended up in the corner of Ray Clemence's net. For years afterwards Evertonians rejoiced in the joke: 'Where's Queen's Drive? It goes from Bootle to Broad Green. Where's King's Drive? In the back of Clemence's net.' We celebrated his goal as if it had just secured the League, FA Cup and European Cup treble.

That it hadn't, that those were barren years for Everton in the silverware department, didn't matter to me; I could not have enjoyed myself any more on the Gwladys Street terraces.

I loved the tribalism, and was in awe of a character known as Fozzie Bear, who used to hang off a stanchion leading us all in song. And what songs they were; what masterly lyrics. 'Bobby Latchford walks on water, tralalalalalalalala!' 'We all agree, Duncan McKenzie is magic!' And of course, the curiously punctuated 'Scotland's, Scotland's, Number One! Scotland's! Number One!' in honour of my pin-up, Georgie Wood.

From time to time, somebody else would try to get a chant going, and all eyes would turn to Fozzie to see whether he approved. On one momentous occasion, my friend Rafe Parker had a go. 'Give us an E,' he suddenly shouted, during a second-half lull in a match against Aston Villa. It was gob-smackingly brave of him, but his bravery, alas, went unrewarded. Nobody gave him an E, not even me, and some years later I thought of Rafe as I stood on the terraces at Murrayfield, watching Scotland's rugby union team play Ireland in a Five Nations match. I was standing among hundreds of Ireland fans, and the occasion – not to mention one or two pre-match pints of Guinness – so went to my head that I decided, the memory of Rafe's humiliation notwithstanding, to have a stab at leading the green hordes in song.

Ollie Campbell was playing at fly half for Ireland that day, goal-kicking with his usual panache, so I waited until the crowd was relatively quiet, and then, to the astonishment of my Irish friend Geoffrey alongside me, threw back my head and bellowed 'Ollie, Ollie, Ollie!' There was a split second of resounding silence, time enough for me to wonder whether to slink away in shame or just get paralytically drunk afterwards, and then, gloriously, the crowd responded.

'Oy, oy, oy,' they roared.

'Ollie, Ollie, Ollie,' I cried.

'Oy, oy, oy!'

'Ollie!'

'Oy!'

'Ollie!'

'Oy!'

'Ollie, Ollie, Ollie!'

'Oy, oy, oy!'

In the hubbub of laughter and appreciation that followed I could not have been prouder of myself had I delivered the Gettysburg Address.

But such bravado was out of the question at Goodison Park, where I was cheerfully a follower in the tribe, not a leader. To be any part of the tribe, however, I had to adapt. Coming from Southport I was a creature known disdainfully in Liverpool 4 as a 'woolly back', a term which also applied to folk from the Wirral, and apparently had its origins in the outsiders who carried sheep on their backs to sell at market in Liverpool. So every Saturday I emptied my vowels, so to speak, of any Southport inflections. I became a Scouser, and I wore a denim jacket on to which my mother, bless her, had sewn a variety of Everton motifs. I fancied that the jacket made me look hard, the sort of lad you wouldn't want to mess with. But I have photographs of myself wearing it and I was obviously quite seriously deluded. I still looked like the sort of lad you would quite like to punch in the nose.

3

Ian Botham's Bottom

Ian Botham nearly did punch me in the nose, once. Although on that occasion I was wearing a quite different jacket: a brown, rather elegant wool/cashmere mix number from Marks & Spencer. Here's what happened. From 1994 to 1999 I worked for the *Mail on Sunday*, not as a sports writer but as the newspaper's television critic. I also wrote a weekly interview feature called Brian Viner's 'Telly People'. This embraced all kinds of people off the telly – actors, comedians, quiz show hosts, TV chefs, newsreaders, even the occasional weather forecaster – but it was also a perfect opportunity to meet some of my childhood sporting heroes, many of whom, by the mid-1990s, were working as commentators or studio analysts.

Botham had just become the top cricket pundit for Sky Sports, who were then anxious for all the publicity they could get. He was persuaded to do an interview with me, probably much against his will, and I was duly informed that it would take place while he was off air during an England v. South Africa Test match at Edgbaston.

For a cricket lover, it was not exactly a hardship to be obliged to spend forty-five minutes in the company of I. T. Botham at a Test match. Nevertheless, I was more than faintly apprehensive. There had recently been one or two stories of Botham losing his rag with journalists and I was fairly anxious that Botham's rag did not go missing in my presence. Therefore, as a) a token of my respect for one of England's greatest cricketers and b) a blatant bribe to keep him sweet, I spent £25 of the *Mail on Sunday*'s money on an excellent bottle of Puligny-Montrachet. I knew about Botham's fondness for fine wines, encouraged by his mentor John Arlott, and naively thought that he might be disarmed by my munificence into being nice to me. Alas, it did not work out that way.

A Sky press officer met me and led me to the Edgbaston commentary box, where Botham was just completing his first stint of the day. We were introduced, and I handed him the Puligny-Montrachet, mumbling my thanks to him for giving me his time. He accepted it, if not exactly ungraciously, then not exactly swooning with gratitude either, and suggested that we proceed to a couple of seats in the stand, where he could keep tabs on proceedings in the field. Throughout this exchange he kept his wraparound sunglasses on, and I gradually realised that he had no intention of removing them. This was disconcerting, to say the least. It is curiously difficult to interview someone wearing sunglasses; without eye-contact there is hardly any chance of establishing even the semblance of a rapport.

Whether he was actively trying to intimidate me, or simply not bothering to conceal his lack of enthusiasm for spending forty-five minutes with a Sunday newspaper hack, I wasn't sure. Either way, I did feel intimidated, and tried to draw solace from the knowledge that he had had the same impact on much tougher men than me. At least he wasn't about to chase me round a car park threatening to flatten me, as he once had the former Australian cricket captain Ian Chappell.

We took our seats in the grandstand, and as we did so the flap of my Marks & Spencer jacket somehow got lodged beneath the great man's substantial posterior, with the result that I found myself leaning towards him at an angle of about thirty degrees. My jacket flap was well and truly trapped; not for nothing did the Indians call him Iron Bottom. Anybody in even vague possession of their dignity, however, would have tugged it free, or perhaps asked him to rise slightly. Pathetically, I found myself unable to do either, and so commenced the interview at this slight listing position, which became doubly uncomfortable when I made the mistake of asking him about his son, Liam.

At that time, Liam Botham was on Hampshire's books, hoping for a career as a county cricketer. He subsequently became a rugby union and then a rugby league man, of course, enjoying a measure of success in both codes and happily immersing himself in sports with which nobody associated his father. As a cricketer, however, he was doomed to be compared unfavourably, and that was my dreadful mistake.

'How good a cricketer is Liam at the age of nineteen, compared with what you were like at the same age?'

It seemed like a reasonable question. There had lately been a good deal of speculation that Liam might just have the talent to follow his old man into the England team, and it would have been journalistically irresponsible not to follow this up. But I realised immediately that I had detonated a time bomb. Botham half-turned to glare through his sunglasses at me, and as he turned, his backside somehow annexed more of my jacket, which had the effect of making me list towards him even more. 'It's hard enough for that lad without people like you putting more fucking pressure on him,' he growled, menacingly. I would have backed away except that I couldn't; my head was almost on his shoulder. 'How is he ever going to make his own way when prats like you keep comparing him with me?'

I kept quiet. It was, I sensibly judged, a wholly rhetorical question. Botham then turned back to focus his attention on the match. I squeaked an apology, he grunted something, and the rest of the interview passed under conditions of distinct *froideur*. Eventually he glanced at his watch, said he needed to get back to the microphone, and rose from the seat, mercifully liberating my jacket. Half-heartedly he shook my hand, while I wondered whether I might redeem myself by jokingly asking if I could have my bottle of wine back. I decided against.

'I hope that was OK,' said the Sky press officer, gaily, when Botham had returned to his post.

'Not entirely,' I replied. 'I asked him whether his son Liam was as talented a cricketer as he was at the same age, and I don't think he liked the question much.'

'Really?' said the Sky man. 'I would have thought that was a fair enough question. I must remember not to ask him that myself.'

I smiled wanly – devilishly wishing that I'd said, 'You must ask him about Liam's talent compared with his own, it's a subject he really enjoys talking about' – and left Edgbaston, suddenly bereft of the appetite to stay for the afternoon's cricket. A few years later, after I had joined the *Independent*, I interviewed Botham again, at the Oval. Thankfully he was in a warm, expansive mood that day, and daringly I reminded him of our encounter at Edgbaston. He chuckled. 'I expect I gave you a hard time, didn't I? Sorry about that. I used to be a bit sensitive about Liam and his cricket.'

Someone, it occurs to me now, should write a manual for

journalists with a section on those seemingly innocuous questions that elicit an explosive response. Another of the projects I gave myself during my time on the *Hampstead & Highgate Express* was to ring well-known people and ask them to name their favourite Beatles songs. I suppose there must have been a reason, an anniversary of some sort, and there were certainly plenty of people in our circulation area who'd had some kind of association with the Beatles, among them Hunter Davies, who had not only spent a season with Tottenham Hotspur but had also written the authorised biography of the Fab Four around the time they recorded the *Sergeant Pepper* album, lucky blighter.

Hunter was his usual obliging self on the phone, which gave me the confidence to call Jane Asher, actress and cake-making doyenne, who famously was engaged to Paul McCartney in the 1960s. She didn't live in the area but I happened to have her phone number, just as I had Denis Healey's. In fact I think I might have asked the former Chancellor of the Exchequer to name his favourite Beatles song, too, slightly to his surprise. Anyone remotely famous whose number I had was fair game for just about any question: one Valentine's Day I did a ring-round getting people to recall their first kiss, a question that rather wrong-footed Bruce Kent, chairman of the Campaign for Nuclear Disarmament and former Catholic priest.

Anyway, Asher was as sweet as icing sugar until I asked whether there was a song that swept her back in time to her romance with McCartney. 'For God's sake,' she snapped. 'It's been almost thirty years. I've been happily married to my husband [the cartoonist Gerald Scarfe] since 1981. Can't you people move on?'

Too late, I was told by someone that Asher, though a perfectly charming woman most of the time, is well known for losing her temper with anyone who drags up the McCartney connection. It could almost be a cruel initiation for a journalism trainee. Just as my father-in-law, on becoming an apprentice engineer at a Yorkshire colliery nearly sixty years ago, was ordered to go to the supplies office and ask for a long weight (he was told to hang on and didn't twig that there was anything amiss until after forty-five minutes, when someone said, 'Reet, yer've 'ad yer long wait, yer can bugger off now'), so fresh-faced youngsters in newspaper offices could be instructed to phone Jane Asher to ask her about some detail of her relationship with Paul McCartney.

There are lots of these incendiary questions in sport; the questions asked guilelessly yet deeply resented. In fact I thought of my Edgbaston experience while watching the 2004 *BBC Sports Personality of the Year* show. When Ian Botham stepped up to receive his lifetime achievement award, Gary Lineker chirpily asked him whether he thought Andrew Flintoff might be 'the next Botham'. By the end of the following summer, with the Ashes back in English hands, there were people wisecracking that Botham had become the first Flintoff more than Flintoff had become the next Botham, but at the time it was a reasonable question. Not that Botham thought so. The slightest flicker of a shadow passed over his face, enough for me to know that a journalist asking him the same thing, away from the television cameras, would have felt the gale force of his disdain. It was clearly a question he thought idiotically trite, but because it was Lineker, and because it was live telly, he had to rein in his irritation.

A lifetime achievement award was a long way away – almost a lifetime, in fact – when Botham first started to make a name for himself, as a Somerset all-rounder, in 1974. Henry Blofeld, a former colleague on the *Independent* and, of course, a cornerstone of BBC radio's *Test Match Special*, likes to recall that he first saw Botham on 12 June 1974, at the county ground in Taunton where Somerset were playing Hampshire in the Benson & Hedges Cup.

Botham was eighteen, a year younger than Liam was when I got into trouble by inviting comparison. The events that day make it clear that there was no comparison. Hampshire were bowled out for 182, and it was Botham who claimed the wicket of their most dangerous batsman, clean-bowling the South African maestro, Barry Richards. He then batted at nine, and walked to the crease with Somerset in trouble at 113 for seven, which later in the same over, with the dismissal of the veteran Tom Cartwright, became deeper trouble at 113 for eight. When the youngster promptly tried to hook a vicious Andy Roberts bouncer – and it should be remembered that Roberts was probably the fastest bowler in the world at the time – Blowers sat up and took notice. Unfortunately, Botham mistimed the stroke and, in those pre-helmet days, copped the ball directly in the mouth. Medical assistance was called for while he spat blood, and two teeth, on to the Taunton square, but he adamantly refused to retire hurt. He then continued to take Roberts on, and scored a thrilling forty-five not out, which included two towering sixes, to lead Somerset to victory by one wicket.

It was three more years before Botham was picked to play for England. Despite his heroics in the county game, he was looked upon for some time as a chancer with the ball and a bully with the bat. His bowling in particular wasn't taken seriously, not least because he had the useful ability, which he never lost, to take wickets with bad balls as well as good ones. When he did make his Test debut, against Australia at Trent Bridge in July 1977, it was entirely typical that a) he should take five for seventy-four in Australia's first innings, that b) the first of his victims should be the masterly Greg Chappell, and that c) it should be with a long-hop. England won that match by seven wickets, and a fortnight later Botham took five for twenty-one at Headingley to help secure the win, by an innings and eighty-five runs, that regained the Ashes. Geoffrey Boycott chipped in as well, I should add, with his hundredth first-class hundred.

By 1977 I was as nuts about cricket as I was about football. These days, I am able to attend the occasional Test match and one-day international in the line of professional duty, which is fantastic, but in those days it was easier to indulge my love of cricket, because as a slothful teenager I felt entitled, if not downright obliged, to spend the entire five-day duration of a Test match watching the telly. I looked upon the BBC's cricket presenter Peter West, puffing on his pipe, like a favourite uncle. And every time he got some doddery old player from yesteryear to fill a tea break with his reminiscences, I was as riveted as I was by the actual cricket. Once, during tea at the Oval in a series against the West Indies, West chatted to the old Surrey and England batsman Andy Sandham, who by then was pushing ninety and nearly blind. They were talking about great captains, in particular Don Bradman. Then West asked the old boy how highly he rated the captaincy skills of his BBC colleague Richie Benaud. Sandham peered at him myopically. 'Benaud?' he said. 'Don't think I know anything about him.' It was a delicious moment. Benaud had retired in 1964, but it was still long after Sandham's time.

The day that is seared into my memory as if it were yesterday, however, or maybe the day before yesterday, is Tuesday, 19 August 1975. I was thirteen, and rose, as was my wont during the school holidays, long after my parents had departed for work. My dad was in the 'job business' in Liverpool, also known, euphemistically, as the import-export business. He would buy end-of-line job lots from manufacturers, and sell them on to retailers. He'd persevered with the betting shop for a while but had learnt, to his cost, that it is nigh-on impossible to make money out of one betting shop; you need several if you are to succeed. So it was back to job lots, which for some reason were mostly vast consignments of women's underwear. The soundtrack of my adolescence was not just Slade, Wizzard and Suzi Quatro, it was also my dad talking on the phone about 100,000 camiknickers, whatever the hell camiknickers were. And my mum's job was to sort them into colours and sizes at a rented warehouse in Argyll Street, Liverpool, a row of gloomy Victorian buildings just off the supremely misnamed Paradise Street. So they would depart the house at around eight each morning, leaving me to fend for myself.

We didn't know it, of course, but by August 1975 my dad had entered the last six months of his life. He was fifty-nine, and had been suffering from angina for a few years, which had put an end to his cigar habit. For some reason, though, he could never quite bring himself to chuck away his cigars, which were kept under lock and key – the rather glaring security flaw being that the key was always in the lock – in the bottom drawer of the dining-room sideboard.

So whenever the fancy took me, and there was no one else in the house, I used to lock myself in the bathroom, open the window, and light up a Villager cigar. I would then lie in the bath like a pubescent Winston Churchill, or perhaps Jimmy Savile, contentedly puffing away. And on that particular Tuesday morning the Villager tasted especially sweet, because it was the fifth morning of the third Ashes Test at Headingley, and I was looking forward to switching the telly on just in time for the BBC's stirring cricket theme, 'Soul Limbo' by Booker T and the MGs, before spending the rest of the day watching England trying to square the series. Australia had finished the fourth day at 220 for three requiring a highly improbable 425 to win, having been skittled out in their first innings for a paltry 135.

It was rare, then as now, to skittle Australia out cheaply. The previous winter, with Dennis Lillee and Jeff Thomson joining forces as devastatingly as Field Marshal von Blucher joined forces with the Duke of Wellington at Waterloo, if that's not too fanciful an analogy, England had been comprehensively thumped in Australia. It was not the happiest of tours on which to make your international overseas debut, although that was the lot of David 'Bumble' Lloyd, who, of course, went on to coach England and whose marvellous tales once kept me entertained for the best part of a rainy Manchester afternoon. While batting at Perth, Bumble told me, he copped a direct hit in the privates from Thomson. It was a story he started dining out on as soon as he got his voice back.

'I was wearing a pink Litesome,' he said, in that glorious Lancashire accent made in Accrington. 'You know, them flimsy pink cricket boxes that looked a bit like soap holders. They had these holes around the edge, and when Tommo hit me, the force inverted the damn thing and pushed one of me knackers through the holes. From time to time you hear people asking "Is there a doctor on the ground?" That day they had to send for a welder.'

There is another self-deprecating story Lloyd likes to tell about the same painful incident: apparently, in trying to downplay the prospect of facing Australia's turbo-charged pace battery, he had blithely remarked to his England team-mates that Lillee and Thomson would be so easy to deal with that 'I'll be able to play them with me dick.' Somehow, even through his pain he retained his sense of humour, because when his worried team-mates checked on his wellbeing as he was being carried off the pitch in agony, he croaked, 'Told yer.'

It was, then, with quite a reputation that Lillee and Thomson arrived in England the following summer. With the formidable Chappell brothers also in the side, to say nothing of such marvellous players as Dougie Walters and Rodney Marsh, Australia were clear favourites to retain the Ashes. Yet it was still a shock when they steamrollered England in the first Test at Edgbaston by an innings and eighty-five runs, with a squeaky-voiced debutant by the name of Graham Gooch bagging a ten-ball pair. The England selectors reacted with predictable agitation, sacking Mike Denness as captain and appointing Tony Greig. Not that Greig seemed to have much of a secret weapon to withstand Australia's fearsome pace attack; his recommendation that the 34-year-old, bespectacled, prematurely grey Northants batsman David Steele be inserted into the England top order seemed to have a ring of desperation about it.

Yet Greig had done his homework. He had phoned a couple of dozen county bowlers and asked them which batsmen they found hardest to get out. Again and again, he got the same answer: Geoff Boycott and David Steele. With the enigmatic Boycott serving a self-imposed exile from Test cricket, that left only Steele.

Whether or not the tourists knew how well Steele was batting at county level, the sight of him striding to the middle in the second Test at Lord's, to make his debut with England at ten for one, was definitely not one to strike fear into Aussie hearts. 'Who the fuck is this, Groucho Marx?' was his warm welcome to the middle from Jeff Thomson. It was as well that Tommo and his team-mates didn't know why Steele was late getting to the wicket. In trotting down the stairs after leaving the dressing room he had trotted one flight too far, much to the surprise of an Irish doorman, who, unaccustomed even at Lord's to being confronted by a man in pads, gloves and holding a bat, asked him where he was going. 'To the wicket,' said Steele. 'You've come down too far, these are the toilets,' said the doorman. 'Right, I'll just nip back up then,' said Steele.

It was a wonderfully prosaic start to a cricketing summer which would win Steele the *BBC Sports Personality of the Year* award for 1975. It wasn't as though he ran up double centuries, nor even that he helped England win the series, which was drawn, enabling Australia to keep the Ashes. But the sheer doughtiness he embodied in scoring 45 and 50 at Lord's, 73 and 92 at Headingley, and 39 and 66 at the Oval, hugely endeared him to the British public. And can you imagine any batsman now facing bowlers of the pace of Lillee and Thomson not only without a helmet, but wearing specs? Moreover, his heroic status with Middle England was somehow compounded by the offer made by a Northampton butcher following his debut at Lord's. The butcher said he would give Steele a lamb chop for every run up to fifty that he scored in each of his remaining Ashes innings, and a steak for every run over fifty.

There was something charmingly old-fashioned yet faintly absurd even in the mid-1970s about a Test cricketer being rewarded in lamb chops, and the absurdity intensified when someone at the Inland Revenue contacted Steele to enquire about the value of the meat he'd been given, whereupon he indignantly offered to meet his tax liability in chops. There were certainly plenty of them. 'When I got that seventy-three in the first innings at Headingley,' Steele later told me, 'the butcher sent me a telegram saying, "Go easy in the second innings, I'm running out of lamb."'

I met Steele in the summer of 2004, in fact we played

cricket together in a Lord's Taverners match in Cheltenham and I unwittingly contributed to his decision never again to pull on his whites. I had joined the Taverners the summer before, partly because it would enable me to do worthwhile things for charity and partly because it would give me the chance to play cricket with my boyhood heroes. Naturally, I was motivated *much* more by the former than the latter, but even so, it was a thrill to find myself at third man in front of a paying audience and against a so-called Ashes XI captained by Mike Gatting, which comprised, among other former England and Australia players, the perennial overgrown schoolboy Derek Randall.

Overgrown schoolboys have always been popular with genuine schoolboys, and so it was in the 1970s with Randall, who lent some much-needed puckishness to the England team at a time when the likes of Dennis Amiss, Mike Brearley, Bob Woolmer and Peter Willey exuded stolid respectability. In fact it always tickled me that Willey, who seemed such a strait-laced sort of chap, gave his name to one of the funniest and most famous of all commentary-box gaffes, when Brian Johnston on *Test Match Special* observed, as Michael Holding purred in at the Oval, that 'the bowler's Holding, the batsman's Willey'.

My all-time favourite story of cricketing nomenclature, however, dates from 1948, when Alec Bedser and the sublimely named Jack Crapp, who had been playing against one another in a county match, travelled together to a hotel in Leeds to join the rest of the England players. When they got there, the receptionist didn't realise that they were part of the England party. 'Bed, sir?' she enquired of one of them. 'No, Crapp,' came the reply. She didn't bat an eyelid. 'Through those doors and first on the left,' she said.

To return to Randall, I quite frankly worshipped the

ground he walked on, which he sometimes did, when he was in the outfield, on his hands. Or I would have done if he'd ever stayed in one place for long enough; Dennis Lillee once quipped that his own problems against Randall stemmed from the difficulty of hitting a moving target. Certainly, Randall was like no other cricketer I'd ever seen before, resembling a cat on hot bricks whether at the crease or in the field, but in both areas capable of sheer brilliance. And he was cheekiness personified; once, when Lillee was roaring in to bowl, Randall stopped him just so that he could turn round to Australia's beefy wicketkeeper Rod Marsh to say, 'It's no wonder Santa Claus didn't visit our house this Christmas, Marshy, you've eaten him.' On another occasion enshrined in the anecdotage of many a seventies cricketer, Randall arrived at the crease and chirruped: 'How're you doing, Marshy?' From behind the stumps there was a glowering silence. 'Not talking today, Marshy?' added Randall. 'What do you think this is?' snapped Marsh, eventually. 'A fucking garden party?'

That was the same Rod Marsh, as definitive an Aussie as Lillee and for a long time the proud holder of the record number of tinnies consumed on a flight from Australia to England, later hired by the England and Wales Cricket Board to establish the national cricket academy at Loughborough University. He was even made a selector, which entitles him to some of the credit for England winning back the Ashes in September 2005. What might the odds against that have been thirty years earlier? What, moreover, would have been the odds against me one day being called on to bowl my spectacularly innocuous off breaks at my hero Randall, in a competitive game of cricket? At Cheltenham I got the nod from my captain, Andy Stovold, just after Randall had come loping in to bat. But he didn't clobber me all over the park, as he easily could have done. Instead, clocking Steele at shortish mid-wicket, he contented himself with lofting every shot teasingly just over the poor man's head, and roared with laughter as Steele tried without much success to haul his 63-year-old body into the air. When he got his aching limbs home that evening, Steele resolved that he was too old to play cricket again.

But in August 1975 he was on top of his game, and top-scored in both innings in Leeds. The stage was duly set on that fifth morning for a fascinating day's cricket. Rick McCosker was ninety-five not out for Australia, but would be facing another England debutant in spinner Phil Edmonds, who had finished the first innings with five for twenty-eight, on a wearing pitch. I finished my Villager, got out of my bath and ambled down the stairs into the lounge, where I switched on the TV to find scenes of utter consternation and bewilderment at Headingley. Some people campaigning for the release of George Davis, a convicted East End gangster whom they believed to be innocent, had somehow broken into the ground overnight and vandalised the pitch, pouring oil not on troubled waters but on a good length.

There was a sporadic IRA bombing campaign in England at the time, yet few bombs caused greater shockwaves than the destruction of the Headingley pitch. It is hard now to remember, still less to understand, what an impact it had. Brian Johnston, for whom cricket was an essential part of a world which comprised nothing more unsettling than finding the odd fruit cake without sultanas, was seen wandering around Headingley in a state of almost catatonic shock. To him, to everyone inside and even outside cricket, it seemed like a terrible act of desecration, although it certainly achieved its short-term objective, which was to garner some publicity for the impressively energetic, if morally dubious, 'George Davis Is Innocent' campaign. A cartoonist in a national newspaper drew a placard, immortalising the joke 'Free George Davis . . . with every gallon of petrol.'

Strangely enough, the tenuous connection between cricket and Davis – whose own affection for the game, or lack of it, is not on record – continued some years later when he was found guilty of murder and sentenced to life imprisonment by, of all judges, Henry Blofeld's brother, John. One hopes that Mr Justice Blofeld sent him down with a single raised finger.

But all that was yet to come on that August morning. While I was smoking my Villager in the bath in Southport, blissfully unaware of the drama unfolding across the Pennines, David Steele in Leeds was trying to ascertain whether, if the match was abandoned, his runs would count in the record books. His team-mate John Edrich, in the car on the way to the ground, had mischievously told him that they wouldn't, and Steele's first act on arriving at Headingley was to seek out Alec 'Bed, sir?' Bedser, the chairman of selectors, to thrash out this particular point. Neither of us, in our very different ways, gave two hoots about who George Davis was and whether he had been the victim of a miscarriage of justice. Steele was aghast at the thought that he might have scored that defiant ninety-two for nothing, while I was aghast at being deprived of a day of watching Test cricket on television. In the event it rained fairly steadily in Leeds that Tuesday, so the match would have petered out into a draw anyway. But that was beside the point. I hated the idea that there were people out there who did not hold Test cricket as sacred as I did.

And hold it sacred I certainly did. If 1970 was the perfect year to be an eight-year-old getting interested in football, so, too, was it an excellent time to be a boy on the threshold of a love affair with cricket. The 1970s was the decade of the first cricket World Cup, the decade of the great West Indian pace batteries, the decade in which Botham, Randall and David

Gower all glittered for England. But more than anything, it was the decade of England v. Australia.

The Centenary Test in Melbourne in March 1977, in which Randall scored a scintillating second-innings 174, was one of the greatest matches anyone, let alone a 15-year-old schoolboy, had ever seen. It was the 226th Test in 100 years of cricket between the two countries, and England, after dismissing the Aussies in the first innings for 138, were themselves bowled out for a lamentable ninety-five, with the peerless Dennis Lillee taking six for twenty-six. England were ultimately set 463 to win, a total far greater than anything achieved not only in the previous 225 Test matches between England and Australia, but in any Test matches anywhere, between anyone.

In the event they fell just forty-five runs short, which by joyous coincidence had been Australia's precise margin of victory on the same ground in the first Test in 1877. As for Randall's remarkable performance, it was notable mainly for the way he got under the skin of the mighty Lillee, who at one point hit him on the head with a bouncer, only for Randall to give the sore spot a cursory rub and chirp, 'No good hitting me there, mate, there's nothing to damage.' When another Lillee bouncer cannoned off his unprotected head, he staggered about for a moment or two, then ceremoniously doffed his cap to the bowler, calling out, in his broad Nottinghamshire accent: 'That were a good one, Mr Lillee.'

The Centenary Test in which Randall performed so heroically was a marvellous one-off, but there were also seven Ashes series between 1970 and 1980, and the hallowed urn changed hands, at least metaphorically, no fewer than four times. Until the late summer of 2005, when England reasserted bragging rights over Australia during probably the most enthralling Test series in the entire history of the game, there were people in their late twenties for whom the Ashes seemed an Australian possession no less than Sydney Opera House. But the venerable contest, thrillingly as it was revived in 2005, was never more competitive than in the 1970s.

Moreover, we might have Freddie Flintoff and Kevin Pietersen to entertain us now, but I doubt whether any leading cricketer now or in the future will ever be as entertaining as Randall. How the Barmy Army would have loved him. He finished with a disappointing Test average of thirty-three, but then he was credited with saving at least twenty runs per innings with his wonderful agility in the covers. Also, the England selectors did him no favours, never quite trusting in his ability and shuffling him absurdly in the order. He batted at one, at seven, and at most points in between.

Gloriously, he saved his best for Test matches against the Aussies. In the fourth Test in Sydney in January 1979, with England in trouble and Geoff Boycott, back in the fold, having just registered his first international duck for a decade, Randall batted for almost ten hours in dangerously intense heat to score 150. It was a match-winning innings, and an Ashes-winning match, making Mike Brearley the first England captain since Len Hutton in 1954–5 to retain the hallowed urn. It also showed that Randall could be Athos or Porthos as well as D'Artagnan, and to keep The Three Musketeers analogy alive, I have no doubt that when he finally made it back into the pavilion he neded a goodly squirt of Aramis.

Despite his heroics in 1979, however, it is his 174 in the Centenary Test that will be for ever remembered, and in particular his duel with Lillee. There was one shot, a remarkably cavalier stroke with which he swatted Lillee for four, that inspired Reg Hayter, writing for Wisden, to heights of lyricism rarely associated with the name Reg. 'Once,' wrote

Hayter, 'when Lillee tested him with a bouncer, he tennis-batted it to the mid-wicket fence with a speed and power that made many a rheumy eye turn to the master of the stroke, the watching Sir Donald Bradman. Words cannot recapture the joy of that moment.'

Nor can words quite recapture the joy of the moment, in August 1972, when I took my seat at my first Test match, between England and Australia at the Oval. I was taken by my older cousins Daniel and Jonathan, and we set out from Southgate underground station, near their home in north London, on what, for me, could not have been a greater adventure if we'd just pushed off from the banks of the Orinoco on a bamboo raft.

I remember cheese sandwiches and being carefully instructed, for the first time in my life, in the art of eating a tomato like an apple. Until Danny's mum, my Auntie Rose, put one in my packed lunch, I had only ever eaten the raw tomato sliced in sandwiches or quartered in salads. But most vividly of all, I remember playing cricket on the outfield during the lunch interval. That doesn't happen now, alas, yet there are other things to lodge in boys' memories. Almost exactly thirty-three years after that day at the Oval I took my son Joe to his first Test match. He was ten years old, as I had been in 1972, and his first Test, like mine, was England against Australia. On 15 August 2005 we got up at 4.30 a.m. and drove from Herefordshire to Manchester where we joined an epic queue to see the last day of the third Ashes Test at Old Trafford. Thousands were locked out, but we made it in, and watched a captivating day's cricket, one of the most captivating even by the standards of an astonishing series, which culminated in Brett Lee and Glenn McGrath stoically batting out the last four overs to secure a draw. Later, as we drove back down the M6, I asked Joe what his favourite moments had been.

'Getting up so early in the morning and the Mexican Wave,' he replied, unequivocally. 'Especially the Mexican Wave.'

'And what about the actual cricket?' I asked.

'Yeah, that was good as well,' he conceded.

I allowed myself a rueful smile. Dennis Lillee had taken five for fifty-eight on the day I went to the Oval in 1972, but it was the lunchtime cricket on the outfield that stuck with me. No sooner had the umpires picked up the bails, than hundreds of boys scurried on to the pitch to set up their own mini-Test matches. For a ten-year-old it was unbelievably exciting to be part of this spontaneous festival of cricket, and, of course, to tread the same turf as Lillee and Derek Underwood, Alan Knott and Ian Chappell. Just as the names of the footballers who illuminated the 1970 World Cup – Pelé, Jaïrzinho, Riva, Boninsegna, even Brian Labone – make my eyes mist up with nostalgia, so, too, do the names of the cricketers who featured in that 1972 series. Indeed, I must be one of the very few men to feel a slight romantic frisson on hearing the word Raymond next to the word Illingworth.

My hero, because he opened the batting for Lancashire as well as England, was Barry Wood. I had other Lancashire cricket heroes too, and took great delight in the heady exoticism of the name of the wicketkeeper, Farokh Engineer, but Wood was the guy I liked most. He never sparkled in international cricket as he did in the county game, averaging just 21.61 for England in twenty-one innings, but by heavens I admired the cut of his jib, whatever that meant. To be a supporter of Everton Football Club and Lancashire County Cricket Club seemed, in the summer of 1970, like having picked a winning ticket in the lottery of life. Everton were League champions and that summer Lancashire won both the John Player League and the Gillette Cup, the start of a remarkable run in which they contested the prestigious Gillette Cup final in six out of seven years.

The most memorable of those years was 1971. First of all they pulled off an improbable victory against Gloucestershire in the semi-final at Old Trafford, when, in rapidly fading light and with all the lights ablaze in the neighbouring Warwick Road railway station, David Hughes smacked spinner John Mortimore for twenty-four in an over, leaving Jack Bond to score one to win, which he did, off the mighty South African Mike Procter. And then, in the final against Kent, with Asif Iqbal seemingly winning the match single-handedly for Kent, who had already reached 197 in pursuit of a modest Lancashire total of 224, Bond himself delivered the *coup de grâce*, leaping like a prima ballerina in the covers to take an extraordinary catch. Asif was out for eighty-nine. Kent then plunged dramatically from 197 for six to 200 all out, and I spent at least the next two days trying to replicate Bond's catch, throwing a tennis ball into the air and then diving on to the couch to catch it.

As the 1970s wore on, my dad remained resolute in not letting me go to Goodison Park, but he was perfectly happy to let me go to watch Lancashire on the few occasions, once or twice a season, that they played at the Southport & Birkdale cricket ground on Trafalgar Road. I used to cycle there, with a rucksack full of sandwiches, fruit and a flask of soup that always got broken. I must have cost my parents a fortune in Thermos flasks. I used to take a packed lunch to school as well, and practically every time I took a flask I would unscrew the lid to find mushrooms or bits of chicken or whatever floating on the surface alongside little silver glass shards. Incidentally, for some curious reason my mother also had a habit of giving me sandwiches that, in 1970s Southport, verged on the avant-garde. My friends got plain cheese or salad or Sandwich

Spread sarnies, and I got chicken with pineapple. I still don't even begin to understand why.

The last time I went to watch Lancashire play in Southport was a fixture against Warwickshire on Wednesday, 28 July 1982. I can date it with absolute certainty because it was the first day of one of the most remarkable county matches ever. It was also the first time I had taken a woman to a cricket match, and a highly sexed Californian at that.

Her name was Robyn, she was two years older than me, and I had met her on a train travelling between Nice and Paris. My friend Mark Sutcliffe and I had spent a month that summer inter-railing round Europe, and we were on the final leg of the adventure when Robyn – slim, tanned, blonde, pearly-teethed and unmistakably Californian – asked if she could share our compartment. I must have been a great deal more forward at twenty than I am now, because by the time we got to the Gare de Lyon, Robyn and I were an item looking for a cheap hotel in Paris and Mark was contemplating the rest of the journey back to England on his own. I would have felt worse about it had I not been 100 per cent sure that Mark would have done exactly the same had Robyn come on to him rather than me.

This has nothing much to do with sport, I know, but I don't think any sports memoir is complete without a spot of sex. We spent two energetic nights in a grotty hotel in the unprepossessing 19th arrondissement and then Robyn decided to alter her plans to hook up with a girlfriend in Amsterdam, choosing instead to come with me to Southport. My mother had remarried the December before and moved to London, so the house in Lynton Road was on the market but still not sold. We stayed there for a week, until the day before Robyn was due to fly back to San Francisco, and then I drove her to London in my mum's Ford Escort, which Mum had generously, or possibly foolishly, left at my disposal. Meanwhile, Robyn's friskiness knew no bounds; not the Ghost Train at Blackpool's aptly named Pleasure Beach, not a photo booth at Southport's Chapel Street Station, not the outside lane of the M6, not a cramped toilet on the train from London Victoria to Gatwick Airport.

But there was one day when my libido came up against my love of cricket, and, like Lillee and Thomson coming up against David Steele in the summer of 1975, simply could not find a way through. I wanted to introduce my American girl-friend of precisely six days to a typical English county cricket match, although Lancashire v. Warwickshire turned out to be anything but typical. As an astonishing game unfolded at S&B cricket ground, Robyn kept suggesting that we might find a quiet spot for what she charmingly called 'intimacy', while I kept insisting that the cricket was too thrilling to leave. 'You mean this counts as unusually thrilling,' she said slowly, and not a little petulantly, watching as the ball was gently lobbed from wicketkeeper to slip, from slip to gully, from gully to cover, from cover to extra-cover, from extra-cover to mid-off, from mid-off back to the bowler. 'I see.'

Except that she didn't see. And I think I realised at that moment that, despite protestations from both of us that we would remain true to each other even when separated by the width of both the Atlantic and the continental United States, my lustful romance with Robyn was destined to be a short-term thing. There were simply too many cultural differences for us to be truly compatible, and rare as it was for me to encounter a woman who wanted my body so much, a 470-run partnership in 293 minutes between Alvin Kallicharran and Geoff Humpage was even rarer.

At Trafalgar Road that day, Kallicharran and Humpage established a fourth-wicket record in English cricket, the high-est for any Warwickshire wicket, and the fourth biggest stand in the history of the county championship. Moreover, Humpage scored thirteen sixes in his 254, which was the most an Englishman had ever scored in one innings. At the end of the afternoon Warwickshire declared at 523 for four, with Kallicharran on 230 not out. And yet, amazingly, Lancashire would win the match by ten wickets. They declared 109 behind after their first innings, bowled Warwickshire out cheaply, and then Graeme Fowler and David Lloyd, the same David Lloyd later to regale me with the story of one of his knackers sticking through the holes of his pink Litesome, scored 226 without loss in the second innings. Robyn was unimpressed; I was agog.

Six or seven years earlier, when I was a chubby, spotty teenager who could only dream of women like Robyn – and, to my mother's despair, quite frequently did – I let off steam physically by playing as much sport as I could fit into a day. My main cricketing buddy was a lad called Andy Boothman, who had moved into Lynton Road with his mother and step-father. My friendship with the Sykes brothers had cooled slightly since I had gone to grammar school, but in any case they weren't big cricket enthusiasts. Andy and I, by contrast, used to play for hours on my drive, using a tennis ball and the middle panels of the garage doors as notional stumps.

He was usually England and I was usually Australia, which suited me, because I liked the Aussie names more: Rick McCosker, Max Walker, Gary Gilmour, Dougie Walters, Rodney Marsh, Ashley Mallett and, of course, Lillee and Thomson. We had a complicated scoring system dictated by the narrow confines of the drive, which can't have been more than three yards wide. A nudge on to the wall of the house or the wall which divided our drive from that of Mrs Evans and Miss Oddy, two elderly sisters who lived next door, was a single. A straight drive which passed the bowler without hitting either wall was two, or four if it went through the gateposts, or six if it crossed the road and hit the garden wall of the house opposite. But an edge on to the garage doors, or a mistimed drive into Mrs Evans and Miss Oddy's front garden, was out.

We played entire Test matches that way, scrupulously keeping score, and trying to avoid following through too far on flamboyant cover drives, which would have bashed our precious Gunn & Moore bat against the wall. We had bought it jointly, at the Aladdin's Cave otherwise known as Fay's sports shop on Houghton Street, Southport. It was a size five, and it cost £6, of which I paid £4 and Andy paid £2, which meant that it was kept at my house, where I rubbed enough linseed oil into it to sink the royal yacht *Britannia*. A couple of years later, when Andy's interest in cricket began to wane (and with it our friendship) on account of his growing interest in Emerson, Lake and Palmer, I bought his stake in the bat, giving me 100 per cent ownership.

I was never, it has to be said, a talented cricketer. I was in my house team at school but then so was Roderick Butterfield, who was a celebrated brainbox but whose hand-eye co-ordination was a thing of wonder. You could throw a cricket ball to Roderick and he would bring his hands together about a yard from where it landed, and at least thirty seconds later. We therefore threw cricket balls to Roderick quite a lot. It was an immensely popular pastime.

Unfortunately for Roderick, you didn't have to be co-ordinated to play house cricket, you just had to be at school that day. Consequently, the standard of play was not high. There was always someone fielding at third man in an anorak, and in our team that someone was always Roderick. Moreover, King George V School had twelve houses, so with even half of them playing cricket on any given day, the already dilapidated boxes of kit had to stretch a long way. We wore threadbare batting gloves with curious green plastic needles attached to the backs of them, and generally had to bat wearing only one pad. Which wouldn't have mattered except that there was always someone who arrived at the crease having buckled his solitary pad to the wrong leg, and that someone, too, was always Roderick. 'Roderick, you knobhead,' was a common refrain during house cricket matches. Even one or two of the teachers manifestly thought that Roderick was a knobhead. They called him Roderick, too. As was established in chapter 1, we normally eschewed first names at KGV, and sometimes didn't even know them, but 'Roderick' seemed altogether too silly a name to ignore.

I have no doubt that Roderick is now a multi-millionaire captain of industry giving employment to at least one of his boyhood tormentors, so he gets the last laugh. On the other hand, he is a lot of laughs in deficit. At KGV, and I suppose at most schools of its type, brainpower plus sporting ineptitude was deemed even more risible than sporting ineptitude alone. Boys could be merciless even to their elders if they were known to prefer chess to cricket or rugby. I remember being a lowly second-former, and being corralled into the school hall one wet dinner time by a bunch of prefects, one of whom was a friendly but weedy fellow called Bernard. To pass the time in the hall, we had devised a game with coins loosely based on shove ha'penny, which we played on a narrow ridge on the backs of the chairs and which for some reason had been outlawed by the school authorities. That day, Bernard decided to get tough. It was a bit like Mr Barrowclough getting tough in *Porridge*. 'You boys,' he said. 'Stop playing hay pushpenny!'

We cracked up. In fact I'm cracking up now just thinking about it. And, of course, poor Bernard was never allowed to forget his slight faux pas. From that day forward, he could not hurry from one end of a corridor to the other without at least one boy, and more usually five or six boys, asking him if he was late for a hay pushpenny match.

Our other wet dinner time pursuit was the cricket game 'Owzat. Most cricket-lovers of my generation will remember it; two hexagonal lumps of metal on one of which were stamped numbers, denoting runs scored, and the fateful word 'owzat, while on the other were modes of dismissal. You kept rolling until you got an 'owzat, and then rolled the other one to find out whether you'd been caught, bowled, stumped or whatever, or indeed whether it had been a no-ball, in which case you could resume 'batting'. And if your 'Owzat was confiscated, or if you'd swapped it with Jeff Brignall for two much-thumbed copies of the naturist magazine *Health & Efficiency*, you could use two HB pencils, scoring the marks on the side with the point of a compass. Either way, with a little imagination, a careful scorer and plenty of paper, you could stage an entire Test series, which frequently we did.

But there was no substitute for playing the game. In 1978 I joined Southport Trinity Cricket Club in Roe Lane, partly in the hope of playing regularly, and partly to avail myself of a pleasingly liberal policy at the pavilion bar, where a pint of bitter cost 35p and nobody appeared to care whether you were old enough to drink it. Southport & Birkdale CC was much closer to my house, but seemed like an altogether more sober establishment. Besides, several of my schoolfriends were already members at Trinity, so I started going to Tuesday-night nets and duly found myself picked for the third XI under the captaincy of a dapper, grey-haired little man called Duncan Hodge, whose son Alec was a quick bowler for the first team.

The Trinity third team was an interesting assortment of impressionable teenagers, worldly twentysomethings and middle-aged family men. We played in division three of the South-West Lancashire League, and so, every other Saturday from April to September, not yet able to drive, I found myself in the back of a Ford Capri belonging to one of the worldly twentysomethings being driven at breakneck speed to such cricketing meccas as Billinge, or Standish, or Skelmersdale, where we always seemed to play in light drizzle.

I loved it. I loved the cricket, which was of a sufficiently patchy standard for me to acquit myself not with honours, exactly, but without embarrassing myself. I usually batted at number five or six and eked out a handful of runs before playing down completely the wrong line and losing my off stump. During the 2005 Ashes series, Geoffrey Boycott, commentating with his usual waspishness for Channel 4, memorably observed of one particular batsman, I forget who, that he had played along the Piccadilly Line when the ball had travelled down the Bakerloo Line. I was even more errant; when the ball travelled down the Bakerloo Line, I was on the Paris Metro. But it didn't really matter because even more than the cricket I loved the craic. I was sixteen, still chubby, still spotty, and my experience in sexual matters amounted to watching Jenny Agutter getting her kit off in the film *Walkabout* (for which I checked the television listings on an almost daily basis), so the thirty-five-minute drive to Standish in the company of moustachioed roustabouts, with their own girlfriends, jobs, flats and cars, was thrillingly educational.

One of them, whom for the purposes of this book I had better anoint with a pseudonym, was a lanky, cheerful Scouser called Roly Kimmage. I liked Roly immensely. He had a devil-may-care attitude to cricket of which I didn't entirely approve – and which on more than one occasion, following a couple of mid-afternoon pints, resulted in him relieving himself without actually bothering to depart the field of play. For

Roly, a slash outside off-stump meant a piss at second slip. But what he lacked in decorum he made up for in ebullient charm. He was at least ten years older than me and my contemporaries, but never treated us with the slightest condescension. And when I was appallingly sick just by the bar billiards table after seven pints of Tetley's bitter one night, it was Roly who drove me home. That he had probably had at least seven pints himself didn't seem, at the time, to detract from the nobility of the gesture; it was a long way from Roe Lane to Lynton Road.

In the company of Roly and others, I began to lose the slightly deferential reserve with which I had been brought up to treat my elders. That may or may not have been a good thing, but it certainly helped me to become part of the boisterous Saturday night scene at Trinity, and before long I was treating even members of the club executive to my particularly fine and assiduously practised impersonation of the BBC television cricket commentator Richie Benaud.

This, I should add, was some years before Benaud was a staple part of the impressionist's repertoire. We had never heard of Rory Bremner or Alistair McGowan in those days, and so my Benaud impression, complete with inscrutable side-long gaze into an imaginary camera, was considered rather a novelty. I even had a set monologue, written by me and a couple of schoolmates, in which I humorously – at least it seemed humorous at the time – summarised a day's play. And I mention this for two significant, if starkly differing, reasons. The first is that, three or four years after I joined Trinity, the pavilion was broken into and a fair amount of money stolen from the till, as well as three boxes of salt-and-vinegar crisps and, bizarrely, two bags of cockles. The police were called and cleverly worked out that it was an inside-job made to look like a break-in, whereupon it transpired that the culprit, to everyone's horror, was my friend, everyone's friend, Roly Kimmage.

Whether he was prosecuted I can't remember. Naturally he was expelled from the club and few of us ever set eyes on him again, but one night, when I was called on to do my Richie Benaud routine, I looked sidelong at my audience and said in my, or rather his, unemotional New South Walian accent: 'It's been a terrific day's cricket, with some quite wonderful performances, but it was Roly Kimmage who stole the show [a long, stagey pause] . . . not to mention three boxes of crisps and two bags of cockles.' Everyone fell about, but, satisfying as it was to provoke such mirth, I couldn't help feeling a stab of disloyalty. I didn't know why Roly had felt compelled to rob the club, but he had always been perfectly lovely to me.

The other reason I mention my Benaud impression is that, at the 1986 US Masters golf tournament, I was wandering through the Georgia pines at the breathtakingly beautiful Augusta National, when who should I almost literally bump into but the great man himself. I said a nervous hello and explained to him that I was there as a Robert Tyre Jones Jnr Memorial Scholar, on a scholarship named after Bobby Jones, the legendary amateur golfer whose conception the Masters was. Benaud expressed considerable interest in this and we had a conversation for ten minutes or so, during which I asked if he had heard how England's cricketers had got on that day in the West Indies. 'Yes,' he said, fixing me to the trunk of a pine tree with his penetrating sidelong stare, 'it's been a terrific day's cricket, with some quite wonderful performances, but it was Ian Botham who stole the show . . .'

Or words to that effect, anyway. Basically, I was being treated to my own personal Benaud monologue, the real thing, after years of dispensing an ersatz version. I didn't know whether to laugh, cry or dance a little jig of joy.

4

Maurice Flitcroft's Cheek

My love affair with golf started about the time I became besotted with football and cricket; like a man with a wife and two mistresses, I hardly knew which way to turn.

In Southport, at the heart of perhaps the finest stretch of links country in England, it was perfectly normal for kids to start playing golf at around ten or eleven. There was certainly no question of it being a snobby or elitist pursuit, which is not to say that there was no snobbery or elitism around. I can't comment on what things are like these days, but it's not wholly unfair to suggest that in the 1970s many members at Royal Birkdale, ritziest and most famous of the Southport clubs, would no sooner have welcomed a black, Asian or Jewish member than collectively urinated into the eighteenth hole. And had they been presented with the choice, the hole would have been full in no time. More recently, not least of the pleasures afforded by the dominance of Tiger Woods was the slap in the face it administered to those who even now believe that golf should be the exclusive preserve of the white middle classes. At a club I know in Yorkshire there is a member who objected when a cardboard cutout of Woods was placed outside the pro's shop. Whether his objection was sincere or tongue in cheek makes no difference; he should have been expelled forthwith, or at the very least been encouraged to sport a small swastika logo on his polo shirt.

There are certainly misconceptions about the degree of race, class and gender prejudice in golf, largely propagated by those who do not play the game. There is, in fact, rather an honourable tradition of bad-mouthing golf. Mark Twain started it, and the dyspeptic American journalist H. L. Mencken added that if he had his way, 'any man guilty of golf would be ineligible for any office of trust in the United States'. Even Winston Churchill called it 'a game whose aim is to hit a very small ball into an even smaller hole, with weapons singularly ill-designed for the purpose'.

But at least they sneered with wit, unlike those who think they're being original by taking pot shots at Pringle sweaters and Jimmy Tarbuck. That man in Yorkshire embodies an unpalatable truth, however, that the sneers aren't completely unwarranted. There is another story, quite possibly embroidered but quite possibly not, about a golf club somewhere in the Home Counties where a female member found herself sitting on the terrace overlooking the eighteenth green as a men's foursome concluded its match. One of the men had a six-foot putt to win, but missed and let off a loud volley of industrial language which so offended the woman that she complained to the club committee. The committee agreed that it was an intolerable state of affairs and something had to be done, so promptly barred women from the terrace.

Another story, which I know to be true because I was there, concerns Aldeburgh Golf Club in Suffolk. On a warm summer's day in 1999 I turned up there with a bunch of mates, intending to have a light lunch in the clubhouse before playing eighteen holes. There was hardly anyone else around, yet we were politely but firmly informed that we would not be permitted in the lounge until we were all wearing jackets and ties. Had we turned up in T-shirts, faded denims and flip-flops, then we might have expected censure. But we were all in regulation golf wear, presentable polo shirts and trousers, and moreover about to present the club with some £400 in green fees.

Anyway, there ensued a marvellous farce, in which those of us without jackets and ties in our cars were obliged to borrow from a clothing reserve kept in the secretary's office. Thus, having arrived in a pale blue polo shirt and complementary dark blue trousers, did I sit down to my leek and potato soup additionally wearing a green kipper tie, and a checked brown jacket two inches too short in the arms. We had arrived looking neat and smart and now we looked preposterous. I was reminded of an excellent cartoon by Jak, published in the *Evening Standard* in 1975, and now in the museum at Lord's. A bunch of monocled and/or moustachioed MCC members are socialising in the sacred Long Room. They are all naked but for their MCC ties. Another chap is entering the room, wearing a smart blazer over his cricket flannels, but no neck-wear. Several of the assembled throng are barking furiously in his direction, and the caption says simply: 'TIE!!!'

Like all the best cartoons it contains a kernel – or perhaps in this case a colonel – of truth. After all, sport is essentially a frivolous activity. It might borrow military phraseology – rear-guard actions, attacking formations, pincer movements, flak flying and the like – but nobody gets shot or blown up. Discipline matters less in sport than it does in the army, because sport matters less than war. Yet no regimental sergeant-major was ever as pernickety about standards of dress as some of the golf club secretaries I have come across, and the chap at Aldeburgh was a perfect example, perfectly satisfied once we had obeyed the regulations even though the eight or so of us tucking into our soup and sandwiches must have cut an eccentric spectacle. Anyone wandering into the lounge might have been forgiven for assuming that we were a convention of circus clowns on our annual golf day, about to walk splay-footedly down the fairway in a contest for the Fred Karno Cup.

Happily, such sartorial constraints did not apply at Southport Municipal in the early 1970s. It was there that I took my first ungainly swipes at a Penfold Commando golf ball, with a driver handed down to me by my cousin, David. And there, too, that I had my first golf clubs bought for me, whenever my dad had a sizeable win on the horses. Thanks to the 2.45 at Uttoxeter one Saturday afternoon in 1974, I became the proud owner of a Lee Trevino Accurist four-iron, six-iron, eight-iron and pitching-wedge. The 3.20 at Newton Abbot several months later yielded a sand wedge, and the 2.15 at Wincanton sometime in early 1975 added a three-iron, five-iron, seven-iron and nine-iron. Oddly, although the Accurists have long since been consigned to the darkest corner of the cellar (I'm far too sentimental actually to throw them away), I am to this day more comfortable with a four-iron in my hands than a five, more comfortable with an eight-iron than a nine, simply because they were the numbers I acquired first, in the pro's shop at Southport Muni more than thirty years ago.

As for the decision to buy clubs endorsed by Lee Trevino, my dad – who knew little about golf – was influenced partly by the fact that they were cheap, but also by the recollection that Trevino had won the Open Championship at Birkdale, within earshot if not quite sight of our back garden, just three years earlier. The star of that 1971 Open, however, had been Liang Huan Lu from Taiwan, who finished just one shot behind Trevino and endeared himself to the galleries by politely doffing his blue pork-pie hat in acknowledgement of their applause. He won even more friends with his second to the eighteenth hole on the final day, which hooked wildly and poleaxed a spectator, Mrs Elisabeth Tippings. Not because Mrs Tippings was unpopular, I should add, but because he was so manifestly distraught. Still, it all finished happily for Mr and Mrs Tippings, if not for Lu, who recovered from his distress but not sufficiently to make the birdie he needed to tie Trevino. Three years later, at Royal Lytham, he ran across the Tippings again and invited them to visit Taiwan at his expense. What a splendid chap.

During that 1971 Open he was known for some reason as Mr Lu, which struck me, aged nine, as immensely funny. It couldn't happen today; it would be considered condescending or even racist. Maybe it was, although Peter Alliss, who eventually succeeded his mentor Henry Longhurst as the BBC's so-called Voice of Golf, would continue unashamedly to talk about 'wily Orientals'. As recently as the 2004 Masters, blissfully oblivious to the forces of political correctness, Alliss was still referring to a golfer from the Far East, K. J. Choi, as looking 'inscrutable'.

He was thirty years too late; the heyday of crass racial stereotyping was the 1970s, when boorish Eddie Booth in the ITV sitcom *Love Thy Neighbour* could cheerfully refer, on primetime family television, to the 'nig-nogs' next door. And within a year of *Love Thy Neighbour* being pulled off the air, ITV came up with *Mind Your Language*, about a night-school class for foreigners learning English, among them a sexy Frenchwoman, a humourless German, and a libidinous Italian. Priceless. But, lest I seem too judgemental in this forensic analysis of 1970s sensibilities, I should add that I was among the thousands of kids who took home from the school playground the ditty about one of the few black men then playing top-flight football – 'Clyde Best, Cadburys took him and they covered him in chocolate!' I don't recall a rebuke from my mum or my dad, either. They probably laughed.

By the time the Open next came to Birkdale, in 1976, my dad had opened his account with the celestial bookmaker. He died in the February and the Open arrived in July, with a first-time defending champion in the quintessentially Midwestern form of Thomas Sturges Watson, a tousled Kansas City boy with a gap-toothed grin. I suppose my mum and I were still mourning my dad, whose death had been so sudden, but I don't remember setting out for Royal Birkdale to watch the Open with anything other than a song in my heart and a spring in my step. I was crazy about golf, and for the first time in my life I was going to watch the greatest players on earth in the flesh: Jack Nicklaus, Tom Watson, Johnny Miller, Lee Trevino, Gary Player and Arnold Palmer.

Some purists might contest the inclusion of Palmer in this list of the world's greatest golfers as it looked in 1976. He was forty-six years of age and more than a decade past his best. At forty-six, his great rival Jack Nicklaus would still be good enough to win the 1986 US Masters, the last of his eighteen major championships, but there was never any chance of Palmer enduring as a competitor in the way that Nicklaus would.

In three magical years from 1960 Palmer had finished second, first and first in the Open, and his swashbuckling presence had done much to restore the venerable tournament's dwindling prestige. But not since 1962 had he finished any-where near the top of the Open leaderboard, and he hadn't won any of the four majors since the Masters in 1964. His swing, never a thing of beauty and once memorably described by the novelist John Updike as looking like someone wrestling with a snake, was less comely than ever. But he remained one of the very greatest, all the same. Of all the autographs I collected at Birkdale that week, and I have them still – Arnold Palmer, Hale Irwin, Doug Sanders, Peter Oosterhuis, Nick Faldo, Ray Floyd, Tom Weiskopf, Hubert Green, Jerry Pate – Palmer's was the one I cherished most. That might have been largely because the crazy golf course in the shadow of Southport pier was named after him, and I liked the Arnold Palmer crazy golf course very much, but it was also because he was plainly the very definition of a sporting superstar.

About twenty years later I got to meet him properly. I then worked for the *Mail on Sunday*'s *Night & Day* magazine, and the editor, bless his heart and editorial budget, sent me to Florida to interview Palmer for an all-American issue he was planning. Someone else went off to interview Bruce Springsteen, and another writer was dispatched to interview Woody Allen, but I couldn't have been happier with my assignment. I went to Bay Hill, the country club in Orlando which Palmer owned, and spent a day with the great man, marvelling at the degree of reverence shown to him. It was like spending a day on Mount Olympus in the company of Zeus. In the Bay Hill dining room, I watched three middle-aged men standing in the doorway with expressions close to rapture, simply watching Palmer eat his lunch. And afterwards, as I walked the golf course with him during his regular fourball with three friends of his called Peter Kessler, Norton Baker and Sam di Giovanni, I watched a young woman come over carrying three golf clubs and visibly trembling.

'Excuse me, Mr P . . . P . . . Palmer,' she said. 'W . . . w . . . would you sign these clubs for my grandaddy in W . . . Wisconsin. It's his ninetieth birthday.'

'I'm not Arnold Palmer, honey,' said little, white-haired, sixteen-handicapper Sam di Giovanni. 'Arnie's over there.'

'Oh my God,' she shrieked. 'I can't believe I just did that. It's just that I'm so n . . . n . . . nervous.'

She looked as though she wanted the ground to open up and swallow her, and, more pertinently, as if she believed that Palmer, by snapping his fingers, could make it happen. Reassuringly, when I later phoned some of the people who knew him best, to get some more material for my article, I found that this man revered like a deity was prey to some distinctly mortal weaknesses. In his younger days, at any rate, his roving eye had been almost as famous as his Popeye arms. I called the ABC golf commentator and former Ryder Cup player Bob Rosburg, who confirmed the truth of a story I had heard but thought might be apocryphal.

Rosburg told me that he and Palmer had often shared a motel room in the early years of the US tour, and that he recalled one night in Texas being woken up by the phone ringing at about 2 a.m. Sleepily, he answered it, to hear a voice that could only be emanating from an angry redneck sitting on a rocking chair, chewing tobacco and cradling a loaded shotgun.

'Is that son of a bitch Arnold Palmer there?' snapped the voice.

Rosburg looked across to the other bed in the room. It was empty.

'Er, no, he isn't,' he said.

'Well, when he do get in, you tell him that ah'm on mah way down there, and ah'm goin' to teach him a lesson, a lesson that'll teach him not to play aroun' with mah wahfe!'

Rosburg was by now fully awake. 'I'll be sure to pass that on as soon as Arnie gets back,' he said. 'But before you do come down here to teach him a lesson, can I just say that mine's the bed by the window.'

It's a cracking story, and of course does nothing to diminish

Palmer's stature as one of the great he-men of sport. But to return to Royal Birkdale in the sweltering summer of 1976, there was a teenager playing in only his second Open Championship, having missed the thirty-six-hole cut the year before, who would, in time, eclipse even Palmer for raw charisma.

It is strange writing with hindsight about the thrilling emergence of a handsome, 19-year-old Spaniard called Severiano Ballesteros, when the same hindsight also encompasses his sad decline. In July 2002 I went to the San Roque Club near Gibraltar to interview him. It was little more than a week since he had returned an eighty-nine in the first round of the Irish Open, and to add insult to indignity, he had then been disqualified after signing for a ten that should have been, God help us, a twelve.

Before the interview he gave me a twenty-minute chipping lesson beside a practice green, first demonstrating how it ought to be done. His short game was still remarkable; it was his long game that had imploded. I watched him flip the ball maybe twenty feet high with a nine-iron, bringing it to rest as if by remote control about eight inches from the hole. Then, with the same club, he clipped the ball low, hardly more than a foot above the ground. It seemed to be shooting past the hole and I felt fleetingly embarrassed for him, but then it checked sharply and stopped almost next to the first ball. It was like watching Picasso paint, Nureyev leap, or Ted Rogers do that 3-2-1 thing with his fingers. Genius at work.

Later, he spent the first five minutes of my private audience talking about how I might improve my short game, maybe to divert the conversation from what I wanted to discuss, which was his disintegration as a golfer, not my improvement. But eventually I was able to broach it, and he told me that he and his brother Vincente thought they had solved the problem, explaining at some length how. As it soon turned out, alas, they hadn't.

Ballesteros also gave me a fascinating insight into games-manship on the golf course, telling me that Tiger Woods intimidated other players much as he had in his heyday. 'Tiger has that hard look in his eyes that I used to have. In matchplay, or medal play, when you say "good luck", you look straight into their eyes, and give them a kind of message. Your deter-mination, your desire, your willpower, it is all in the eyes. And you know on the first tee whether the other guy feels intimi-dated. Some, like Raymond Floyd, Jack Nicklaus, Tom Watson, Paul Azinger, never did. But others you keep an eye on, looking for their weaknesses. For example, if he is a quick player, you walk slowly.'

In 1976, such ploys were not yet part of his repertoire. Nor was the pronunciation of his name part of ours. It is strange to recall that what is now so familiar then seemed so bewilder-ingly foreign, like Martina Navratilova's name around the same time. But Severiano Ballesteros was clearly a name that we were all going to have to learn. After two rounds of sixty-nine he led the Open by two shots, and held the same advantage, despite a third-round seventy-three, going into the final day.

Little-known players have led and even won the Open since then – notably Ben Curtis at Royal St George's in 2003 – but not at the age of nineteen, not as dashingly or as fearlessly, and not so obviously as a presage of things to come. Few people in any sport have burst into the limelight quite as spectacularly as Ballesteros did that week. And any suggestions that it might have been a fluke were obliterated a week later when he won the Dutch Open, swiftly followed by the Lancôme Trophy (in which, symbolically, he resisted a final-day charge by Palmer in one of the veteran's last hurrahs). Seve – as we would mercifully learn to call him – won the Order of Merit that year having effectively given the rest of the European Tour half a season's head start.

But it was on the last day at Birkdale that he announced his genius. He was paired with Johnny Miller, who overtook him in the course of a brilliant final-round sixty-six and eventually won by a comfortable six-shot margin. Ballesteros would shoot a seventy-four, his worst round of the week, but for twelve holes, more significantly, it seemed certain to be very much worse; he played the last six holes in five under par and arrived at the tough par-4 eighteenth needing a four to tie for second place with the great Jack Nicklaus.

The odds were very much against him when, like Mr Lu five years earlier, he erred with his second shot, leaving it short and left of the green, with two bunkers between him and the flagstick. A lofted wedge-shot seemed like the only option, but it would be fiendishly difficult to stop the ball close to the hole. Everyone thought that he would have to settle for joint third place, alongside Raymond Floyd.

Everyone but Ballesteros. The youngster sized up his situation, and then hit a low bump-and-run chip so audacious and unexpected that those of us in the crowd immediately groaned, feeling sure that he must have mis-hit it. He hadn't, of course. It was merely the first significant demonstration of a startling talent around the green that, as I saw for myself at San Roque, would survive even years later when the rest of his game was assailed by demons. The ball skipped forward between the two bunkers, almost as if tugged by a piece of string, and came to rest about four feet from the hole, leaving a holeable putt that was duly, boldly, holed.

'It's not possible,' grunted Henry Longhurst in the commentary box. But by the time Seve won the Open, three years later at Royal Lytham & St Annes, we knew that impossible shots were his speciality. It wasn't like the arrival of Tiger Woods on the scene two decades later; from the very beginning we knew the Spaniard's game had imperfections. But nobody has ever thrilled the crowds quite like Seve did.

At Birkdale, he received his runners-up cheque for £5250 with me watching, admiringly, from the grandstand. I had been at the Open throughout the championship and on the practice days too, scrounging tickets from those leaving early. It was a school week but my mate Andy Boothman and I got home as soon as we could and legged it to the course, even giving up the opportunity to watch telly coverage of the third Test match between England and the West Indies forty miles away at Old Trafford. This was perhaps as well, because England's cricketers were thoroughly humiliated in Manchester, losing by 435 runs after being bowled out for a miserable seventy-one in their first innings. Michael Holding did most of the damage, taking five for seventeen in less than fifteen overs, although England's batting line-up of Edrich, Close, Pocock, Steele, Woolmer, Hayes, Greig, Knott, Underwood, Selvey and Hendrick sadly meant that the bowler was at no point Holding the batsman's Willey. I suppose he might have been Holding the batsman's Pocock, but it doesn't work quite as well.

At Birkdale, England's cricketing shame greatly amused Lee Trevino. Feeling a kind of kinship with him on account of my Accurist golf clubs, I followed him round like a poodle, albeit with several hundred other poodles, and yapped delightedly along with everyone else as he embarked on what was basically a four-hour stand-up comedy routine, mostly aimed at the bewildering game of cricket. On the second tee he buttonholed some spectator – how I wished it had been me – and asked him to explain what was happening at Old Trafford.

'So let me get this straight,' he said, as he teed his ball up.

'England has eleven players who scored seventy-one runs in total and this West Indian guy Greenidge has scored seventy-one all on his own?' He then hit the ball with a resounding thwack, and watched it sail low from left to right, ending up in the middle of the fairway about 270 yards yonder. 'Man, England must be real bad at cricket. But you English invented it, right?' He gave a gleeful cackle, and so it continued for the rest of his round, with scarcely a pause in the chatter even on his backswing. He must have been hell to play with. In fact, the story goes that in some tournament or other he was paired with Tony Jacklin, who arrived on the first tee and said, 'I really don't want to talk today, Lee.'

'That's OK, Tony,' came the reply. 'All you have to do is listen.'

The huddle to hear what is being said on the tee is an essential part of the spectating experience at golf tournaments. But very rarely is anything said that is actually worth hearing, not that you'd know it from the gales of laughter when Phil Mickelson or someone cracks a lame joke. At least Trevino was genuinely entertaining. These days, devoted fan of the game though I continue to be, I sometimes wonder why it is such a popular spectator sport. After all, it is hard to see more than a fraction of what is going on, and any sporting event at which periscopes are on sale just inside the gate is perhaps to be regarded with suspicion.

Mind you, the periscopes have come on a bit since I first bought one, at Birkdale in 1976. My periscope was a flimsy cardboard affair, with two artfully angled mirrors, of the kind my mother used when she applied her lipstick, wedged at the top and bottom. It cost £1 and carried the logo of a tobacco company, I think Benson & Hedges. By contrast, those I saw for sale at the 2002 Ryder Cup at The Belfry cost £30, and were sleek metallic jobs, miniature versions of the kind you might find on nuclear submarines. No matter how sophisticated the periscopes, though, there's no escaping the fact that you're still watching the action through a mirror. And even if you do manage to get to the front of the gallery beside a green or a tee, there is always the nagging suspicion that all the excitement might be unfolding elsewhere. Indeed, to walk across a golf course during an event such as the Open Championship is to overhear meticulous strategies being planned that would not disgrace a military campaign.

'Right, we'll stay by the fourth tee until Darren Clarke comes through, then we'll follow him to the tenth, by which time Ernie Els should be teeing off, so we'll wait for him by the tenth green, then find a slot near those bunkers on the sixteenth, just in case anything happens there, then we'll circle back under the cover of darkness, dynamite the bridge and catch the Boche when the bastards are least expecting it.' Or words to that effect.

As for the phenomenon of spectators laughing fit to burst when a competitor says or does something faintly tittersome, it is not, in fairness, confined to golf. The worst malefactors I have come across in this regard are the crowds at the Wimbledon Lawn Tennis Championships, of which more later in these pages. If an errant pigeon lands on Centre Court for a moment or two, then there is an explosion of laughter such as you might hear at a Billy Connolly show at the Glasgow Empire. And if a player hands his racquet to a ball girl, implying that she might be able to do better with it, then the St John's Ambulance Brigade is put on standby to carry out people who have ruptured themselves by laughing so hard. It's a curious business.

In 1984, just to skip forward a few years, I had a small taste of this myself. I was by then a modern history student at St Andrews University, and had a casual bet with some friends that I could get myself on to the practice ground at the Open, posing as a player. I borrowed a large, professional-looking golf bag, recruited my flatmate Dominic to act as my caddie, affected the right kind of swagger, and got through the main gates without a problem. It was Wednesday, the final practice day before the championship began. With far more care than I ever lavished on essays about the economic policies of Franklin D. Roosevelt, I had constructed a cunning plan. Although there was a security man checking badges at the entrance to the practice ground, I had arranged to have a conversation with a friend close enough for him to hear. My friend had gamely offered to wear a turquoise polo shirt and red trousers, so that he looked passably like either a pimp or a professional golfer.

My caddie and I made our way towards the practice ground; impassively, the security guy watched us coming. Then, just before we reached him, I 'noticed' my friend, and stopped for a chat.

'Hi George,' I said. 'Have you played yet?'

'Yeah, went out with Canizares and Aoki,' he said. 'I had a bit of a problem with my putting stroke, but Aoki helped me out. Said I was taking back the putter head a bit too sharply. How 'bout you?'

'Oh, I'm just going to hit a few medium irons,' I said, breezily. 'I've got a practice round later with Hale Irwin and Nick Price. Maybe see you tonight.'

And with that, the security guard smilingly stood aside, all but tugging his forelock, and allowed Dom and me on to the practice ground. To our right, lining the fence, were hundreds of spectators who were perfectly content just to watch the players hitting balls. Among them was another stooge, my good friend Angus MacLeod, who called me over to sign his autograph book. 'You won't remember me,' he said, 'but we were at school together.' This was a lie; we hadn't gone to school together, although we had gone to the pub together the night before. 'Oh, right,' I said. 'How are you getting on?'

'Not as well as you,' he said, and we bantered, not very amusingly, for the next few minutes, while the twenty or thirty people around him chuckled with delight. It was fascinating to experience life, quite literally, on the other side of the fence. No comedian ever had an audience as indulgent as that enjoyed by a professional golfer bantering with the gallery. Not, of course, that I was a professional golfer. But they thought I was, and that was enough. I suppose that most pro golfers, like most tennis players at Wimbledon, seem so blink-ered in pursuit of glory that the slightest evidence of a sense of humour is seized on by fans like a hungry dog seizes on a bone. It relieves the tension.

I scribbled twenty or thirty autographs, leaving the fans none the wiser as to my identity, then sent my caddie to get a bucket of balls and strode off purposefully to the practice green, which for a glorious few minutes I shared with only two other players: Greg Norman and Bernhard Langer.

After some embarrassingly erratic putting, even for a man who skipped lectures on a regular basis to play golf, I felt a tap on my shoulder. I steeled myself for, at best, a ticking-off. But in fact it was a journalist from an American golfing magazine, wanting to quiz me about my prospects in the Open. Unsurprisingly, he didn't recognise me. He assumed that I was a rank outsider, and frankly he was right, although he didn't know quite how rank. He asked whether I truly thought I stood a chance of lifting the Claret Jug at the close of Sunday afternoon. I smiled. I would, I replied modestly, be happy simply to make the thirty-six-hole cut. 'Absolutely fucking delirious, I should think,' muttered my caddie, with unneces-sary irreverence.

Maurice Flitcroft's Cheek

When the golf writer asked my name I gave him that of David Ridley; I had found him on a list of qualifiers in that morning's paper, and thought him suitably obscure. Dom and I then strolled over to the fleet of courtesy cars, and again I gave my name as David Ridley. He was duly crossed off an official list while we were given a car, with an attractive blonde driver called Carol, who undertook to take us wherever we wanted to go. I wondered how far I might take this student prank. To Edinburgh fifty-odd miles away, perhaps, for a night out? Or just to the Dunvegan Hotel, my local, a thinned nine-iron shot from the eighteenth green? I also wondered what might happen if the real David Ridley turned up to claim his car? Would he be unveiled as an impostor?

Carol chauffeured us slowly out of the practice ground, whereupon Angus, the stooge in the crowd, ran over to the car waving his programme. He was followed, Pied Piper-like, by a small posse of young autograph-hunters, who clearly thought there was someone in the car with a scribble worth having. I buzzed the window down to oblige them. For a minute or two there was quite a melee, and out of the corner of my eye I saw Johnny Miller, whom I had watched winning the Open eight years earlier, walking towards us. He peered into the car, a half-smile on his face, plainly expecting to see Tom, Jack or Seve rather than any Tom, Dick or Harry. The half-smile vanished, and was replaced by a look of puzzlement as this wholly un-familiar yet clearly immensely popular young player whizzed off into the sunset. Or at any rate into the bar of the Dunvegan, where there awaited more free pints of heavy than I care to remember, or indeed, the next morning, could remember.

For years afterwards I told this story to anyone even vaguely interested in golf, one of whom was a very senior man indeed – who had better remain nameless here – on the *Independent*. In 1999, when I was sent by the paper to cover the Open at Carnoustie, he suggested that I might get a decent story out of trying to repeat my prank of 1984.

I was more than a little apprehensive; a student prank is one thing, but by now I was a fully fledged sports writer, who could be summarily stripped of my accreditation and sent home. Moreover, I had grown into a responsible father of three, whose student impulse to cock a snook at authority had greatly receded. Still, an assignment is an assignment, and the notion that every barred entrance represents a challenge is as valid among journalists as it is among students. So, on the penultimate practice day, I borrowed a big bag of clubs from an obliging man at the Callaway stand in the tented village, alerted the *Independent*'s excellent sports photographer, David Ashdown, to my intentions, and set off to storm the practice ground again.

This time I was accompanied by a different caddie, my friend Graham, a well-known Scottish sports writer. Like Dominic in 1984, Graham found the perfect hangdog countenance; professional caddies always look as though they have the woes of the world on one shoulder, perhaps to counterbalance the enormous bag on the other. And sure enough, simply by looking as though we belonged, we strode through the gate and into the company of Ernie Els and José-Maria Olazabal, who were striking balls in the general direction of Norway.

There was a spare bay between them, and Graham urged me to take it. My jolly jape fifteen years earlier had stopped short of actually striking balls. There had been a slot available alongside Seve Ballesteros, who went on to win the championship in typical toreador-like fashion, but I'd convinced myself that my occasional shank, an ugly shot whereby the ball squirts off the clubface almost at right angles, might have given the game away. More seriously, it might also have injured Seve, drastically altering the course of golfing history.

This time, however, egged on by Graham, there was no chickening out. He rolled me a ball and handed me a five-wood. It was metal wood, that great golfing oxymoron, habitually referred to by Seve as 'a mental wood'. I took a long, deep breath and stepped forward between Olazabal and Els. The grandstand overlooking the practice ground was packed, and for all the formidable diversions on offer, there were bound to be some people watching me. I wiggled. And waggled. And swung. There was a resounding 'tink' as metal wood connected with ball. I looked up. The ball was flying, arrow-straight, into the blue yonder. Its course never wavered, and it eventually fell to earth what seemed like minutes later. Graham managed to stifle a cry of amazement, then burst out laughing. He offered me another ball, but I knew that I had been only fleetingly touched by the golfing gods. There would be no repeating that shot. Meanwhile, I heard an elderly Scotsman in the crowd say to his wife, 'It's just incredible how well these guys hit the ball, isn't it?' It was eminently possible that he was referring to Ernie rather than me, but, gloriously, I have never known for sure.

Later that day, I wrote an account of my caper for the next day's paper, setting it in the context of what had happened in 1984. About a week later, a colleague on the sports desk contacted me. 'We've had a phone call from a guy called David Ridley,' he said. 'He wants you to call him.'

The chickens, birdies and eagles had come home to roost. Tentatively, I called Ridley, who was by then the pro at Coxmoor Golf Club in Nottinghamshire. He was graciousness itself, and said he'd been highly amused by the tale of how I had stolen his name. It had also solved a 15-year-old mystery, he told me, because he had indeed been denied a courtesy car on that Wednesday afternoon in July 1984.

'They looked at their list and said "But you've already gone",' he told me. 'I said "How can I have gone when I'm still here?"' But the woman in charge of the courtesy cars was adamant. So in the end, while the fake David Ridley was downing his umpteenth pint in the Dunvegan, before vomiting copiously into a gutter on the way home, the real one was swallowing only his pride by having to ask the South African golfer David Frost if he could share his car.

It was an amusing deception, but nothing like as accomplished as that perpetrated by Maurice Flitcroft, the godfather of golfing hoaxers, in 1976. Somehow or other, Flitcroft, a crane driver from Barrow-in-Furness, managed to slip through the screening process to land a place in the final qualifying round for that year's Open. At least I was a golfer of some modest ability; Flitcroft was an absolute duffer. But once he'd started his qualifying round he was permitted to continue, doubtless in accordance with some arcane rule or other, and eventually completed the eighteen holes – at Formby, a few miles south of Southport – in 121 strokes, a majestic forty-nine over par. According to Pat Ward-Thomas, the *Guardian*'s distinguished golf correspondent, it was a round 'marred by only one par'. For my friends and me, Maurice Flitcroft became an instant hero.

But if the 1970s was the heyday of Open Championship hoaxes, so was it the heyday, rather more significantly, of the Open itself. I have already championed the seventies as the golden age of the FA Cup on the basis that the grand old trophy was captured by several unfashionable clubs, including Sunderland and Southampton of the Second Division. Precisely the opposite applies to the Claret Jug. What made the seventies the greatest of golfing decades was the stature of its Open champions: from 1970, the list goes Jack Nicklaus, Lee Trevino, Trevino again, Tom Weiskopf, Gary Player, Tom Watson, Johnny Miller, Watson again, Nicklaus again, Seve Ballesteros.

All those men, with the exception of Weiskopf, had won, or would win, more major championships. Many more, in most cases. And Weiskopf, at least, was widely reckoned to have the finest swing in the game. With the greatest of respect, there is nobody on that list like a Paul Lawrie, a Ben Curtis or a Todd Hamilton, all unfancied outsiders who undoubtedly played splendidly to win in, respectively, 1999, 2003 and 2004, yet also owed their success, irrefutably, to the mistakes of others (albeit, in Lawrie's case, to the mistakes of another outsider, the hapless Frenchman Jean Van de Velde). In most other sports I am happy to root for the underdog. It was great to see eleven Todd Hamiltons in the form of Sunderland FC winning the 1973 FA Cup against eleven Tiger Woodses in the form of Leeds. But the best and most memorable Opens – such as those in 1970, 1977, 1979, and more recently when Tiger Woods twice won by a street at St Andrews – are those won by colossi of the game.

Of course, there's more to golf than the Open, and from a British perspective it could be argued that the seventies was a thoroughly forgettable decade. It is true that the seeds of future triumph in the Ryder Cup were sown in 1979 when the Great Britain and Ireland team was permitted to include continental Europeans, but the American stranglehold was not broken until 1985. It is also true that Tony Jacklin won the 1970 US Open having won our Open the year before, but that marvellous double represented a rare oasis in a particularly arid wilderness. Jacklin was the only Brit to win even one major between Max Faulkner, in 1951, and Sandy Lyle, in 1985.

In 1973, during the first round of that year's Open at Royal Troon, I watched the television coverage of Faulkner playing with 71-year-old Gene Sarazen on the day that Sarazen, who'd won the competition in 1932 when even Faulkner was only a lad of sixteen, holed out with a five-iron on the par-3 eighth hole, the so-called Postage Stamp. I was eleven years of age and remember thinking even then how marvellous it was that these old-timers should still be playing at such an exalted level, a feeling compounded the following day when tubby little Sarazen, whose height was matched by his circumference, holed his second shot at the Postage Stamp from a greenside bunker. He had taken a total of three strokes to play a par-3 hole twice, and hadn't required his putter at all, an achievement that nobody else in a field that included Nicklaus, Miller, Player and Trevino, even came close to emulating. There are some who consider it one of golf's frailties that those of pensionable age should be able to compete alongside the young superstars: I think it is one of the game's glories.

As for Faulkner, in 2001 I travelled down to West Chiltington Golf Club in West Sussex to interview him, fifty years after he had won the Open at Royal Portrush in Northern Ireland. He was eighty-five years old and in fine fettle apart from a dreadful dose of the shakes, a genetic disease called familial tremors. The barman set a pint of bitter down in front of him which he proceeded to sup like a horse from a trough; then, when he had downed half of it, the shakes miraculously stopped and he was able to pick up the glass by the handle. 'After a pint and a half I'm cured for five hours,' he growled. 'Otherwise I'm wobbling like hell.'

He was wonderful company. I'm often asked what sporting interview I have enjoyed the most from the 300-plus that I have conducted, and my afternoon with old Max Faulkner – now no longer with us, alas – definitely belongs in the top three or four. Not least of the attractions was his defiant political incorrectness. He had been, for example, contemptuous of the decision to allow 'continentals' – initially, two Spaniards and a German – to join the British and Irish contingent in the

Ryder Cup. 'Two from the Armada and one from the ruddy Luftwaffe,' he snorted. Even Peter Alliss would have baulked at that one.

He was in thrall to nobody's reputation. I asked whether he had ever played with Nicklaus, and he looked at me fiercely. 'No, I didn't. Didn't bloody care to, either. In Boston one time he came down the clubhouse steps in such a bloody huff that he knocked into me and nearly knocked me into the flowerbed. I thought, "Christ, you rude bastard." That really made me cross.'

I laughed uneasily, like a courtier at Versailles in the company of a respected sage who was daring to knock Louis XIV. For me, Nicklaus had always been the nonpareil, above criticism. My cousin Stuart had given me his book *Golf My Way* for my thirteenth birthday, and I had made it my bible. I read passages before going to sleep, and passages when I awoke, having dreamt about passages in between. On the cover there was a picture of Nicklaus in his familiar crouched putting style, and behind him a group of about fifteen spectators. I got to know every one of those spectators' faces as well as I knew my own. Better, given the fresh spots that were appearing on my forehead and chin every morning. And I aped the Nicklaus swing in every way I could. The preliminary glance at the spot just ahead of the ball, the little tilt of his head to the right, I copied every nuance of it, which made it all the more mystifying when the ball came to rest behind a tree or in a bush scarcely thirty yards from where I had struck it.

Still, in October 1976, two weeks before my fifteenth birthday, I broke 100 for the first time: a ninety-seven at Southport Muni that could so easily have been a ninety-six if I'd remembered Jack's tip (on page 238 of *Golf My Way*) to keep the head steady over the line of a putt. And the following summer

I went on my first golfing holiday, to Scotland, with my mum and my friend Andy Boothman.

While my dad was alive, we'd always had an annual foreign holiday. Whatever the state of the family finances, and they were often parlous, enough money was always found for a week on the Costa Brava or in Majorca. But after he died, with my mum struggling to keep the business ticking over on her own, resources became much tighter. A holiday in Spain was out of the question. But she decided that summer that she could stretch to a week in Scotland, during which I could play golf with Andy, while she would take herself off for long walks and lose herself in the novels of Georgette Heyer.

But first we had to get there. My mum hadn't driven while my dad was alive because he discouraged her to learn, reckoning in the chauvinist spirit of the times that driving was the husband's job. The term 'male chauvinism' has these days been replaced by 'sexism', but whatever you want to call it, there's no doubt that it is greatly diminished compared with the 1970s. In 1975, for example, Jenny Pitman walked into the Jockey Club's plush headquarters in Portman Square, wondering whether the horse-racing establishment would deign to grant her a trainer's licence. The establishment did, as it turned out, but she'd had good cause to wonder; it wasn't all that long since Norah Wilmot's application had been turned down with the memorable edict: 'Women are not persons within the meaning of the Rules.'

Whatever, my dad's failure to see that there was any point in my mum learning to drive meant that following his death, as well as dealing with her grief, with the business, and with me, which wasn't exactly a win treble, she had also had to learn how to reverse round a corner and perform an emergency stop. She passed her driving test first time and my admiration for her, looking back, is unbounded. But I should also add that she was a rotten driver. When I passed my test a few years later, she told me that I should expect around fifteen minor accidents in my first twelve months behind the wheel, that being the national average. In fact, it was only her average.

In her Ford Escort, though, she somehow got us up to Scotland without having to call on her emergency stop. We stayed in a small hotel in Auchterarder, Perthshire, just down the road from the somewhat grander Gleneagles Hotel. To save money the three of us all slept in one room – which must have been a tricky arrangement, and perhaps gave rise to a few eyebrows behind reception, although I can't say I remember any awkwardness.

The highlight of the week was a trip to the holy of holies, St Andrews, to play the Old Course. My mum had booked us a starting time of 1.10 p.m., but the journey from Auchterarder took us longer than she'd expected, and then she found herself unable to park in the auld (and rather crooded) toun, so by the time Andy and I pitched up at the starter's hut to pay our green fees, a quaint-sounding £7 each, it was five minutes after our starting time. The starter, a large, ferocious-looking man with a cruel moustache, told us with an air of palpable satisfaction that we were too late, we'd missed our tee-off time.

Distraught, we slunk back to where my mum was carefully manouevring the Escort through a thirty-seven-point turn to tell her the bad news. A thunderous expression settled on her face and, leaving the car at an even more eccentric angle to the kerb than usual, she strode purposefully over to the starter's hut. I knew from painful personal experience that she could be alarmingly fierce when she felt the need. On the other hand, the starter looked like someone who ate Sassenachs for break-fast. It promised to be an encounter between an immovable object and an irresistible force, but it turned out that their exchange, which Andy and I watched from a safe distance, was hardly even a contest. She marched back to where we were standing. 'You can play now,' she said, shortly. We returned to the hut, where the man seemed to have been shorn, if not of his cruel moustache, then certainly of his ferocious look. He took our £14 without a word, handed us our scorecards, and then said, almost timorously: 'Next time, tell your mother not to bully the starter.'

So that was the memorable beginning to my inaugural round of golf on the Old Course, a course I would get to know and love, although like many before and since, I wondered on first acquaintance what all the fuss was about. As for that particular starter, he was still there – guarding the first tee as snarlingly as Cerberus the many-headed dog of Greek legend guarded the gates of Hades – when I arrived to study at the ancient university four years later. I often wondered whether I should remind him of the day he met his match, in the form of my furious mother, but sensibly never did. He still looked like he ate Sassenachs for breakfast, and I had no reason to doubt the story I heard about his encounter with a Frenchman who turned up one day desperately hoping for a chance to play the world's most famous links.

'Excuse me,' said the Frenchman, in decent but heavily accented English. 'Ees eet possible for me to play today on ze Old Course?'

The starter looked disdainfully at him, then talked into the microphone which conveyed his voice through a loudspeaker to those waiting on the first tee.

'Play away noo, Mr McTavish,' he boomed. He turned back to the Frenchman. 'Ye'll nae get on the course today,' he barked. 'The R&A have it booked right through.'

'Zen perhaps tomorrow?' asked the Frenchman, brightly.

'Hold on,' snapped the starter, and leant over his microphone again. 'Play away noo, Mr Mackenzie,' he bellowed.

He looked at the Frenchman and sighed. 'There's a starting time at 7.05 a.m. tomorrow. What's your name?'

'Fouquet,' said the Frenchman.

'Play away noo, Mr Kirkbride,' thundered the starter. And then looked suspiciously at the Frenchman.

'How are you spelling that?'

'F-O-U-Q-U-E-T.'

The starter's eyes narrowed even further. 'Right, you've a 7.05 starting time tomorrow morning, Mr, er, Fouquet,' he said. In his strong north-east Fife accent, Fouquet rhymed disconcertingly with bucket. Monsieur Fouquet turned away, delighted.

'But just one thing, Mr Fuckit,' barked the starter.

'Yes?' said Monsieur Fouquet.

'When you come back in the morning, you'll answer to the name of Patterson!'

Whatever the truth of that story, I know for a fact that my mother's confrontation with the St Andrews starter was not the only tussle on a Scottish golf course in the summer of 1977. There was also the small matter of Jack Nicklaus and Tom Watson trading blows, or at least birdies, in the most remarkable Open Championship that anyone could remember. Even now, even in the age of Tiger Woods, the quality of the golf they played at Turnberry beggars belief. And because there were no British players to root for, it being after the decline of Tony Jacklin and before the rise of Nick Faldo, Sandy Lyle and Ian Woosnam, partisanship did not cloud the issue. There was hardly such a thing as a British or European golf fan in those days, we were just golf fans. And here was the greatest player who had ever lived, Nicklaus, playing at the height of his mountainous ability yet still unable to suppress the young pretender to his crown at least as the greatest player of the age, 27-year-old Watson.

A few months earlier, the same pair had grappled for a green jacket. At the Masters, Watson had started the final day three shots ahead of Nicklaus, whereupon Nicklaus shot a sixty-six. It was brilliant stuff, but not brilliant enough. Watson shot sixty-seven to win by two. At Turnberry, over the first three days, both men shot identical scores: seventy, sixty-eight and sixty-five. Only at the very end did Watson nudge ahead, shooting a second consecutive sixty-five to Nicklaus's sixty-six. Who came third is a nice trivia question. It was that year's US Open champion Hubert Green, finishing on 279, a score which had been good enough for Johnny Miller to win at Birkdale the previous summer by six shots. Yet in this Open, Green lagged eleven shots behind Watson, ten behind Nicklaus. So much for 'open', as Green later acknowledged. 'I won the tournament I played in,' he said. 'They were playing in something else.'

In front of the telly in Southport I was riveted. These days, when I watch videos of championship golf in the 1970s, it's hard not to be distracted by the crimes against fashion, even though they weren't considered criminal at the time. At Turnberry that day, Nicklaus wore bright yellow, and Watson pale green, and looking back you can't help thinking that the manufacturers of Opal Fruits missed a hell of a marketing opportunity. But at the time it seemed entirely fitting that bright colours should adorn what quickly became known as 'the Duel in the Sun'.

There are only a handful of events which have so transcended their sport, or even transcended sport itself, that they are known by names which give no particular clue to what was being contested. The 1970s specialised in this phenomenon: the Rumble in the Jungle, the Thrilla in Manila, the Duel in the Sun. But what also lends immortality to these occasions, what makes them a spectacle that those of us who weren't there will never forget, is classic television commentary. And having gently knocked Peter Alliss earlier in this chapter for being, shall we say, something of a reactionary, I crave your indulgence in paying tribute here to his pitch-perfect professionalism.

The seventy-second hole in that 106th Open will be remembered for as long as the Turnberry Hotel stands, and probably beyond. Watson, leading by a shot, was the first to tee off, and knocked an iron straight down the middle. Nicklaus, knowing he needed a birdie to have any chance, pulled out his driver. When uncharacteristically he pushed his shot into the right-hand rough, adjacent to an unfriendly gorse bush, his chance appeared to have disappeared. And while he contemplated his predicament, Watson seemingly nailed him with one of the great Open Championship shots, a superb seven-iron to the side of the hole.

'Elementary, my dear Watson,' remarked Alliss, finding the perfect four words for the moment. It was a line he could have used on any number of occasions that week, but he had held it back, and here was his reward. As a small aside, in July 2005, following the death of James Doohan, the actor who played Scotty, the chief engineer of *Star Trek*'s *Starship Enterprise*, I wrote that *Star Trek*'s most famous catchphrase, worked into every newspaper report of Doohan's death and not a few of the headlines, was 'Beam me up, Scotty.' In fact, although the show certainly yielded many catchphrases, and Scotty himself rarely got to the end of an episode without saying 'She'll not take much more, Captain', not one of the 432-strong crew of the *Enterprise* (strangely we only ever saw about eight of them) ever uttered precisely those words, 'Beam me up, Scotty.' It was an urban or at any rate an intergalactic myth. 'Beam us up, Mr Scott,' was the closest they got.

In response to this a number of *Independent* readers wrote

in with their own favourite misquotes, and the one mentioned most was 'Elementary, my dear Watson.' Apparently Sherlock Holmes said 'elementary' quite a lot, and 'my dear Watson' quite a lot, but not once, in any of Arthur Conan Doyle's stories, did he combine the two. So one of golf's most celebrated one-liners actually celebrates a misquote. Not that it matters in the slightest, but I thought you'd like to know. In any case, Alliss had still picked the *mots justes*, as Monsieur Fouquet might have said: Watson really had made an extraordinarily difficult shot, given the pressurised circumstances, look remarkably easy.

It helped, of course, that Nicklaus wasn't exactly in an ideal position from which to make a birdie. On the other hand, he was the most formidable competitor golf had ever known. He ripped into an eight-iron, tearing the ball from the heavy grass, and somehow muscled it on to the green, albeit at least thirty feet from the pin. When Watson reached the green, he looked at the exceptionally difficult putt confronting Nicklaus, and then he looked at Nicklaus. He knew better than anyone the preternatural mental strength of the man, and told his caddie, Alfie Fyles, that he had to assume Nicklaus would hole the putt. Fyles, a wily old rascal from Southport whom I would get to know a few years later, paying him in ale for his stories, muttered, 'I expect him to, sir.' And, of course, Nicklaus did, miraculously making the birdie he knew he required, thereby leaving Watson with only one putt to win, rather than two. But it was short, and he was fearless, and in it went, to conclude the finest Open Championship since old Willie Park played the twelve-hole course at Prestwick in fifty-five, fifty-nine and sixty to win the inaugural 1860 championship by two from Old Tom Morris. Sadly, Peter Alliss wasn't at the microphone that year. I think it must have been Henry Longhurst.

5

JPR's Sideburns

If I had to pick the most memorable bits of commentary from the most memorable sporting decade, then 'Elementary, my dear Watson' by Peter Alliss would rank highly, and there would certainly be an honourable mention for John Motson's 'That's it! Everton have beaten Liverpool, Andy King the scorer. Seven is his number, and seven years it is since this last happened . . . Liverpool's run of twenty-three league games unbeaten is over!'

But pride of place would unquestionably go to Clifford Isaac Morgan, who, in the course of twenty-five seconds at Cardiff Arms Park on 27 January 1973, uttered, with increasing excitement, the following words: 'Kirkpatrick . . . to Bryan Williams . . . this is great stuff . . . Phil Bennett covering . . . chased by Alistair Scown . . . brilliant . . . oh, that's brilliant . . . John Williams . . . Pullin . . . John Dawes, great dummy . . . David, Tom David, the half-way line . . . brilliant by Quinnell . . . this is Gareth Edwards . . . a dramatic start . . . what a score!'

When you read those words, they don't really add up to

much. When you hear them in Morgan's Welsh lilt, however, getting louder and louder, they still make the spine stiffen and the mind swim with unforgettable images. The occasion was a Barbarians v. All Blacks match still touted as the most scintillating eighty minutes of rugby union ever played. And in January 2003 the approaching thirtieth anniversary of the Barbarians' 23-11 victory struck me as an ideal opportunity for some shameless nostalgia in the pages of the *Independent*.

I phoned Morgan (who'd been an outstanding outside-half capped twenty-nine times by Wales between 1951 and 1958, and was the most luminous star of the triumphant Lions tour to South Africa in 1955, before joining the BBC where he not only rose to become Head of Outside Broadcasts but was also – respect – one of the original team captains on *A Question of Sport*) and asked whether I could use the anniversary as an excuse to interview him. 'Oh, it was nothing to do with me,' he said, adding that he was seventy-two and had nothing of interest to say any more. After some gentle pleading on my part, he finally agreed to meet me, and, of course, it turned out that he had nothing to say that wasn't of interest.

We met at the Landmark Hotel in London, just round the corner from his flat. A regrettable legacy of a dazzling sporting career was a pair of wrecked knees, and he walked with tremendous discomfort downstairs to the bar, sank gratefully into an armchair, fixed me with sympathetic brown eyes that had clearly seen it all, and told me to fire away. 'That match in 1973 . . .' I began. He needed no more prompting. 'I have always regarded that match as one of the great privileges of my life,' he said. Tragically, throat cancer would later claim the glorious Rhondda voice, but at the time, unlike the Rhondda knees, it was still undiminished by age. 'The commentary should have been done by Bill McLaren, the greatest,' he added, 'but he couldn't do it. And the game had everything. It had all the qualities of an exhibition game, yet great toughness, and both sides wanted to win.'

I apologised for asking a trite, predictable question that he had doubtless been asked a thousand times before; on the other hand, it had to be asked. Where did he place the Edwards try in the pantheon of all the great tries he had seen, and indeed scored?

'Well, I suppose it has been watched more than any other try in history,' he mused. 'I have seen other fabulous tries, but this was a great team try, Bennett starting it off in his own twenty-five, with adventure. A famous Welsh writer, Alun Richards, once said that there were two sorts of fly half in Wales, the chapel fly half and the church fly half. Barry John was a church fly half, laid back, plenty of time, melodic movement. Bennett, I think, like me, was a chapel fly half, a bit more wild, nonconformist. Willie John McBride, one of the most unbelievable men you'll ever meet in your life, says Bennett for him was the best. When something wanted to be done, he could do it.'

And what of Edwards, the scorer? Morgan smiled and leant forward fractionally in his armchair. 'The greatest rugby player ever born, in any position, anywhere in the world. Gareth for me represents it all. He was built like a middleweight boxer, he was a great gymnast, and Bill Samuel, who got him into Millfield School from the tiny village of Gwaun-cae-Gurwen, told me that he could have won the pole vault in the Olympic Games. He still holds the record today in the schools 100 metres hurdles, you know. He beat Alan Pascoe, who went on to run for Great Britain. He had all the gifts, including the one thing I always thought about Pelé: the most extraordinary vision. He could look forward yet see over both shoulders. And he played with a sense of fun, as they all did in the great Welsh side of that era, J. P. R. Williams, Gerald Davies, John Dawes, Barry John. Names that still hit you.'

I could have sat listening to Morgan all afternoon, and did my level best to do so, asking question after question, begging anecdote after anecdote, until finally he said that he really had to go and hauled himself uneasily to his feet. He didn't fancy trying to walk up the stairs, so we took the lift. No sooner had he pressed the button, however, than there was a slight jerk, and the lights went out. We were stuck, by jove, and I couldn't help thinking that there was hardly anyone with whom I'd rather be stuck in a lift than Cliff Morgan. I suppose Elle MacPherson might have pushed him close, but I'd heard that her fund of stories about Barry John was on the limited side.

The same, I should add, cannot be said of a younger journalistic colleague of mine, who has asked to remain nameless, although really his name should be shouted from the rooftops, because as a gawky fifteen-year-old he sidestepped Barry John, leaving the great number ten for dead. It did not happen on the field of play, alas, but in the back garden of John's semi-detached house in Cardiff. My friend was on the hammock, canoodling with one of the comely daughters of the house, a spectacle which for some reason greatly enraged the girl's famous father, who came storming into the garden to make plain his discontent.

Now, I know that it can be an unsettling experience meeting a sportsman you revere in his capacity as a father of a girl you fancy, because it once happened to me too, albeit in less exciting fashion. During my year as a Bobby Jones Scholar, at Emory University in Atlanta, Georgia, I learnt that Nancy Nicklaus, daughter of Jack, was a student at the University of Georgia sixty-odd miles away. Not everyone in Georgia was familiar with the Bobby Jones Scholarship and its association with the greatest amateur golfer of all time. Indeed, I was once mistakenly introduced, at a function in Atlanta, as a Bobby Sands scholar. Which was all the more inappropriate given that the IRA hunger striker hadn't been dead for all that long and we were about to sit down to a hearty dinner of southern fried chicken.

But Jack Nicklaus knew all about the Bobby Jones Scholarship because he was one of its trustees, so I decided to use this tenuous connection to ask Nancy on a date, initially for no better reason, I confess, than that I wanted to be able to tell my golfing friends that I had spent an evening – or even a night! – with the great man's daughter. Tracking her down was easy. I had a friend who was an alumnus of the University of Georgia, and knew that girls from wealthy families tended to join one of two sororities. So I phoned the Alpha Beta Blocker house or Gamma Delta Force house, or whatever it was called, and asked if Nancy Nicklaus happened to be there. She was.

I explained that her dad was connected with my scholarship, and could I buy her dinner? Sure, she said. We met, she was sweetness itself, and we had a nice time, and that's about the end of the story, except that at the Augusta National a few months later I was introduced to her formidable father, whose piercing blue eyes might have been designed to intimidate young men with designs on his only daughter. It was 1986, the year that Nicklaus would win his sixth US Masters title, but for one moment, maybe even two, I took his mind away from golf. 'So,' he said, with what sounded to me like a note of faintly menacing disapproval, 'you're the guy who took Nan out.'

This uncomfortable experience helps me to identify with my friend's story about Barry John, who thundered towards him unambiguously intent on discouraging him from spending time in the John hammock ever again. My friend quickly sized up his escape routes, and realised that there was only one way he could go: along the passage to the left of the house. He ran at his would-be assailant and shimmied to the right. John, one half with Gareth Edwards of perhaps the finest half-back partnership of all time, a man nicknamed 'the King' on account of his brilliance during the 1971 Lions tour of New Zealand, shimmied with him. But my friend then jinked to the left, leaving the King clutching at air. 'I knew he'd never been much of a tackler,' my friend reports now. 'But having said that, once I was past him I certainly didn't look back.'

To get back to my own, less threatening predicament with Cliff Morgan in the lift at the Landmark Hotel, I wish I could say that it took three hours for us to be rescued, during which time he gave me the full inside story of the 1955 Lions tour, but the prosaic truth is that there was another slight jerk about thirty seconds later, the lights flickered back on, and up we glided to the ground floor.

As I watched him limp away, I mused on what it was, exactly, that made a great raconteur. Since becoming a journalist I had interviewed perhaps 1000 people, and listened to at least 3000 anecdotes. This didn't make me as well equipped as Michael Parkinson (a three-time interviewee of mine, although he has rather rudely never returned the compliment) to assess the qualities required by the best raconteurs, but nonetheless gave me a pretty clear insight.

A good, preferably great voice is crucial, and a Scottish, Welsh or Irish brogue definitely helps. Obviously, you also need to be able to time a punchline, and have good stories to tell, but just as important is a mastery of words. I once invited Bill McLaren – the greatest commentator not only according to Morgan, but many others besides – to pick his favourite all-time XV, and when he got to inside centre he unhesitatingly chose Mike Gibson, another star of that Barbarians v. All Blacks match, on account of the fact that Ireland's finest 'could sniff a scoring opportunity like a forest animal, and, although a skinny fellow, had a tackle like the crack of doom'. There are novelists who sit hunched over their keyboards for days, getting through hundreds of filterless cigarettes and gallons of strong black coffee, trying in vain to think of similes like that. Yet McLaren, like Morgan, could just pluck them out of the air.

For some reason, rugby union, which can be the most brutal of sports, produces these sensitive wordsmiths by the dozen. Maybe it's because the most eloquent rugby enthusiasts have tended to be Celts, men with poetry in their souls. When Morgan told me about the annual trips to the seaside during his childhood in the village of Trebanog, a dreamy look came into his eyes. 'Ah, the Sunday school trip to the sea,' he said. 'One day a year, one magic glimpse of the sea. We went to Barry Island.' A chuckle. 'Gwyn Thomas used to say it was Baptists to Barry, Congregationalists to Porthcawl, Methodists to Penarth . . . and Buddhists to Aberavon Sands.' To borrow a phrase: brilliant, oh that's brilliant.

But let us return to the year of the greatest game of all, 1973. It was also the year that I passed my 11-plus, left Farnborough Road Junior School and went to KGV. The last days of August were spent gathering all the kit and caboodle I would need as a grammar school boy, starting with the blazer from Rawcliffe's, Southport's official supplier of school uniform, that was a size too big to allow for 'growing-room'. Whatever happened to growing-room, by the way? When my wife buys clothes for our three children, they fit. That was an unheard-of phenomenon when I was a kid. And if I grew out of a coat or a pair of trousers before a school year was up, then a kind of gloom would settle on the household, as if we had all failed in some way; me for growing upwards, or indeed outwards; my mum for not predicting the growth spurt; my dad for not having anything to do with the purchase in the first place.

Obviously, this has partly to do with levels of affluence then and now, but there has also been a significant cultural, or behavioural, or even culturo-behavioural shift. When I was a child I was free to amble to the rec on my own and not come home until dusk, but I was not free to decide that I didn't want to go somewhere that my parents wanted me to go, or to refuse to wear something they wanted me to wear. In one generation, these laws of childhood seem to have been turned completely upside down. It is most odd. Anyway, as a result of my mother's preoccupation with 'growing-room', I commenced my seven years at KGV – in common with plenty of other boys, I should add – with only the last third of my fingers emerging from my blazer sleeves.

The blazer showing only the tips of my fingers, though, was itself only the tip of the iceberg. It had ever been thus. I have a fascinating mail-order catalogue from an outfitters called Bodenhams in Ludlow, Shropshire, dating from 1901, which lists all the items required for a 12-year-old boy going to boarding school. Here's a truncated version just to give you an idea of the social history it represents; the actual list is almost four times as long.

1 Dress Eton Suit . . . from 22/6
1 Rugby Suit . . . from 8/11
1 Overcoat . . . from 8/11
1 Dressing Gown . . . from 9/6
1 Silk Hat . . . from 9/6
1 Felt Hat . . . from 2/11
1 Cap . . . from 6d
1 Hat Brush . . . from 3d
2 pairs Cricket Trousers . . . from 5/11 each

2 Cotton Cricket Shirts, from . . . 1/9 each

4 Flannel Cricket Shirts, from . . . 2/6 each

4 Flannel Nightshirts . . . from 3/3 each

6 pairs Hose . . . from 1/- pair

1 Clothes Brush . . . from 1/-

2 Hair Brushes . . . from 1/- each

1 Tooth Brush . . . from 3d

1 Nail Brush . . . from 2d

1 Play Box . . . from 5/6

The list sent to 'the parents or guardians of Brian Viner' in 1973 wasn't quite like that one. After all, I wasn't going to boarding school, and I certainly didn't need a Felt Hat, or six pairs of Hose, or, regrettably, a Play Box. But the KGV list was almost as comprehensive, and rather worryingly it included some words that were utterly alien to me. A protractor? What the hell was a protractor? A slide rule? I didn't like the sound of that at all. But there was one requirement on the list that excited me, while at the same time filling me with dread: two rugby shirts, the list said; one white, one maroon.

I had never played rugby before, but I knew that KGV had a rich oval-ball tradition, in which I would be expected to participate. The reason for my excitement was that in my valedictory report from Farnborough Road Junior School, the headmaster, Mr Bird, had speculated that I might make 'a good goalkeeper or rugby player', words that I had read and reread at least 100 times. The reason for my dread was a faint suspicion that Mr Bird was just trying to think of activities that would suit my plumpness, compounded by the fact that instead of buying me a pair of rugby boots, my mother had borrowed an old pair from Mrs Watson at number 56, whose grown-up son Giles had played years earlier. I wish now that I'd kept them. Even in 1973 they looked fifty years old, and I don't suppose they would have been the height of fashion in 1923, either. They were huge, unwieldy things made of ancient cracked leather, with steel toe-caps and little hooks around which to wind the laces. They reminded me of Billy's Boots, as worn by the cartoon hero of my favourite comic strip in my favourite comic, *Scorcher 'n' Score*. But the point about Billy's Boots was that every time he put them on, he played like some famous hotshot from generations before. That wasn't likely to happen to me.

In the end, mercifully, even my mum realised that Giles Watson's old boots were museum pieces. It was a narrow escape. Had I unveiled them in my first games session in my first week at KGV, I would have been a laughing stock until the Lower Sixth at least.

My new school, however, was still a decidedly old-fashioned establishment in 1973; several of the senior masters wore gowns, which swished impressively behind them as they strode along polished parquet corridors, but even they did not have the radiance of the members of the first XV, who were feared and revered in equal measure.

It seems bizarre to think that these were lads of only seventeen or eighteen, whom I would look at now as fresh-faced kids with everything still to learn about life. It seems so bizarre, in fact, that I refuse to believe it. Even were I to be transported as an adult back to 1973, I'm sure that I would still be in awe of the likes of Wilkinson, 'big Wilky', who was captain of the first XV and head boy and stood about eight foot five in his stockinged feet. And I'm certain there was nothing fresh-faced about them. Unless my memory is body-swerving me, everyone in the first XV had so much facial hair that you weren't sure whether it all belonged to them or whether they were wearing particularly woolly balaclava helmets. Ah, balaclava helmets. That was another feature of the

1970s; everything was said in full. We talked about balaclava helmets and avocado pears and continental quilts and rubber johnnies, although never, as far as I can recall, in the same sentence.

As one of the first-year intake, I was known as 'a newt'. And for those further up the school, particularly the old-timers embarking on their second years, newts were fair game. If you were a newt who looked hard enough, like Tony Rodwell, or had a brother in a higher year, you were left alone. Otherwise, your life could be made a misery. My own chief tormentor was a weaselly character called Price, who bullied me relentlessly until I had a word with Jem Sykes, my former best friend from Lynton Road, who was in the year above me. Jem grabbed Price by his tie-knot, which handily in those days were about the size of dinner-plates, and informed him that he would kick his miserable fucking head in if he didn't leave me alone. Price took the subtle hint. He never troubled me again.

On the whole, the sixth-formers were above bullying, although prefects could hand out dinner time detentions and some of the power-crazed ones took full advantage of the privilege. I could hardly wait to become a prefect, or a 'D' as they were known, which very wittily was an abbreviation for 'defect'. But what I wanted to become more than anything was a member of the first XV. They were gods, and wore blazers which proclaimed their godliness. Full colours blazers made Joseph's dreamcoat look drab. They had vertical technicolour stripes and were usually worn with smart waistcoats underneath. Occasionally, I would see one of the first XV in town on a Saturday afternoon, perhaps with his mum and dad and little sister, wearing jeans and a knitted sweater. It was distressingly disorientating, like seeing Clint Eastwood in a tutu.

As in the case of big Wilky, the captain of the first XV was invariably head boy as well, which in retrospect seems like an awfully unfair concentration of kudos. But then the head boy needed the respect that was automatically accorded to the school rugby captain. At morning assembly, his job was to bellow 'Quiet school!' to stop the chatter of 600 boys, where-upon the teachers would file in and the headmaster – a stern, remote figure called George Dixon, known as 'the Fez' for some reason that almost certainly had nothing to do with Tommy Cooper – would ascend the stage and lead us in the Lord's Prayer. Occasionally, if the head boy was away climbing the north face of the Eiger or separating warring tribes in the Sudan or something, another prefect would be called upon to do the 'Quiet school!' bit, and would always be roundly jeered until the Fez appeared and raised an eyebrow, delivering instantaneous silence.

It quickly became apparent that my own chances of even-tually making it into the first XV were less than rosy. I played for my house, Woodham's, and like all the fat boys I was made a prop forward, but I soon realised that there was more to being a prop than pre-pubescent blubber and a gumshield. In my third year I was made captain, but that was only because my housemaster, Mr Berry, a German teacher with negligible interest in sport, thought that any boy with shoulders like mine had to be a decent rugby player. Little did he know that my shoulders, following my mum's visit to Rawcliffe's that August, were mostly blazer.

House rugby, like house cricket, could be a joke. I once cap-tained Woodham's to a 64-0 thumping at the hands of Spencer's, and the margin might have been considerably more had not the match been cut short by the referee, our PE teacher Mr Stichbury, on compassionate grounds. But nobody joked about the senior house final at the end of the spring term.

JPR's Sideburns

It was KGV's blue riband sporting event, and the whole school was forced to attend, so that the entire pitch was ringed with boys – some watching, some reading, some playing conkers or slaps or giving each other Chinese burns – but all bodily present. Attendance was a three-line whip. Inter-house rugby throughout the school was taken deadly seriously, even though certain houses seemed to have a monopoly on the best players, while others were full of Roderick Butterfields or, heaven help us, Marc Almonds. Being at KGV must have been a nightmare for the future lead singer of Soft Cell; he must have been dragooned on to the rugby field at some time or another, and whereas I can think of one or two gay men who have thoroughly enjoyed rugby and played to a very high level indeed – not that I'm going to out them here, of course – I don't suppose Wednesday afternoons in the mud were ever his idea of fun. Gay rugby players tend to be jovial butch types rather than highly strung artistic types.

By contrast, I greatly looked forward to my own Wednesday afternoons in the mud. It wasn't the playing that appealed to me, exactly, so much as the manly stuff before and after: the banter in the changing room, the whiff of Ralgex, the taste of the gumshield, the clatter of studs on concrete. Maybe there was something a bit homo-erotic about it. Whatever, someone's boot gashed me just above the right eye one Wednesday, and a spectacular amount of blood cascaded from my head on to my white shirt. I was sent straight to the first-aid room, but deliberately took a circuitous route past the mobile classrooms in the hope that I would be spotted, splattered with mud and blood, looking like a fully qualified member of the Pontypool front row.

I knew about the Pontypool front row, as I knew about many aspects of Welsh rugby, because my Latin master, T. B. L. Davies, was a rugby zealot. I never cared all that much for Latin, could never really tell the difference between nominative, accusative and ablative, but by God I knew the difference between Gerald Davies and Mervyn Davies, although I looked up to neither of them as I did to Thomas Bleddyn Llewellyn Davies, known to every pupil and even some of his fellow-teachers as Blod.

Blod's wife, Mrs Davies, was also a teacher at KGV. She taught French, was inevitably known as Ma Blod, and I hope that wherever she is now she won't mind me adding that she was unrivalled even by Raquel Welch in the thoughts of those of us who fantasised about sexual initiation at the hands of an older woman. Ma Blod was as curvaceous and sexy as Blod was tall and macho; together they were the Richard Burton and Elizabeth Taylor of the parquet corridors. And they both had that indefinable aura that seemed to shimmer around teachers with whom you knew you could not step out of line. Those teachers who lacked it were given miserable lives, but there was no propelling soggies – small balls of paper pulped in the mouth and then torpedoed through an empty biro, usually in the direction of Roderick Butterfield – in any lessons of Blod's or Ma Blod's. In fact, the only time she failed to control an unruly class was when she stormed into room 6 to shout at 4S, whose teacher had left them to work on their own for ten minutes, and who were taking full advantage by staging a minor riot. 'Will you be quiet!' she thundered. There was quiet.

'Have you boys never heard of a four-letter word beginning with W and ending in K,' she added.

It was a perfectly innocent rhetorical question, but an unintentionally ambiguous one to set before twenty-eight thirteen-year-olds, whose testosterone you could practically smell. There was uproar again.

Lessons with Blod, meanwhile, were a joy. He once spent

ages telling us about the film he and Ma Blod had seen at the ABC on Saturday night, *One Flew Over the Cuckoo's Nest*, and by the time we finally got round to the gripping fact that Sextus was a *puer superbus et temerarius*, the bell rang to end the lesson. On another occasion we passed an entire lesson listening to a tape of Max Boyce, who was then – it seems hard to believe now – considered a tyro of stand-up comedy. And if you were interested in rugby then double Latin was a treat. It didn't take much to get Blod rhapsodising about J. P. R. Williams and Gareth Edwards, and once he did you knew that you could leave Sextus, Cornelius and Aurelia on the Appian Way, and that it really didn't matter how Caesar sent a message to Cicero.

The only time I ever felt disappointment in Blod was in February 1976, after my father died. I was kept off school for almost three weeks and when I got back I found that all my classmates were pretending that nothing had happened. Only one, Pete Venables, cementing a friendship which continues to this day, said that he'd been sorry to hear about my dad. I thanked him for the sentiment, and he explained that Blod had advised the class not to mention it, but that his own dad had told him he ought to say something. Blod meant well, of course, but I've always thought it was a misjudgement.

Still, that doesn't make him any less of a hero. In 1999, when I realised that my column was going to fall on St David's Day, I decided, for want of anything better to write about, to pick a Davies XV: fifteen people called Davies who had made a significant impact on sport. After the obvious ones – Gerald, Mervyn, Jonathan and Gareth the rugby players, Kevin and Wyn the footballers, Laura the golfer, Lynn the long-jumper, Dickie and Barry the broadcasters – I found that I was struggling slightly. So I included Blod, wondering whether perchance he might see it and be reminded of a chubby kid from a Latin class long ago.

I wrote that he gave me a lasting appreciation of rugby union and that was undoubtedly true. More specifically, the manifest joy he derived from the pre-eminence of the Welsh dragon rubbed off on me. Through him I formed an attachment to Welsh rugby that I have kept quiet about pretty much until now. Of course, it wasn't hard to support Wales in the 1970s. The Welsh shared the Five Nations championship in 1970 and 1973, and won it outright in 1971, 1975, 1976, 1978 and 1979, of which 1971, 1976 and 1978 were also Grand Slam years. A 34-18 defeat by Scotland in 1982 ended a remarkable run of twenty-seven championship games undefeated at Cardiff Arms Park. For an Evertonian in a decade dominated by Liverpool, it was rather satisfying to go through the 1970s rooting quietly for the Welsh rugby union team, even if a wet weekend in Ruthin with my parents was my only direct experience of the principality's charms.

I wasn't the only one captivated by Blod's enthusiasm. He was a provincial Latin teacher, not a professional broadcaster like Cliff Morgan and Bill McLaren, but there was romance in the way he talked about the latest triumph at the Arms Park, and even now, although England is my country and I love seeing England do well, I have a more visceral affection for the heirs of Phil Bennett and Gerald Davies, and a strong concomitant disdain for 'Swing Low, Sweet Chariot'. When the brogued, Barboured ranks at Twickenham sing it, and especially when they perform the mime version, simulating masturbation when they get to the oddly ungrammatical line 'coming for to carry me home', I always feel an urgent need for a sub-machine-gun. It's quite alarming, really. Maybe I came from Merthyr Tydfil in a former life.

But is it right or fair to refer to Twickenham's brogued and Barboured ranks? I once got into trouble with a reader of my column, a Mr John Bradshaw, for precisely this turn of phrase.

He argued that I was grossly misrepresenting Twickenham regulars, of whom he was one, but only a tiny fraction of whom wore either brogues or Barbours. Rugby was a fantastic sport with spectators from all walks of life, he quite reasonably argued, and if I wanted to huff and puff, I should turn my attention to football. 'You miss all the best stories about football,' he complained. 'That in general it is managed by financial dreamers and incompetents; that its stars are overpaid; that it continues to be the commonest reason for, and the home of, tribal violence; that English football is heading down a cul-de-sac which excludes home-grown talent; that it is corrupt as well as venal; and, most important, that in its present form it is totally unviable beyond the next couple of years.'

There was some prescience in his words, written in October 2003. And although I didn't know that at the time, I admired his vehemence. So I thought of Mr Bradshaw a week or so later when a letter was published in the newspaper written by a man called Bill Finch, a devoted Tottenham Hotspur supporter and confirmed rugbyphobe. It was the middle of the World Cup in Australia, a splendidly provocative time for Mr Finch to write the following:

> If rugby is so good, why has it never caught on? The game only has a kind of foothold in a handful of ex-empire countries. I appreciate that not everybody has the motor skills for proper football, so I guess it makes sense to have a game to cater for the uncoordinated unfortunates. But please don't try to kid me that this is any sort of spectacle.

I admit that I read his letter and chuckled. To suggest that Jonny Wilkinson and Jason Robinson might be regarded as 'uncoordinated unfortunates', or that France v. New Zealand in 1999 or for that matter the Barbarians v. All Blacks in 1973 was 'no kind of spectacle', had to be worth a chuckle. I also wondered whether Mr Bradshaw had read the letter. And it struck me that it might be fun to get them together, so that Mr Bradshaw could deal with Mr Finch's claim that rugby was for the uncoordinated, and Mr Finch with Mr Bradshaw's assertion that, far from being the beautiful game, football was 'the ugliest game in the universe'.

I offered, in my column, to take them both out for lunch, and assured them that I would be an objective referee. 'For the record,' I wrote,

> I follow football more keenly than I do rugby, yet my blood is stirred at least as much by a magnificent try as by a magnificent goal, by a tightly angled Jonny Wilkinson penalty as by an impudent David Beckham free kick. And if match commentaries provided the soundtrack to my adolescence, John Motson bawling as Ronnie Radford's thunderous shot hit the back of the Newcastle net in Hereford United's famous FA Cup win looms no louder than a disbelieving Cliff Morgan bellowing 'What a try!' less than a year later, as Gareth Edwards touched down in the corner for the Barbarians against the All Blacks.

Which was emphatically true, as I have already recorded.

Both men cheerfully agreed to my proposal. So a few days before the Australia v. England World Cup final I met them in Covent Garden and we all went to a restaurant called Belgo Centraal, where the waiters are dressed as monks, not that there was anything monastic, and definitely nothing Trappist, about our lunch, from which here is a extracted transcript.

> *Mr Finch* (a 38-year-old corporate pensions consultant, who had absolutely no intention of watching the impending World Cup final): There was a period in the mid-1980s,

the Will Carling era, when it was fashionable to take an interest in rugby. And I did, very briefly, until I realised that it was a pantomime. I have always half-expected everyone to wake up one day and realise that the emperor is wearing no clothes – that rugby is complete rubbish. What really gets me is that the principal strategy for gaining ground is kicking the ball out of play. And where's the poetry, the elan, in a pushover try?

Mr Bradshaw (the 57-year-old Head of Communications for the Red Cross in the north of England, who could not recall where he was when Bobby Moore lifted the Jules Rimet trophy in 1966, only that he avoided it 'like the plague'): Pushover tries are wonderful to watch. My enthusiasm for rugby grows daily. I recorded the England v. France semi-final and have watched it twice already. I admire hugely the immense subtlety of forward play, whereas soccer seems formless to me. Twenty guys hacking a ball up and down a park. And compare the England captains, David Beckham and Martin Johnson, starting with Beckham's Alice band—

Mr Finch (exasperated): But football is fundamentally a better game. Apart from the back-pass to the goalkeeper, its laws haven't changed in my or my father's lifetimes. There is a purity about them. The laws of rugby seem to change all the time.

Mr Bradshaw: Fine-tuning. The basic laws are very simple. You don't throw the ball forward, and you don't stand in front of the ball. And what's wonderful about rugby is that there is room for every physical type. A whole form of schoolboys can play rugby, even the fat kids who are useless at sport.

Mr Finch (triumphantly): Exactly. That's my point. Even at the top level, football is essentially a game of skill, rugby a game of power. And I don't understand how the team that scores more tries, like Wales against England (in the World Cup quarterfinal), can lose. The equivalent in football would be scoring three goals, but losing because the other team took more corners.

Mr Bradshaw: Ah, but that's all part of the marvellous complexity of rugby. It rewards territorial advantage, and pressure, and penalises mistakes. And the intrinsically better sport is surely the one you can attend in complete safety, without hordes of police to take the opposing supporters to the train station. Indeed, I sat near a man at the England v. Italy match at Twickenham who was loudly applauded for singing the Italian national anthem. Imagine that at a soccer match.

Mr Finch: Yes, but if rugby had the same place as football in our culture, it would have the same crowd problems. And actually I find the singing of a slave song, 'Swing Low, Sweet Chariot', very offensive. Mind you, I was at Wembley for the England v. Germany game in Euro '96, and I found it extremely offensive that the England fans shouted 'There's only one Bomber Harris' and 'Two World Wars and one World Cup'—

Mr Bradshaw: Doo-dah, doo-dah.

It was an engrossing exchange, which ended with a beguiling hint that Mr Bradshaw was perhaps a closet football fan after all. Whatever, I thanked them both for playing ball, regardless of its shape, and left for home musing that, while Messrs Finch and Bradshaw had conversed even-temperedly and sometimes good-humouredly, there had been a palpable underlying disdain for one another's beliefs. And beliefs, it occurred to me, are exactly what they are. It is amazing, and kind of wonderful, that sport can unleash as much angry, blinkered, loquacious passion in people as politics and religion.

And yet, as with politics and religion, the most fierce enmity of all is often to be found between people supposed to be broadly on the same side. Mr Finch's condemnation of rugby union was positively rose-scented next to the rubbishing that rugby union habitually gets from followers of rugby league, who are implacably convinced of their code's innate superiority.

I haven't written much about rugby league in this book because, even though my Eddie Waring impression circa 1978 was as good as anybody's, it has captured my respect but never my devotion. For the same reason, it has rarely featured in my newspaper column. But in March 2005 I found to my delight that I was being busily discussed on rugby league websites following a piece I had written about a man called Peter Howard, who captained the England rugby union team in 1931 and in the same year was recruited by Sir Oswald Mosley to lend some muscle to meetings of his extreme right-wing New Party.

I was positively bombarded with e-mails from rugby league enthusiasts saying that it was no surprise whatever to them to learn that an English rugby union captain had been mixed up in nasty right-wing politics. A large number gleefully quoted Philip Toynbee, who once wryly observed that a bomb placed under the West Stand at Twickenham would set back the cause of British facism by fifty years. Others scornfully cited South African rugby union in the age of apartheid, and French rugby union during the Vichy regime, as further examples of the sport's tainted record.

As for Howard, I then discovered, somewhat to my embarrassment, that he was the father of the eminent *Times* columnist Philip Howard, himself the father of a guy I was friendly with at university. I duly talked to Philip, who was the soul of kindness and clearly felt deep ambivalence himself about his late father's convictions. But by any standards Peter Howard was an intriguing character, who in 1939 featured in Great Britain's world championship-winning bobsleigh team, and after the war was a leading light in the Moral Rearmament movement. Philip also told me that Peter's sporting deeds were all achieved with a withered leg, which he'd had since birth and which, during international matches, he tried to conceal with copious bandaging. Once, as Peter ran in a try for England at Cardiff Arms Park, the bandaging came undone and much to the crowd's delight according to Philip, 'was flying behind him like a Jack Russell chasing him'.

All of which has taken me a long way from my schooldays, but at least it has whisked us back to the Arms Park, scene of that January spectacular in 1973. There was a great deal of needle before the match. It was only eighteen months since the Lions had won a Test series in New Zealand for the first time, and the All Blacks arrived in Britain with a score to settle, which their fearsome prop Keith Murdoch attempted to do partly by flattening a security guard in a Cardiff hotel. Murdoch was promptly sent home by the embarrassed All Blacks management – a huge story back in New Zealand – and dozens of reporters gathered at Auckland airport to greet him, only to find that he'd taken the strategic decision to disembark in Australia.

So keen was he to avoid the opprobrium waiting for him at home, that Murdoch seemingly disappeared off the face of the earth, and wasn't discovered until years afterwards, when a Kiwi rugby writer eventually tracked him down to a remote mining town in the Outback. According to one version of the story, instead of sniffing out the world exclusive interview he was hoping for, the writer wound up sniffing both barrels of a loaded shotgun, and quite reasonably decided that it would be better to depart with his tail between his legs than with his brain on his shoes. The question 'So Keith, if you don't mind me asking, do you still feel a terrible burden of shame for letting your country down?' sensibly went unasked.

Murdoch or no Murdoch, at Cardiff Arms Park the mutual antipathy intensified the pressure on both teams, and Bennett, acutely aware that he was trying to fill the boots of the great Barry John, felt it more than most. But Carwyn James, Bennett's coach at Llanelli, a brilliant operator who had also orchestrated the Lions victory in 1971, had dispensed exactly the right kind of pep talk. 'I remained convinced,' J. P. R. Williams later said, 'that the whole thing really was Carwyn's try. He soothed us, told us to enjoy it. And I'll never forget his last words – to insist to Phil, who was full of trepidation, to go out and play just like he did for Llanelli.'

Which is precisely what Bennett did. The sensible option, when he collected the New Zealander Bryan Williams's long kick upfield, was to boot the ball into touch. But James had told him that he could 'sidestep this lot off the park' and his instinct was to do just that. The try that followed seems almost preordained when you watch it now, in just the same way that Carlos Alberto's epic goal for Brazil in the 1970 World Cup final looks preordained. When the move begins, you cannot believe that the participants don't know how it's going to end, so utterly confident and seemingly telepathic is their movement.

Of course, sporting memories are always rose-tinted; according to the *Sunday Times*'s rugby correspondent Stephen Jones in an excellent book called *The Sporting Century*, the video of the match 'now reveals a good deal of dire ball-retention and aimless kicking'. Similarly, I quite recently watched England's victory in the 1966 World Cup final from first whistle to last, and was shocked by how many tedious longueurs there were between bursts of exciting action. But Jones checks himself, adding that the dire and aimless bits were 'mere punctuation marks between some sumptuous rugby. The try by JPR in the second half passed through more pairs of hands and had more twists and turns than even the Great Try itself.'

In the end, I suppose it's pointless even to debate whether the Edwards try was the best in the history of the game. But, as Cliff Morgan said to me, it is surely the most watched of all time, the most talked about, the most celebrated. Eight years later, when I got to university, I found to my great satisfaction that I was by no means the only one who knew Morgan's commentary by heart. Indeed, whenever my friends and I walked home from the pub intoxicated – which happened once or twice or perhaps six or seven times a week – it only took one person to cry 'Kirkpatrick . . . to Bryan Williams . . . this is great stuff' for the try to be simulated, with an empty beer can or some rolled-up chip paper as the ball, and if we were really drunk then the person steaming along the outside of the pavement would launch himself into a full horizontal dive to an exultant chorus of 'this is Gareth Edwards . . . a dramatic start . . . what a score!' Albeit followed swiftly by 'Oh shit . . . are you all right, Dom?'

For the last three of my four years at St Andrews, these closing-time larks amounted to the only rugby I played. In my first year, however, I had joined the university rugby club, and played quite a few games for the third XV before a punch thrown in a ruck by a brutish police sergeant – in a match between students and the Fife Constabulary that by a savage irony had been intended to improve the relationship between undergraduates and the local police force – broke a bone in my nose and with it my enjoyment of playing the game.

So I left the rugby club and joined the football club, not particularly sorry to be leaving behind the post-match culture of drinking a pint of snakebite through the captain's jockstrap, and being forced to drop your trousers if you spilt any, while everyone bellowed, 'I zig a zumba-zumba-zumba . . . get 'em down, you Zulu warrior!' Even in my cups I recognised the absurdity of anyone in our team being referred to as a Zulu warrior, though I could appreciate that it was a more uplifting lyric than the technically more accurate 'Get 'em down, you fat arse.'

The post-match frivolities in the university football club were less boorish, but animosity towards students was no less manifest on the football field than it had been on the rugby field. The North-East Fife Football League was full of tough little men from tough little towns such as Auchtermuchty and Methil, who rarely uttered the word 'students' without the prefix 'fucking', and whose idea of a disappointing game against the 'varsity' was one that ended without any skin stuck to their studs. Occasionally we played mid-week friendlies against these teams. These were, of course, anything but friendly, which duly increased the pleasure we all felt when one of our players, a biochemistry postgraduate from Iran called Araz Ali, who spoke only broken English, asked one day what time he needed to report for that afternoon's 'lovely'.

But I am getting ahead of myself again. The reason I pursued rugby at university was that at school I actually had managed to get into the first XV, very briefly, although by then the boys' grammar school had been transformed into a co-educational sixth-form college. Those spectacular colours blazers weren't awarded any more, the Fez had retired, and there were no prefects, nor a head boy to bellow 'Quiet school!' A place in the first XV was nothing like the Holy Grail that it had been when I was an impressionable newt. Still, compensation arrived in the form of dozens of gorgeous creatures from Southport's High School for Girls.

I was in my final year when girls arrived in KGV's Lower Sixth, which I've always thought should have been taken into consideration by the Joint Matriculation Board when they marked my year's A-level papers. Moreover, the influx of girls did nothing for my rugby career. I had quickly figured out that I was deficient in the three male virtues sought by 17-year-old schoolgirls in Southport in 1979 – namely a car, an unblemished complexion, and a car. So I decided, in similarly traditional style, to woo them not with my non-existent Morris Minor but by making them laugh, an offensive that included a ruse developed with my friends Andy Coughlan and Mark Sutcliffe, whereby we fell over a lot.

I can see now that this lacked an element of sophistication, but at the time we thought we had uncovered the secret of comedy. What happened was that we would designate a particular 'greasy' spot in the sixth-form common room, then Andy would walk in and take a spectacular tumble there, and a few minutes later Mark would follow suit, followed after a moment or two by me. Most girls, quite rightly, thought this ridiculous slapstick routine beneath contempt, but the laughs we got from a few of them encouraged us to develop it even further. We became remarkably adept at falling headlong down flights of stairs, and even found out which girls had Saturday jobs in which shops in Southport town centre, just so that we could go and fall down the stairs. Rare was the Saturday afternoon at Dorothy Perkins or Freeman Hardy Willis that did not, at some point, find Mark Sutcliffe or me lying in a crumpled heap at the foot of the stairs, with a gaggle of horrified elderly shoppers asking if we were OK, and one sales girl crimson with embarrassment.

The reason why the duration of my time in the first XV was limited to precisely nine minutes was because the constant falling-down had exacted a terrible toll on my ligaments and tendons. As I went to jump up in a line-out, my right knee buckled and I collapsed in agony. 'Something shot out of my knee,' I screamed, and indeed it was my severely dislocated kneecap, which twanged fully three inches out of place before twanging back. Later, my tendency to fall down for laughs was cited as a cautionary tale even by my good friend, The Boy Who Cried Wolf. Everyone assumed that I was play-acting, including the referee, Mr Peach, who invited me to stop 'dicking around'. Even when I went to Southport Infirmary to have a badly broken leg set in plaster, the captain of the first XV, Chris 'Stoffer' Stitson, refused to believe that I wasn't taking a familiar joke an extra mile or two. When after eight weeks the plaster was removed, revealing a spindly white limb that was a miserable shadow of its former self, Stoffer still wasn't convinced.

And so a KGV rugby career that had started in uncertainty, ended in ignominy. But on the somewhat bigger stage, the sport had never had it so good. It is no coincidence that two-thirds of the all-time world XV selected by Bill McLaren in his 2003 book, *Rugby's Great Heroes and Entertainers*, played all or part of their international rugby in the 1970s. They were Andy Irvine, Gerald Davies, Mike Gibson, Gareth Edwards, Mervyn Davies, Fergus Slattery, Frik Du Preez, Colin Meads, Graham Price and Fran Cotton, and those of us who quibbled with McLaren's choice of Du Preez at number 5 did so only in favour of Willie John McBride, who captained the Lions in twenty-two games unbeaten on the epic tour of South Africa in 1974, the same year in which the mighty Ulsterman inspired the Irish to their first championship victory for twenty-three years.

McLaren's other contentious choice for his notional team of all-time greats was a fellow Scotsman, Irvine, to play at full-back. Most of us would agree with him that the 1970s yielded the greatest fullback since young William Webb Ellis first picked up a ball and ran with it, but our choice would not be Irvine, it would be J. P. R. Williams. I would be prepared also to countenance the claims of a thrilling Frenchman, Serge Blanco, but JPR epitomised the halcyon years of British rugby like nobody else, not even Gareth Edwards.

He was a remarkable character, who was so fiercely proprietorial about 'his' part of the field that he once gave Edwards a furious lambasting when the latter committed a rare error, allowing the opposition to score a try. It should be added that Wales were 32-0 up against Ireland at the time. It was March 1975 and the Irish had arrived at Cardiff Arms Park in contention for the Five Nations championship, only to be humiliated by a Welsh XV playing at its glorious best. Wanting to give the crowd a little flourish just before the final whistle, Edwards flicked a reverse pass to Bennett, except that it was intercepted by the Irish number eight, Willie Duggan, who lumbered forward twenty-five yards to score his team's only try of the afternoon in what was practically the last move of the match. Edwards and Bennett were chuckling while they waited for the conversion to be taken, but Williams went ballistic. 'You've allowed them to cross my line!' he roared at Edwards, who recorded in his autobiography that he felt like an errant pupil being bawled out by the headmaster. And this chastened pupil was the man summed up for me by Cliff Morgan as the greatest rugby player ever born, in any position, anywhere in the world.

But then reputations meant nothing to JPR, who a year later gave perhaps the definitive demonstration of his gifts. This was the famous occasion in 1976 when his single shoulder charge all but won the Grand Slam for Wales, and McLaren recalled it neatly in his book.

> He shoulder-charged a flat-out Jean-François Gourdon, the French full-back and wing, with a form of engagement that shook the rafters, sent Gourdon flying into touch, and gave that big son of France the impression that the sky had fallen in. Of course nowadays that would be regarded as danger-ous play and open to penalty. But it saved the Grand Slam for Wales and put Monsieur Gourdon into the third row of the National Stadium.

Moreover, not only was JPR utterly fearless and strong whether on the counter-attack or in defence, not only was he blessed with preternatural positional sense, he also had marvellous sideburns, which looked as if someone had glued a sample of shag-pile carpet to each cheek. We continue to poke fun at the sideburns and perms and flares of the 1970s, but the fact is that no other decade has so many fashion emblems fixing it in the mind's eye. And if there was a single sporting star with an absolutely definitive pair of sideburns then, give or take the odd female East German swimmer, it was J. P. R. Williams.

In addition, he had those wondrous initials. Jaypeeyar. Written down, it could be the name of an unremarkable Sri Lankan seam bowler. Spoken, I can't think of any other com-bination of letters that roll off the tongue quite so felicitously, nor any that evoke an entire era. But that wasn't the best thing about him. The best thing about him was that he was a doctor. It seemed too wonderfully ironic to be true, that the man responsible for the Gourdon shoulder-charge should be a healthcare professional, and it lent him a kind of mystique. I used to fantasise about what it might be like to have him as a GP.

'Er, Mum, I've got a slight headache, I think I need to see Dr Williams again.'

'Really dear, but that's the fifth time this week!'

If JPR's sideburns symbolised the 1970s, his status as a medical practitioner perfectly symbolised the amateur ethos of rugby union. When Cliff Morgan told me that the great Welsh team of the 1970s played with a sense of fun, I ventured that the sense of fun had been rather sapped by professionalism. I didn't expect him to disagree and nor did he. 'I never believed that rugby union was meant to be professional,' he said, forlornly. 'Rugby league was professional, and I love rugby league, but rugby union was about relaxation after the day's work, an opportunity to meet the fellows, have a beer.' When he joined Cardiff, in 1949, he trained only on Tuesdays and Thursdays. 'And I went mainly because I knew I'd get a free pint of beer and a kipper. There was a big box of kippers in the dressing room. We had a fork and would hold them in front of the electric fire.'

By the 1970s the only kippers in rugby union were the club ties, and the writing was already on the dressing-room wall as far as amateurism was concerned, with certain clubs more or less openly rewarding their players with homes, cars and even, in the notorious case of a beefy north-of-England farmer, a brand new career as a City of London broker. Professionalism was bound to come, if you think that the reason Gareth Edwards didn't tour New Zealand with the 1977 Lions (the tour that yielded one of the most memorable of all sporting images, the photograph of a mud-caked Fran Cotton rising like some horrible, primordial creature from a swamp) was because he was reluctant to ask for time off work.

Similarly, the reason why Mike Ruddock, the man who coached Wales to the 2005 Grand Slam, had to quit playing the game altogether in 1985 was because his ladder was knocked from under him while he was carrying out electricity board repairs at the top of a telegraph pole. Patently, that was an unacceptable state of affairs. But has the professional game in which Ruddock would later distinguish himself ever produced a greater try than that scored by Edwards on a January day long ago? You know what I think.

Bobby Moore and Pelé after England's group game against Brazil in Guadalajara, June 1970: two footballing titans, neither with quite the six-packs of some players nowadays, although I'm sure their lunchboxes matched up. And how many modern players could equal them for skill and sportsmanship?

Goodison Park's Gwladys Street End had its own Pelé in the somewhat burlier form of Bob Latchford. This was the day – 29 April 1978 – on which Latchford scored his 30th goal of the season to bag a £10,000 prize. My own excited digits are in this picture somewhere, and 'Fozzie Bear', the Street End's cheerleader, is standing just to the left of the stanchion.

Former Chelsea hero Alan Hudson reflects on signing for Arsenal from Stoke City in December 1976, while also considering the impending operation to reduce the size of his massive left hand.

Here's Stan Bowles playing for Queen's Park Rangers in 1974, probably also with size on his mind; the size of his next bet. His own mother once said of his tendency to gamble on 'dead certs' that failed to win, that he had only to become an undertaker for people to stop dying.

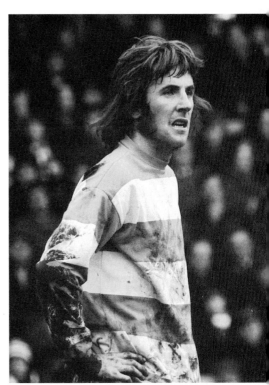

On the day Bob Stokoe died I was shocked to learn that I was the same age as he was when Sunderland won the 1973 FA Cup. I remembered thinking of him as an old geezer in a trilby. Here he is, aged forty-two, shortly after the final whistle, with Vic Halom (left) and Billy Hughes.

The peerless Dennis Lillee playing for Australia against Middlesex in June 1975. At The Oval in 1972 I had watched him take 5 for 58 against England, although was far more excited about my own game of cricket on the outfield during the lunch break.

While these men considered whether to abandon the England v. Australia Headingley Test in the wake of the 'Free George Davis' protest in July 1975, David Steele wondered whether his 92 would count in the record books, and I wondered what I was going to do all day.

With the 1977 Ashes won, Bob Willis wears his customary expression of barely containable glee. He always looked as though he had the cares of the world on his mind, not to mention most of the world's hair. With him are (left to right) Geoff Miller, John Lever, Graham Roope, and my hero, Derek Randall.

The motliest of motley crews: Southport Trinity third XI circa 1979. I'm sorry to say that I'm the one in the front row wearing a beanie hat and a stupid expression. My mate Jonny Cook (front row, extreme left) by contrast appears coiled and ready for action, though he assures me that the intense look was more to do with trapped wind.

The great Jack Nicklaus and Tom Watson walk off the eighteenth green at Turnberry following their Duel in the Sun in the 1977 Open Championship. For three days they shot identical scores of 70, 68 and 65, then Watson pipped Nicklaus with another to a 66. Who came third is a good trivia question. It was a bemused Hubert Green, 0 shots adrift. Yet his score of 279 had been good enough for Johnny Miller to win the previous year's Open by 6 shots.

If sport in the 1970s was about anything, it was about mud. Whatever happened to all that mud? Here, Fran Cotton of the British Lions rises like a primordial beast from a swamp during the 1977 tour of New Zealand, the tour Gareth Edwards missed because he was reluctant to ask for time off work.

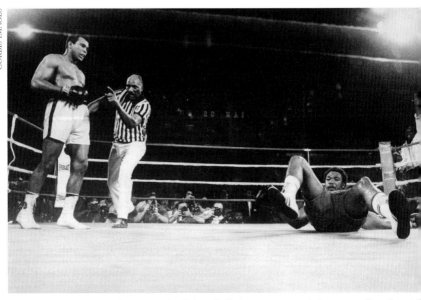

It wasn't the greatest heavyweight fight of all time, or even of the 1970s. But the 197 Rumble in the Jungle is unarguably the most talked-about, the most written-about, a here's its defining moment, Muhammad Ali decking George Foreman in the eighth round. 'I was devastated afterwards,' Foreman told me thirty-odd years later. And y defeat, paradoxically, was the making of him.

Tracy Austin dries her braces between games at Wimbledon in 1979. The poor girl was almost as famous for her dental work as for her excellent tennis. These days she has perfect teeth but a serve that couldn't crack an egg, at least according to my colleague Richard Edmondson. It was a jibe that reduced her to tears.

e greatest moment of my own tennis-playing career, partnering John McEnroe against John Inverdale and James Allen at Queen's Club in 2001, was marked by a cruel *Independent* sub-editor with the caption: 'Brian Viner shows his doubles partner, the slightly bored John McEnroe, just how unorthodox a serve can be.'

Romania's Nadia Comaneci becam
the first Olympic gymnast to reco
a perfect 10 at the 1976 Games. T
scoreboard operators, who only ha
two digits at their disposal, had to
record it as 1.0. Comaneci, born
barely a fortnight after me,
subsequently left Montreal with
three gold medals. I, meanwhile, h
three merit cards in French.

Southport's biggest sporting
celebrity by far, Red Rum,
shortly before he won the first of
his three Grand Nationals. There
is a statue of him in Southport,
but the town couldn't raise quite
enough money for a life-size
model, which is why a visiting
foreigner might reasonably
wonder what an Alsatian named
Red Rum did to deserve
immortality in bronze.

6

George Foreman's Fists

Suddenly Ali looks very tired indeed. In fact Ali, at times
now, looks as though he can barely lift his arms up . . . oh,
he's got him with a right hand! He's got him! Oh, you can't
believe it. And I don't think Foreman's going to get up. He's
trying to beat the count. And he's out! Oh my God, he's
won the title back at thirty-two!

If anyone's words rival Cliff Morgan's as the most powerfully
evocative of the greatest sporting decade of all, they are surely
Harry Carpenter's, bellowed over the hullabaloo that broke
out in Kinshasa, Zaire, shortly before dawn on 30 October
1974, when it became apparent that George Foreman had
failed to beat referee Zack Clayton's count and Muhammad
Ali had become heavyweight boxing champion of the world
for the second time.

There are several contenders for the most momentous
sporting event of all time, by which I suppose I mean an event
that transcended sport. The Bodyline cricket tour in 1932–3
threatened to fracture an entire empire; the successes of Jesse

Owens in front of Adolf Hitler at the Berlin Olympics in 1936 cocked a snook at the twentieth century's most repugnant political philosophy; the triumph of Francois Pienaar's Springboks in the 1995 rugby union World Cup, in front of Nelson Mandela, symbolised the rebirth of a nation.

In terms of its wider significance, the Rumble in the Jungle cannot stand comparison with those historic episodes. Nor, as a spectacle, was it in the same league as the Thrilla in Manila between Ali and Joe Frazier nearly a year later, which was probably the greatest, and most primal, heavyweight fight of all time. And yet, if you were to ask ten veteran sports writers what they consider to be the ultimate sporting event that they have ever attended, I would wager that almost all of them – even if they were also at the football World Cup finals of 1966 and 1970, and at Wimbledon for the Borg v. McEnroe final in 1980, and there when Red Rum won the Grand National for the third time and when Steve Redgrave won Olympic gold for the fifth time, and when the Ashes were won in 1981 and 2005, and when Marvin Hagler fought Tommy Hearns and when Roberto Duran fought Sugar Ray Leonard, and indeed when Ali fought Frazier in Manila – would pick Ali v. Foreman in Zaire.

And while I'm in a betting mood, I would also wager that more print in more books and magazines and newspapers has been expended on that fight than on any other single sporting event. Norman Mailer managed to get an entire volume out of it in 1975, and all he had to do was call it *The Fight*. No further elaboration was needed. Years later, it inspired an Academy Award-winning documentary, Leon Gast's compelling *When We Were Kings*.

In the year of the Rumble in the Jungle I kept a diary, which I still have. It is a Letts Pocket Diary and its vintage can be determined, apart from the 1974 clearly embossed in little gold numbers on the front, by the densely printed page on Metrication. Oddly enough, the word metrication isn't even in the dictionary now; it was junked in favour of the longer and somehow more satisfying 'metrification'. But in 1974 it represented the future, the unknown, and I can still remember reading my diary's helpful explanation and trying to understand it.

'The change to metric measurements in this country is, as yet, voluntary, although officially encouraged by the Government,' explained my diary.

> Metrication in industry is being phased over ten years and should be complete by 1975. Britain will be using SI units (*Système International*), a simplified version of the continental system. Millimetres and metres will replace inches, feet and yards. The metre is slightly more than the yard and will be used to measure your height or the length of a room. The kilometre will replace the mile. Small weights will be in grammes. The kilogramme will replace pounds, stones and hundredweights; half a kilogramme is just over a pound. Larger weights will be in tonnes.

Well, more than thirty years on the kilometre has still not replaced the mile, and most of us can judge instantly whether a man is closer to five foot eleven than six foot three, without having a clue what his metric height might be. As for metric weight, my wife tells me that she recently went into a butcher's shop in Leominster, our nearest town, and asked him how much his sausages were. 'Five twenty a kilo, love,' he said. 'Right, I'll have a pound, please,' she said, and, not batting an eyelid, he duly started measuring them out. All of which must be a grievous disappointment to whoever compiled the 1974 Letts Diary, and of course shows that Britain is an essentially conservative nation, rushing to embrace change like a tortoise with a gammy leg.

Yet in other ways things have changed considerably. For example, in the last week of 1973, as I sat down painstakingly filling in the 'Forward Engagements' section of my new diary, I wrote 'Frazier v. Ali, 28 Jan. '74'. I wonder how many twelve-year-olds now would carefully log the dates of forth-coming world heavyweight title fights in their diaries? It wasn't as if I was that much keener on boxing than the next boy; it was just that world title fights, especially if they involved Muhammad Ali, were major cultural occasions.

He was, without the slightest doubt, the most famous man on the face of the earth. In 1998 we had a family holiday on the Caribbean island of Virgin Gorda, one of the British Virgin Islands, and a couple of locals started telling me with almost breathless excitement about the time Ali had visited. They talked as though it had happened a month earlier; in fact, it had been more than twenty years. They also told me that every house on the island – every single one, they assured me – had on a wall or a table a picture of Ali posing with some member of the family. Who else in sport, or indeed any walk of life, could visit a small Caribbean island nowadays and have the kind of impact still likely to resound two decades later? David Beckham? Michael Jordan? Madonna? Paul McCartney? Brad Pitt? I doubt it. In recent years maybe only Nelson Mandela comes close.

My interest in Ali v. Frazier, then, was by no means unusual. More unusual were the kids not interested. But it helped having a father who enjoyed boxing. Although my dad's first sporting passion was horse racing, he adored a good fight. Sometimes, he would go to charity boxing nights at the Adelphi Hotel in Liverpool, and I loved listening to him telling my mum about them the following day, reporting with a chuckle that Liverpool's biggest villains always seemed to be seated at the same tables as the city's top-ranking policemen. 'They're probably in the same lodge,' he used to say, scornfully.

My dad had a dim opinion of Freemasonry. 'Overgrown boy scouts,' he called the masons, and I haven't been given much reason in the many years since his death, having received a number of disconcerting handshakes, to think that he got it wrong. On the other hand, there were certain things about which he was as blinkered as one of his beloved racehorses, in fact he might just as well have worn a sheepskin noseband to make the comparison complete.

For some reason, he loathed the actor Stewart Granger with fierce intensity. He thought him an utterly incompetent actor, and a more or less reprehensible human being. Hitler, Stalin, Mussolini and the Moors Murderers I never heard him criticise, but Stewart Granger got it in the neck regularly. It is a streak of irrationality that he seems to have bequeathed me. My own *bête noire* is Richard Gere, a decent enough cove by all accounts, but with his visits to the Dalai Lama and all that carry-on he gets my goat, or maybe my yak. I also think he's a crap actor. I once became quite friendly with a well-known actor in *Coronation Street* who bitchily summed up the woodenness of another leading actor on the show by saying that 'He might as well be sponsored by the Forestry Commission.' I feel the same way about poor old Richard Gere. Still, he's a multi-millionaire and he used to share a bed with Cindy Crawford. He should worry.

Besides, I can't honestly claim that I feel as ill-disposed towards him as my dad did to the star of *Beau Brummell*, among other forgettable films. I never got to the bottom of his Stewart Granger loathing. I guess it's possible that their paths crossed at some time or other, because my dad was remarkably good at smooth-talking his way into the best racecourse enclosures, the best restaurants, the best casinos. He struggled to make much profit out of bras and camiknickers, and what profit he did make was often lost on the horses or at the poker table, and home was a three-bedroomed semi overlooking the Liverpool–Southport railway line. Yet he somehow had the comportment of a wealthy man. He was handsome, too. Allen Viner, I frequently heard it said, looked like a heavier version of David Niven. And he also had something of Niven's debonair charm.

I don't remember him ever sitting me down and giving me tips on how, just by looking the part, one can gain access to places that might otherwise be prohibited, but it was obviously a lesson I absorbed. That was how I pulled off the Open Championship caper, and it was also how I wound up at a reception at the North British Hotel in Edinburgh on Saturday, 4 February 1984, held by the Scottish Rugby Union in honour of 'The English Fifteen', on the day of the hundredth Calcutta Cup match.

Now, there's nothing more tedious than tales of someone else's wacky student japes; at least, that's the knowing, self-deprecating way in which I like to introduce tales of my wacky student japes. And this one seems relevant in terms of my father's influence on me, even though, or just possibly because, on 4 February 1984 he had been dead for eight years to the very day. That 4 February anniversary has always weighed heavily on me, but never have I marked it as memorably as I did in 1984.

The idea had taken root in the Guildford Arms, an ornate Victorian pub close to Princes Street, where on Saturday afternoons after Scotland had played at Murrayfield in Five Nations matches, both teams habitually turned up for a pint or six, before trooping over to the North British for the official post-match dinner. My friends and I used to travel down from St Andrews for most of Scotland's home matches, and quickly got wise to the knowledge that if we could get ourselves to the Guildford Arms before the doors were locked, there would be a chance of some beer and banter with the marvellous, muddied oafs we'd just cheered out on the Murrayfield greensward.

But in the Guildford Arms after the 1983 Scotland v. Ireland game – the one at which I had fleetingly led the massed Irish fans in song with my 'Ollie, Ollie, Ollie' chant – it occurred to me that there were several men I recognised as players only because they were wearing bow ties and dinner suits. In fairness, some of them also had squashed noses, cauliflower ears and missing teeth, which more than hinted at a top-level rugby career, but there were others who were unmarked and roughly my age. All it would take for me to sign lots of autographs and receive some veneration along with some free drinks, I calculated, was a dickie-bow and a dinner jacket.

The plan was put into action on the day of the following season's Calcutta Cup match. My friend Angus had an uncle who lived quite close to the Guildford Arms, so I changed into my dinner suit at his flat and made my way, with five or six friends in ordinary clothes, to the pub. When we got there, however, there was a large, hostile bouncer on the door, refusing admission on account of the fact that the place was 'fuckin' heavin''. I pushed to the front of the group, offered a silent prayer to the memory of my father, and said: 'I know the pub's full, but these people are friends of mine. Would you mind very much letting them in with me?' I almost flinched in anticipation of being told to fuck off, but 'fuck off' came there none. As soon as he clocked the black tie, the bouncer's expression changed immediately. 'Sure, no problem, in you come,' he said, respectfully. And as I passed him he held out a match programme. 'If it's nae bother, would you mind signing this?' he said. Heart thumping, I scrawled my own signature alongside the list of replacements. There was no point trying to pass myself off as Bill Beaumont.

Inside the pub I studiously avoided the other players, but signed plenty more autographs, and was plied with drinks by admiring strangers as well as friends. I then took the decision, ignoring the advice of several mates to quit while I was ahead, to make my way across the road to the reception and dinner at the North British Hotel. Once again, the formal attire got me over the threshold. I circulated cheerfully at the reception, thrilled to find that drinks were free, getting drunker and drunker, and even admitting my deception to England's gigantic second-row forward Maurice Colclough, who indulged me by chuckling, albeit over his shoulder as he moved swiftly away to talk to somebody else. By the time dinner was announced, however, I had forgotten there was any deception. Rather like that conman a few years ago who pretended to be the film director Stanley Kubrick until he firmly believed he was Stanley Kubrick, I had become convinced that I was there perfectly legitimately, and complained vehemently and noisily when I failed to find my name on the table plan. This led in due, inevitable course to my ejection at the great big hands of two enormous doormen, who actually held me up between them with my feet off the ground, before forcefully propelling me out on to Princes Street very much in the manner of a John Ford Western.

Somehow or other I managed to stagger back to the Guildford Arms, where my first act was to throw up over the shoes of the bouncer whose programme I had signed, which rather gave the game away. Happily my friends were still there to dissuade him from thumping me, and to shepherd me back to someone's cousin's girlfriend's Edinburgh flat. Wherever it was, I remember waking up on an unfamiliar floor the next morning – feeling as right as rain, having so comprehensively expelled all the poisonous substances in my system – and wondering whether, if my father had been looking down, he would have felt proud or ashamed. Perhaps, I decided, a little of both.

He might also have been relieved that I hadn't been beaten up. After all, when he so abruptly departed this life on 4 February 1976, I was a flabby fourteen-year-old with few resources in the self-defence department. Two years earlier, when I came home from school reporting that I was being bullied, by Price and one or two others, my dad had even suggested that I take boxing lessons, from a man he knew called Sam who'd been an amateur middleweight champion in Liverpool during my dad's youth, and now lived in Southport. I remember Dad being positively taken aback and slightly hurt when my mother pointed out that Sam was now a frail old man, whose uppercutting days were probably about half a century behind him. Rather sweetly, Dad still looked at Sam and saw the champion he had been, not the elderly and, as I recall, slightly smelly man that he had become. Nevertheless, the instinct was the right one, to teach me how to deal with bullies myself rather than storming in to talk to my teachers.

It was perhaps for that reason that my parents did not discourage the boxing matches that took place in our front garden. Jem and Chris Sykes had each been given a pair of boxing gloves one Christmas, perhaps in the hope that they would refrain from thumping each other with bare fists, and my small garden, with a fat privet hedge most of the way around it, seemed like a natural boxing ring. Nige Evans used to come down from number 92 to join in, and we all loved it when it was our turn to wear the gloves: they were red leather, lined with a kind of yellow felt, just like the ones Muhammad Ali and Joe Frazier wore.

The trouble was that all our fights were dreadful mismatches, since Chris was older and tougher than Jem, Jem was older and tougher than me, and I was older and marginally tougher than Nige. Therefore, Chris v. Nige was like Joe Frazier v. Leslie Crowther. Indeed, when I had my reunion with the Sykes brothers in November 2004, Chris told me that he still gets unpleasant flashbacks in which he is battering Nige Evans into a stupor in my front garden, knowing that he should stop and yet somehow unable. He and Jez (formerly Jem) also remembered Margaret Evans, Nige's mum, telling their mum one day that Nigel was 'extremely interested in the inauguration of President Ford'. It's funny how these things linger in the mind. Nige, meanwhile, wherever he might be now, will perhaps read this book and let me know whether he, too, gets flashbacks to those boxing sessions. I guess his might be even more unpleasant. It would also be nice to know how much he recalls of President Ford's inauguration.

Before and after big televised title fights, a lot of boxing took place in my garden. Just as Hillside rec was filled with boys and footballs moments after the final whistle blew in the FA Cup final, and every court at Hillside Tennis Club was full during Wimbledon, and the first tee at Southport Municipal was booked solid during the Open, so were the red leather gloves hardly off whenever boxing was at the top of the sporting agenda, as it was in January 1974. I couldn't wait for Ali v. Frazier, as my Letts diary showed. But I wasn't at all sure which of them I wanted to win. It seems downright treasonable to say it now, but Ali was almost a hate-figure back then, and for those of us too young to appreciate the marvellous theatricality of his pre-fight braggadocio, or to be seduced by

162

his extraordinary charisma, he was that unacceptable animal: a boaster.

Funnily enough, that's one thing that hasn't changed; my children now consider boasting to be virtually unpardonable. They can do all sorts of unspeakable things without ratting on each other to their mother and me, but boasting is beyond the pale. And I suppose I took the same childlike view of Muhammad Ali, that he was an intolerable bighead.

As I saw it, the only sporting figure as outrageously big-headed as Ali was the former Derby County manager Brian Clough, which is why I had watched open-mouthed in 1973 when Ali, after a fight in Jakarta against a guy called Rudi Lubbers, televised by *World of Sport*, suddenly turned to camera and cried: 'Brian Clough – I hear you talk a lot! Well, Clough, that's enough!' ITV's Reg Gutteridge had put him up to it because Clough was due on the programme, even though Ali didn't have the slightest clue who Clough was. I didn't know that at the time, of course. I thought Ali meant every word. Whatever, it is interesting now to reflect on how, in retirement and poor health, both men were later venerated. At the peak of their powers they were loathed at least as much as they were loved.

Still, more than I loathed a bighead, I loved a winner. Which man, Ali or Frazier, was going to win? Frazier had won their epic first meeting, in March 1971, on points. But since then, in January 1973, Frazier had been pulverised by Foreman, the new world champion, while Ali had been beaten by, and had then beaten, Ken Norton. I hate to keep banging the drum about golden ages, but this was truly the golden age of heavyweight boxing. At any rate, I can't think of any other era when a fight as huge as Ali v. Frazier could have taken place at Madison Square Garden, with so much hype sur-rounding it, yet without a world title being at stake.

As in the later case of Jack Nicklaus and Tom Watson's Duel in the Sun, the fact that there was no British interest didn't bother me at all. The strange thing is that I only had eyes for heavyweight boxing even though in other divisions, the 1970s had started auspiciously for Britain. No British boxer had won a world championship in a foreign country for fully fifty-five years when Ken Buchanan captured the world lightweight championship in San Juan in September 1970, a feat equalled by John H. Stracey in Mexico City a few years later, when he became world welterweight champion. Jim Watt and Maurice Hope also won world titles in the seventies, as did John Conteh. Moreover, I had particular cause to celebrate Conteh's light-heavyweight world title, because he came from Liverpool and in fact moved his numerous siblings up the road to Southport when he started making decent money. I knew his sister Angela slightly, and always treated her with studied politeness. 'I'm going to set my big brother on you,' was a common enough threat in local parks, but it wasn't one I ever wanted to hear from her.

My dad, meanwhile, had got Conteh to sign my autograph book at one of his Adelphi boxing nights. I also had the signatures of the jockey Terry Biddlecombe, and of a man who'd played Widow Twanky in an amateur production of Aladdin that I had greatly enjoyed, which represented a precious enough collection for me to hide my autograph book on top of my bedroom wardrobe whenever we went on holiday. But Dad never got me the autographs I really craved: Pelé, Benny Hill and, boaster or not, Muhammad Ali.

As January wore on, I could hardly contain my excitement over the forthcoming Ali v. Frazier fight. My diary entry for Tuesday, 21 January 1974, reads: 'Woke up at 6.45. Dressed. Had breakfast. Went to school on bus. Did homework during assembly. Had lessons. Borrowed 1p off Munoz at break.

Lessons. Had lunch. Hit Taylor. Had lessons. Got early bus home. Washed. Went to Simon's party with Dexter. Had tea there. Driven home. Watched TV. Had rice pudding. Saw more TV. Ali v. Frazier one week away. Went to bed at 9.30.'

And for Wednesday, 22 January: 'Woke up. Dressed. Went to school on bus. Bought sweets. Had lessons. Munoz bought me wafer at break. Had lessons. Played football with 3rd formers. Lost 6-4. Had lessons. Top French mark. Had fight with Bryan in maths. Got black eye. Lost key. Went home on bus. Did homework. Watched TV. Ali v. Frazier 6 days away. Went to bed at 9.15.'

And for Friday, 24 January: 'Woke up. Dressed. Went to school on bus. Bought sweets. Did recessitation exam with Ridgeway. Had lessons. Went to shops with Sutton. Had fight with Venables. Got 100 lines from Whittaker. Swapped poker dice for magic trick with Shearer. Played rugby. Scored 2 tries. Went home. Had bath. Phoned Mahoney. Saw interview with Ali and Frazier.'

I'm sure you get the picture; that I wasn't Samuel Pepys or even Glenn Hoddle, that I couldn't spell resuscitation, and that it never occurred to me that waking up and getting dressed every day could perhaps be taken as read, without having to be faithfully recorded in my diary. For a boy whose excitement could not be contained, I was leading a pretty humdrum life. I also appear to have been a much more pugnacious child than I remember, but maybe that was because it was the week preceding the big fight, which clearly weighed heavily on my mind.

The following Tuesday went as follows: 'Woke up. Did homework. Dressed. Went to school on bus. Heard Ali v. Frazier result from "big gob" Munoz. Drat! Had lessons. Got crisps at break. Had audition for play. Flask was broken. Sewell bust it more. Went home on 15 bus. Jem had mud in eye thrown by Rodwell. Watched TV. Had lovely supper. Did homework. Saw Ali fight. Nicked biscuits. Went to bed.'

Obviously it was my intention to go the whole day without hearing the Ali v. Frazier result so that I could watch it fresh that evening, although I don't suppose there would have been much chance of that even if Munoz – who had kindly lent me 1p and bought me a wafer the week before, you'll notice – had kept his big gob shut. The funny thing is that I have a vivid memory of my dad waking me up in the middle of the night to watch the Ali v. Frazier fight, but perhaps that was their next meeting, the famous Thrilla in Manila in October 1975. There were certainly several occasions when he did wake me up in the small hours for live television coverage of world title fights, and padding downstairs in my dressing gown, trying not to wake up my mum by treading on the particular creaky stair three from the top, was one of the thrills of my young life. The same, alas, cannot be said of the time he woke me up in July 1969, to watch the Apollo 11 moon landing. All I can remember of that is being unutterably bored, and not being able to make head or tail of the snowy pictures. I've always rubbished those conspiracy theories which hold that the moon landing was a CIA-perpetrated hoax, and insist that it actually all happened in a Burbank television studio, if only on the basis that CIA hoaxers would surely have made the thing more fun to watch.

Anyway, the result relayed by 'big gob' Munoz was that Ali had beaten Frazier on points. It was a fantastic fight, maybe even better than their first encounter in 1971. In the second round, Ali sent Frazier reeling with a devastating right, but was prevented from following it up, and perhaps finishing the fight there and then, by a serious blunder from referee Tony Perez. Apparently thinking he'd heard the bell, Perez parted the two men about ten seconds early, which would doubtless have had people crying fix had Ali not eventually prevailed. That he did so was remarkable enough. In the third, seventh and eighth rounds, Frazier hit him hard enough to finish off any other fighter. Or more accurately, any other fighter except Foreman, the most interested spectator of all, who was perhaps still smarting at being loudly booed by the Madison Square Garden crowd before the fight, having been grandly introduced as world heavyweight champion.

Foreman did not get the respect he deserved partly because he was considered to be a champ less in the mould of Ali or even Frazier than Sonny Liston or, later, Mike Tyson: a nasty, brutal demolition expert, with a wrecking-ball of a punch. This was unfair. He wasn't just a puncher, although he certainly had a hell of a punch. 'Of all the people I've seen hitting the heavy bag, including Sonny Liston, none ever hit it like Foreman,' said Norman Mailer in *When We Were Kings*, adding that for all the arrogance of the challenger, there was, for the first time, fear in Ali's eyes. 'He had to know that he had not done nearly as well against two fighters, Frazier and Norton, whom Foreman had demolished.'

As for the depths of Foreman's talent, Hugh McIlvanney – who often gets called the doyen of British sportswriters and I see no reason not to echo that here – later explained it with characteristic eloquence. 'Foreman was a master at shrinking the ring,' the doyen wrote. 'Against Norton in Caracas there was a deadly geometry in his footwork, which employed a perfectly timed sideways step to shut off escape routes and leave his man trapped under the bombardment of his huge arms.'

But at Madison Square Garden that night the Norton fight was yet to come. The crowd's other reason for booing Foreman was because he had defended the title only once in his twelve-month-reign, a first-round slaughter of a relative nobody, Jose Roman.

It wasn't, of course, that Foreman had anyone to fear, not after the fearful battering he had inflicted on Frazier a year earlier in Kingston, Jamaica. 'Smokin'' Joe had been a worthy world champion, and just before the Foreman fight had signed for the rematch with Ali that almost everyone assumed would be a title fight. Foreman took less than five minutes to reduce that title fight to a mere eliminator. The champ was decked six times, in as ferocious an assault as I had seen since Chris Sykes last fought Nige Evans in my front garden. Awesome has become a devalued word, but that's what Foreman's punching power was. Yet Ali, in his post-fight press conference, threw down the gauntlet. 'If George Foreman wants to fight, we can get at it,' he said. 'I think he will meet me because his people want him to be number one and nobody can be that if he doesn't fight me. He's got the title, but I'm the people's champion.'

It was true. In the *Sunday Times* on 22 September, Keith Botsford recalled of Foreman's victory in Jamaica that 'two hours after the fight he was alone in his bedroom looking out of the window and not quite able to believe it. No god, he, why should he believe it? No-one has treated him like the champ; he has no nicknames, no following; he can't even get his share of his own purses. Between performances, which are the only times he's got all his attributes about him, he's almost determinedly neuter, breeds dogs, and dwells in Livermore, California.'

At the Twentieth of May Stadium in Kinshasa, on 30 October 1974, nine months after the Ali v. Frazier rematch and one month after the fight was originally meant to take place but was postponed when a sparring partner's flying elbow cut Foreman's right eyelid, Ali got his wish. Unfortunately, my 1974 diary had petered out by then. It stopped abruptly after the entry for Sunday, 3 March, and I suppose that when it is found in some attic 200 years from now, it will be assumed that, tragically, I just stopped waking up and getting dressed one morning.

I did better the following year; my 1975 W. H. Smith pocket diary gets as far as Sunday, 17 August. But the missing months include the Ali v. Foreman fight, which for the purposes of this book is a shame, because I would like to be reminded of how much I looked forward to it, and indeed whether I was allowed to watch it as it unfolded in the early hours of an African morning. I have seen it so many times since that the memories I have of sitting there watching it live with my dad might just be wishful, and indeed wistful, thinking.

Happily, since becoming a sports writer I have got to know several people who not only watched the fight live, but watched it live at ringside. So at least I have a kind of vicarious sensation of having been there, experienced partly through the recollections of an esteemed colleague on the *Independent*, Ken Jones. Indeed, while I'm sticking to my conviction that there was no better decade than the 1970s for a sports-mad kid to go through adolescence, I don't mind conceding that there was also no better time to be at a typewriter, charged with filling the sports pages of a national newspaper (albeit in the heyday of misprints, such as the one about Mulhearn stopping a rocket of a shit from Greenhoff, and another favourite: 'Little, all 55ft 8ins of him, is on the fringe of the England team').

While I was writing this book I phoned Ken and asked him the question that I pondered earlier in this chapter: what do you consider to be the transcendent moment of your long career as a professional spectator? I gave him no steer; if he'd said the 1983 National Hay Pushpenny Championships in Budleigh Salterton, I would have had to accept it. But he didn't. Perhaps he couldn't make it to Budleigh Salterton that year. 'In football, I suppose England v. Brazil in 1970,' he said. 'Or maybe the 1966 World Cup final. But overall, it would have to be Ali–Foreman in Zaire, in 1974.'

'That,' I said, 'was just what I was hoping you'd say.' It was also, of course, what I was fully expecting him to say, or else I wouldn't have made the call. I knew that if one of the talents of sportswriting is being in the right place at the right time, then Ken had to go down as one of the two most talented sports writers in the history of the business, the other being Hugh McIlvanney. For some reason, while the rest of the press pack was housed in Kinshasa, Jones and McIlvanney stayed forty miles away at N'Sele, the location of Ali's training camp. And five or six hours after the fight, still too wired to sleep, they took a stroll, only to encounter the man himself, similarly wired. Ali invited them back to his villa, where they sat – for one hour in Ken's recollection, two in Hugh's – while he talked them through the fight. The only other two people present were Ali's bodyguard and his cook.

'I remember that he had his feet up on a low table,' Ken recalled, 'and it was almost as though he was only just beginning to realise the magnitude of what he'd done. He said to us, "I done fucked up a lot of minds", which was an extremely usable quote. I'd never heard him swear before. Hugh was able to use it in the *Observer*, I remember, but in the *Sunday Mirror* they changed the "fucked" to "screwed" or something, which took away all the impact.'

In *The Sporting Century*, McIlvanney described the same remarkable audience. 'Of all the abiding impressions left by an extraordinary monologue,' he wrote,

> the strongest was the reminder that greatness, for those who are capable of it, is always a practical matter. What seems impossibly bold and unconventional to the rest of us,

strikes them as the only rational course. When Ali leaned
far back over the ropes, stretching his head away from murderous blows, covering the vital areas of his body with his
arms and disdainfully absorbing the vicious punches that
did land, we were sure he was acting courageously and
courting disaster. According to his criteria, he was merely
being sensible.

'Truth is I could have killed myself dancin' against
him,' Ali said in the villa. 'He's too big for me to keep
movin' round him. I was a bit winded after doin' it in the
first round, so I said to myself, "Let me go to the ropes
while I'm fresh, while I can handle him there without
gettin' hurt. Let him burn himself out. Let him blast his
ass off and pray he keeps throwin' . . ." There he was
swingin' away and all the time I was talkin' to him, sayin'
"Hit harder, George. That the best you got? They told me
you got body punches but that don't hurt even a little bit.
Harder, sucker, swing harder. You the champion and you
gettin' nowhere. Now I'm gonna jab you." Then pop! I'd
stick him with a jab . . . I'd jab, then give him a right cross,
then finish with a jab. Nobody expects you to finish a com-
bination with a jab. Those punches took the heart away
from George.'

McIlvanney added that being there 'with my friend and colleague Ken Jones . . . was the supreme privilege of my time in
sports writing'. Understandably so. I, meanwhile, have a far
less exalted career from which to pick my privileges. But one
of them was an interview, in a London hotel room in
November 2002, with George Foreman, who, of all the people
mentioned in this book, must be the one who has made the
greatest journey in terms of public perception. And not just
because there is a whole generation now who know him not as

a great boxer but, thanks to his Big George Lean Mean Fat Grilling Machine, simply as the grill man.

It is by no means unique in the world of sport to be unpopular, even demonised, as a participant, only to be treasured later in life and clutched to the collective bosom. To a greater or lesser extent, John McEnroe, Martina Navratilova, Jack Nicklaus and, indeed, Muhammad Ali have all gone through that process. But in those instances, what we cherish now was plainly there all along.

With Foreman it's different. Years ago he really was a nasty, brutish piece of work. In his youth he was a thief and a mugger of old ladies. Now he is a preacher in Houston, Texas, at the Church of Our Lord Jesus Christ, Soul of Eternal Lovingkindness or something like that; considerate, companionable and engaging to a fault. As for the 'almost determinedly neuter' man described by Keith Botsford, he ended up with ten children, five daughters and five sons, the boys all called George Edward Foreman on the basis, he explained, that when he succumbs to amnesia, as ex-boxers do, he will stand a half-decent chance of remembering their names. The man who told me this with a twinkle in his eye was the man who, as a teenager in Houston, used to get blind drunk on a cheap wine called Thunderbird, then went out looking for houses to rob. He gave up crime after he took up boxing, but he didn't exactly become a pillar of the community. 'Ali is everyone's friend,' wrote Botsford in Zaire, 'Foreman only his own.' Yet now, it is only Ali who would beat Foreman in a popularity contest for ex-heavyweight champions. And what changed him was the Rumble in the Jungle.

'After that knock-out,' said Mailer in *When We Were Kings*, 'he went for two years through the deepest depression, and he almost didn't come out of it. To see the way in which he reconstructed his personality until you'd be hard pushed to find anyone in American life more affable . . .' Mailer's sentence, unusually, petered out; such was his admiration, he was lost for words.

I was excited about meeting Foreman. I approach most interviews not quite with the dry cynicism of a world-weary old hack, but nor quite with the perky enthusiasm of a schoolboy. It's a job of work, for which I prepare diligently but with professional detachment, whether it's Freddie Flintoff I'm interviewing, or Zinedine Zidane. With those two in mind, by the way, I once invited readers of my column to submit twenty-six alliterative sportsmen, and was duly impressed when a guy called Jon Russell, a football trader at Sportingbet.com, produced a list consisting entirely of footballers, from Alan Ainscow to Zlatko Zahovic. He even found a Q (Qu Qing of Adelaide United) and an X (Xu Xiang of Shanghai Zobon). There's nothing like writing a sports column in a national newspaper to be reminded on a regular basis that there are people out there with significantly wider sporting knowledge.

Anyway, as I took the lift up to the sixth floor of a Knightsbridge hotel to meet Foreman, my usual professional detachment was missing. I couldn't suppress a feeling of childlike exhilaration. I was even looking forward to shaking his hand, the right hand that had flattened Frazier, and almost defeated Ali.

A word here about handshakes. At a party years ago, long before I became a journalist, I shook hands with a decidedly eccentric man whose curious surname, I remember, was Ing, and who collected handshakes. Eagerly, Mr Ing asked me whether I'd ever shaken hands with anyone who might have shaken hands with Albert Einstein. Einstein was the big gap in his collection, he explained, adding that he collected handshakes either directly or by proxy, so that to shake hands with someone who'd shaken hands with Einstein, say, would be 'to have Einstein in two'. The more direct the link, he told me, the more valuable the handshake as a collector's item. He had Hitler in three, he claimed, and Beethoven in seven.

To his obvious disappointment, I was unable to oblige with Einstein, and he seemed unimpressed that I could offer him Ronnie Corbett, although there was a flicker of interest when I mentioned having the original Lassie in two, via a relative who'd worked at MGM and shaken the celebrated paw. Anyway, before he wandered off to meet someone else, arm outstretched in keen anticipation, Mr Ing briefly explained how this unusual hobby had started.

His grandfather had known Neville Chamberlain, he said, so he'd shaken the hand which shook the hand of Adolf Hitler. This idea so excited him that he started his collection, always asking of anyone he met whether they'd ever met anybody famous. It's an intriguing business when you think about it. And, of course, my own handshake collection became pretty impressive once I started interviewing famous people, although on the six degrees of separation principle, it's my guess that half of the population could claim the other half in six handshakes or fewer. When I worked for the *Mail on Sunday* I wrote a feature about this, and contacted the anthropologist Desmond Morris, who told me that handshaking had been around as a salutation for at least 200 years, so if you could be reasonably certain that two people had been introduced since about 1800, they would probably have shaken hands. I duly worked out that I had Abraham Lincoln in nineteen.

I also phoned round a few celebrities I knew, and invited them to have a go. Bob Monkhouse, bless his dear, departed soul, was brilliant. 'I've shaken hands with Noël Coward, who shook hands with all the Mitfords,' he said. 'Unity Mitford shook hands with Hitler, who embraced and shook hands with

Mussolini. And Mussolini shook hands with the great tenor Enrico Caruso. I know that because Caruso tried to have the photograph suppressed. So I've got Caruso in five.' Which gave me, through Monkhouse, Caruso in six, Mussolini in five, Hitler in four, Unity Mitford in three, and Noel Coward in two. It gets quite compulsive, especially if you start thinking about the other things hands are used for. For example, I once shook hands with Arthur Miller, so I've caressed Marilyn Monroe in two. And a similar thought passed through my mind when I shook hands with Foreman: that I'd flattened Frazier in two, and therefore Ali in three, Liston in four, Floyd Patterson in five, Ingemar Johansson in six, and so on back through the annals of heavyweight boxing.

But enough of such whimsy. I talked to Foreman about his remarkable punching ability, and he agreed that he'd had quite a pile driver. 'I'd be in trouble sometimes,' he said, 'and the fight would look like it was going the other way. But then I'd hit the guy and he'd be on the canvas. Brute strength, that's all it was. Did you hear the story about the greatest archer in the world? He was travelling the countryside, and saw a bull's-eye, and perfectly in the middle of it was an arrow. He measured it, he had never seen anything that direct. He was the greatest of all time, but he'd never seen that kind of marksmanship. Finally he met the guy, and said: "Tell me, how did you get to be that accurate?" The guy said: "It's easy, I shoot the arrow first, then I paint the bull's-eye"'.

Foreman gave a huge chuckle. 'My career is like that,' he continued. 'I got those knock-outs, now I go back and tell how they happened. The truth is, I don't know how they happened.'

I knew this huge man was being disingenuous, that he had been a much more skilful fighter than he let on. On the other hand, his self-confidence as a fighter was so bruised on that night in 1974 that perhaps it never fully recovered. Maybe that's why he went on fighting for such an absurdly long time, winning a version of the world title at forty-five and even threatening another comeback ten years later. Maybe he wasn't displaying his self-confidence, but searching for it, still trying to come to terms with the crippling stigma for any proud sporting professional of being famous more as a man who lost, than a man who won.

'I was devastated afterwards,' he told me. 'I'd wake at night jumping up, thinking I was still in the fight trying to beat the count. I had to live with that man standing over me screaming: "I told you never to doubt me, I'm the greatest!". And I tried to smear his defeat. For years I said this happened in Africa, that happened in Africa. I even said I was doped. But he defeated me fair and square. And later, I tried to make up for what I had said. He became like my brother. I love him. I want to protect and take care of him.' A huge smile lit up Foreman's cherubic face. 'Although when he sees me he worries because I try to convert him to Christianity all the time.'

Clearly, I said, it must have crossed his mind that perhaps his own punches contributed to the tragic physical decline of this man he loved. Foreman's big smile faded.

'Yeah, well, you can't throw that out the door. I remember beating him up pretty good about the third round, and when the bell rang he looked round and said: "I made it." He came back out and said: "I've weathered the storm, you can't do that to me again", and he was right. He used his rope-a-dope strategy and it worked. I got tired. But the mistake he made was, because he weathered the storm with me, he started to let everyone beat up on him, figuring they couldn't hit him like that all night. So I don't think I did damage to him, but because he defeated me that way, I think that's what did the damage.'

Ali fought four more times within the next twelve months – unimaginably prolific for a heavyweight boxer these days. One of the fights was against Britain's own Joe Bugner, not that the British had ever warmed to Bugner. This was partly because a highly controversial refereeing decision had given him victory over the much-loved Henry Cooper in 1971, and partly because his origins were slightly closer to Budapest than to Bournemouth.

Only in cricket, it now occurs to me, do the British unequivocally embrace those sporting stars who hail from elsewhere but ally themselves with the country of Lord Nelson, Sir Winston Churchill, Sir Anthony Eden, Clement Attlee, Henry Cooper and Lady Diana, as an overexcited Norwegian football commentator once so famously put it. As soon as Basil D'Oliveira, Tony Greig, Allan Lamb, Graeme Hick, Robin Smith and Kevin Pietersen started scoring runs against the Aussies, we were more than happy to accept them as our own. But we never felt the same way about Zola Budd, for example, and while we don't mind the fact that Greg Rusedski comes from the West Country, we'd rather the West Country in question wasn't Canada.

I can even remember some question marks over Virginia Wade, on account of her clipped South African vowels. In 1977, when both she and Sue Barker reached the semi-finals of the ladies singles at Wimbledon, there was no doubt that Middle England was firmly rooting for Barker. That changed, of course, when good old Virginia, bless her pink cardie, beat big, butch Betty Stove, Barker's conqueror, in the final. Suddenly Virginia was as British as jellied eels, her formative years in South Africa dismissed as merely a long holiday. I suppose the same thing might have happened to Bugner. It was hard to whip up much in the way of patriotic frenzy when he fought Ali – which he did for a second time in July 1975 after losing on points in 1971 – but we probably would have managed it if he'd won.

Whatever, the fight that everyone wanted to see was a third showdown between Ali and Frazier, and it did not disappoint. An even greater fight than the Rumble in the Jungle, it took place in the Philippines on 1 October 1975. Ali won when Frazier's corner nobly decided at the end of the fourteenth round that their man couldn't continue, but the champion too had taken some more appalling punishment. In retrospect, that was the time for him to retire, after the Thrilla in Manila. On the other hand, that would have denied Richard Dunn, a navvy from Bradford who'd somehow found himself British and European heavyweight champion, his slightly surreal shot at Ali's title in May 1976. And it would also have denied me one of the odder experiences of my interviewing career, which took place in February 2001, in a café, in a gloomy little town called Moreton, near Birkenhead.

I had heard, to my amazement, that Earnie Shavers, the boxer from Alabama who challenged Ali for the title at Madison Square Garden in 1977, now lived on the Wirral and was working as a 'greeter', that splendid euphemism, a couple of nights a week at Yates' Wine Lodge in Liverpool. I remembered watching his fight with Ali; Ali only just won on points, and Shavers, he later said, hit him harder than anyone else ever had, Foreman included. A couple of years later, another great champion, Larry Holmes, said the same thing about Shavers. This had to be a man worth meeting. If nothing else, it would be another good hand to shake.

Fortuitously, it turned out that Shavers was writing his autobiography and was keen for publicity, so he agreed to meet me in a greasy-spoon café in Moreton. He was there when I arrived, shorter than I expected, but wider, and I remember him turning round slowly, like an oil tanker, to greet me. He was accompanied by a mate, Kenny Rainford, a hard-as-nails light-heavyweight from Liverpool; the thought struck me that it was the perfect moment for an accident-prone scally to burst into the café and demand the takings.

Like me, Rainford had watched Shavers fighting on television in the 1970s. Unlike me, he was a pretty decent young boxer himself, who later fought in America and met the man he'd seen years before on *World of Sport*. They became friends, and Rainford invited Shavers to Merseyside to speak at a boxing dinner. During his visit, Shavers was sitting in Rainford's kitchen when Rainford's aunt dropped in for a cup of tea. Rainford chuckled as he recounted the tale. 'After she'd left, Earnie turned to me and said, "Pretty soon you'll be able to call me uncle."'

Shavers's enormous shoulders heaved with laughter. 'And that's how I ended up here,' he told me. 'The love of a good, honest woman. She doesn't want children, which is perfect with me, because I already have eight daughters and a son [not to mention five ex-wives]. And with the money I make from this book, we're gonna travel the world. You know, when my mother died she left all the money I gave her to enjoy life. So I'm gonna enjoy life. Which is why I want you to tell your readers to buy my book. The proceeds go to underprivileged children and old ladies.' Shavers paused, with the timing of a stand-up comedian. 'I have nine underprivileged children and one old lady.' The small café could not contain his laughter, which erupted out of the door and down the street.

We talked for ages, but I particularly wanted to know about the fifteen punishing rounds with Ali. After I asked Ken Jones to name the greatest sporting occasion he had ever attended, I had put the same question to another highly respected veteran scribe, the *Independent*'s chief sports writer James Lawton. Jim hadn't been in Kinshasa for Ali–Foreman, so I thought he'd choose an epic football match or a stupendous 100 metres final or a thrilling Derby. But no. 'The magic moment, the one more memorable than anything else,' he told me, 'was Muhammad Ali against Earnie Shavers in Madison Square Garden. That was an extraordinary thing to see, fifteen rounds that seemed to last about four minutes. And after it you could hear Ali screaming from inside his dressing room that he wanted it dark. The lights of the dressing room were like needles in his eyes. It was then that his doctor, Ferdie Pacheco, said he'd never go in his corner again. The damage was beginning to show.'

On the Wirral, Shavers had altogether different recollections of that New York night. 'That was the pinnacle of my whole career,' he said. 'Ali didn't want to fight a puncher so he put obstacles in my way. He said: "If you beat Roy 'Tiger' Williams I'll give you a shot." That was a life-or-death fight but I finally beat him in the tenth, and then Ali made me fight another guy, Norton's sparring partner. I beat him, too, so then Ali had to fight me. I'd already fought it 100 times in my mind. I knew he wouldn't hurt me. He wasn't a damaging puncher and he was not so fast any more, and he couldn't psych me because we were friends. But I still underestimated him. I was too relaxed. I had him in trouble in the second round, but I backed off because I was programmed to go the distance. He kept talking, saying, "Throw some punches, man, the crowd's come to watch you." He wanted me to punch myself out.'

Not surprisingly, Shavers agreed with me that the 1970s were heavyweight boxing's golden age, even ahead of the eras of Jack Dempsey, Joe Louis and Rocky Marciano.

'You would never have heard of guys like Holyfield back then, because there were so many great fighters. It was so competitive. And you had to compete in every way. Everything they did, you did. Ali wouldn't dream of doing drugs, so you didn't. They eat raw eggs? Gimme one. They go to bed at seven? I'm going at 6.30. And Holmes was the most under-rated of them. He had a much more damaging jab than Ali, and he always found the strength to get up. I hit Holmes in the seventh round with an overhand right – boom! – and he fell like a ton of bricks. He said that if I hadn't hit him so hard I would have won, because hitting the floor like that brought him round. I couldn't believe it when he got up. I thought: "Lord, gimme a gun."'

I left the café with his laughter ringing in my ears. Not until I met George Foreman did I come across anyone who seemed happier, or more contented with life, than Earnie Shavers. Maybe they were just counting their blessings that they hadn't ended up like Ali. On the other hand, they both told me that Ali, whenever they saw him, was the embodiment of content-ment too. Furthermore, I left Henry Cooper's company one December afternoon, after a couple of hours with him and his wife, positively replete with the milk of humankindness. As I left, his wife even pressed a Christmas present into my hand, a bottle of chianti.

'This is for you and your family, from my hubby and me,' she said.

Her hubby smiled, indulgently. I wanted to hug them both, and not merely to avail myself of the Great Smell of Brut (note for younger readers: this is a reference to a particularly pungent aftershave advertised in the 1970s by Henry Cooper and Kevin Keegan). I've also heard that Lennox Lewis is a lovely fellow, and they say that Joe Louis, in retirement, was a sweetheart. It seems odd that a career having your lights punched out, or punching other men's lights out, should breed such . . . pleasantness. Which is not, frankly, a word I would ever attach to the star of the next chapter.

7

John McEnroe's Scowl

This book makes no pretence at being a comprehensive record of sport in the 1970s. There are plenty of sports not covered at all, just because they didn't particularly light my fire then, even if they do now. And I give coverage to other sports that is as notable for what is left out as what is included. Thus, I haven't written much about professional golf away from the Open Championship, hardly anything at all about rugby union beyond the international scene, and very little about boxers other than the big, bruising heavyweights. Similarly, I don't remember being remotely interested in top-level tennis except during Wimbledon fortnight, which I suppose was a tendency I shared with 90 per cent of Middle England. Even the other grand slam events, the US, Australian and French Opens, hardly registered on my consciousness. I was no more interested in them than I was in the outcome of the Bingham Trophy at Hillside Tennis Club. Considerably less interested, in fact.

Yet when Wimbledon came round, I turned into a tennis nut. When I wasn't watching, I was playing. And if I was neither watching nor playing, then I was either at school or asleep. Or possibly both, if it was one of Mr Ashworth's physics lessons.

The male player I liked most was Ilie Nastase. He was a rascal but a born entertainer, the Derek Randall of tennis, and in particular I liked watching him playing doubles with Jimmy Connors. Actually it was less a doubles partnership than a vaudeville act, albeit still good enough to win the Wimbledon title in 1973. They had a kind of Harlem Globetrotters approach, trying to win but horsing around at the same time, and when they sent a series of lobs into orbit, as they did in most matches, I practically hugged myself with delight. Only the Globetrotters, whose matches were occasionally transmitted by *World of Sport* in the slot normally reserved for swimming from Sheffield or badminton from Guildford, had the capacity to thrill and amuse me simultaneously, like Connors and Nastase did.

In 2003 I interviewed Nastase and was pleased to find him no less rascally than he had been in the 1970s. I had done my research beforehand, learning that his parents were caretakers at the Progresul Club in Bucharest, where he grew up watching the elite of the Romanian Communist Party playing tennis. Communist Party rallies, I suppose. But he didn't acquire his first racquet until he was twelve. Before that he simply hit a ball against a wall with a piece of wood, over and over again, and it struck me that the so-called 'feel' players in sports considered the preserves of the affluent middle classes, notably tennis and golf, are more often than not those who grew up poor, learning with makeshift equipment. In which respect, Nastase had plenty in common with Lee Trevino and Seve Ballesteros.

Whimsically, I invited him to name the five most famous Romanians of all time. 'Ceauşescu,' he said. 'Nadia Comaneci.

Vlad the Impaler. Brancusi, who was a fantastic sculptor, better than Rodin. And me.'

We both laughed at that. 'But not necessarily in that order,' I presumed. 'No,' he said, grinning. 'Me, then Vlad the Impaler.' I told him that his epic match against Stan Smith in 1972 – which Nastase lost 6-4 3-6 3-6 6-4 5-7 – was the first men's singles final I saw. He rolled his big, brown eyes. 'You make me feel old,' he said.

The following year Nastase was perhaps the highest-profile player to defy the boycott of Wimbledon called by the Association of Tennis Professionals for long-forgotten political reasons concerning the Yugoslav Tennis Federation's decision not to let Nikki Pilic play in its Davis Cup team. Everyone remembers miners, steelworkers and operatives on the Ford assembly line going on strike in the 1970s, but hell, it was a decade when even tennis players took industrial action. And thirty years on the episode still rankled with Nastase.

'It wasn't my decision,' he said. 'The Romanian Tennis Federation called me and said I had to play Wimbledon. The Minister of Sport was a general in the army, and there was pressure from Ceauşescu. At the time he was very well received in the West because he was a little bit against Russia. Two years before he was here in England being greeted by the Queen. I couldn't say to Ceauşescu, "The ATP don't want me to play." He didn't know what the ATP was. He didn't even like tennis, he liked volleyball. So I played, and the ATP fined me five thousand dollars, and Wimbledon didn't give me membership, so I was shafted by everybody.'

He flashed me a dark look, as if he expected me to shaft him, too. 'You have to win Wimbledon to become a member, but there are sometimes exceptions. They made other finalists members but not me. So I played in 1973 and then I was shafted by the All England Club. They say to me "you have to wait" and I waited, and now it's been thirty years. I might get a chance one day if I see one of those old guys at Wimbledon and push him down the stairs. Then there might be room for me. Because I think I did a lot for Wimbledon.'

I can second that. But Nastase was not the only thrill in the BBC's television coverage. If I am brutally frank, and I think you'd like me to be, then part of the attraction for me was the opportunity the cameras afforded of looking down, or for that matter up, women's dresses. I went to an all-boys school, remember, and had to get my kicks however I could. In common with many schoolboys of that era, my favourite spectacle was Evonne Goolagong, whose name change from the aboriginal Goolagong to the prosaic Cawley, in 1975, I found most regrettable. Not that it robbed her of her prettiness, but it did seem disturbingly non-exotic after Goolagong, and, of course, the implication that she now only had eyes for her husband, some bloke called Roger Cawley, further reduced the already remote chance that she might turn up in Lynton Road one day asking for me.

Still, long after she became Mrs Cawley the BBC commentator Dan Maskell quite rightly persisted in calling her 'the former Miss Goolagong', either because he enjoyed saying the name as much as I did, or to distinguish her from another Mrs Cawley, the former Helen Gourlay, whom Miss Goolagong had defeated in the 1971 Australian Open singles final. That there should have been two of them showed just how prosaic the name Mrs Cawley was, but, of course, everyone was frightfully amused when as married women they met again in the final of the 1977 Australian Open, Mrs Cawley defeating Mrs Cawley in straight sets.

As a player the former Miss Goolagong was marvellous to watch. She was effortlessly graceful, wonderfully deft at the net, a brilliant improviser of tightly angled shots, and the owner – forgive me – of a delectable bottom and a quite phenomenal pair of legs. I sometimes find myself snorting in a superior manner when I read about teenage boys these days lusting after Maria Sharapova, or before her Anna Kournikova. My generation lusted with much greater discernment, indeed to have a crush on Miss Goolagong during Wimbledon fortnight, rather like having a crush on Ma Blod at KGV, was almost a rite of passage. So it always came as a bitter disappointment when she was knocked out, as she so often was, leaving only Chrissie Evert, as it invariably did, as the main object of fancy. Miss Evert was attractive too, but somehow lacked the former Miss Goolagong's snub-nosed, gamine qualities, as well as her glorious (former) name.

Now, before you tire of this deeply sexist perspective on Wimbledon during the 1970s, let me add that these libidinous stirrings were by no means exclusive to boys; girls had them too. I knew this because the older sister of my friend Philip not only had a poster of Björn Borg on her bedroom wall, and not only kissed it passionately before she went to sleep every night, but had even, according to Philip, sent Borg a pair of her knickers. At least I hadn't sent my underpants to the former Miss Goolagong, for which mercy she ought even now to be profoundly grateful.

There was even a word coined, presumably by the tabloid press, to convey the intensity of Borg's attraction to teenage girls: the Borgasm. Yet I could never really understand what girls saw in him. Those round shoulders, that almost spookily calm demeanour, those close-set eyes. Clive James got it right in his unmissable television column in *The Observer*, which, by the way, was another of the pleasures of living in the 1970s. In his review of an ITV documentary unambiguously titled *Borg*, James noted that 'the young champion strings his rackets so tightly that they go "ping" in the night, thereby waking up his manager. Borg runs a taut ship. He likes his headband tight too, to bring his eyes closer together. He likes them touching.'

Still, touching eyes or not, Borg was a remarkable tennis player. So, like Philip's older sister, albeit in a different kind of way, I was positively vibrating with excitement as I stood in the Centre Court crowd in 1978, waiting for the defending champion to play his first-round match with the enormous, hard-serving Puerto Rican, Victor Amaya. It was my first time at Wimbledon. I had gone with my cousin Danny, who with his brother Jonathan had also accompanied me on my trip on a bamboo raft down the Orinoco, or at any rate its equivalent in terms of adventure, the visit to the Oval in 1972.

By 1978 I wasn't much more worldly than I had been six summers earlier. The trip across London from Danny's house in Winchmore Hill still seemed like a thrilling undertaking, the more so as I knew that without Danny to tell me when and where to get off one tube and on to another, I would end up in Wimbledon, if at all, via Woking, Winchester or Weymouth, or possibly all three. These days, by contrast, my *savoir faire* in the business of getting to the All-England Lawn Tennis and Croquet Club is second to none. I am dispatched there every June by the *Independent*, and every June I remind readers of my column that the best underground station at which to alight is not the officially recommended Southfields, where there is a more or less permanent multitude of people shuffling along the platform towards the exit, but the next stop on the District Line, Wimbledon Park, where hardly anyone gets off, and where there awaits a pleasant, stress-free amble to the All-England Club, across Wimbledon Park Golf Course.

So there we are; if this book is good for nothing else, it is at least good for advice on how best to access the world's premier tennis tournament by London Underground. On which subject, I heard once that someone had written an entire manual specifically to explain where to get on to each Underground train according to whatever journey you were making, just so that you would be opposite the appropriate exit when you stepped off. If, for example, you were travelling from Russell Square to Pimlico, the manual would tell you how far along the platform you should stand at Russell Square, so that you could get off the Piccadilly Line train at Green Park directly opposite the Victoria Line exit. The only reason I mention this manual is that the author, apparently, was the 1924 Olympic 100 metres champion Harold Abrahams. Can that possibly be true? And if so, is it not time for a sequel to *Chariots of Fire*, in which Harold, having achieved his ambition to be crowned the fastest man on earth, descends the escalator at Ealing Broadway with a pencil and jotter?

I digress. When Danny and I arrived at Wimbledon, on a chilly, overcast day more suited to late autumn than early summer, we queued for what I recollect as being just under a month to get Centre Court standing-room tickets. The only queue I had known that was anything like it was the one snaking up and down the pavements outside the British Museum waiting to get into the Tutankhamun exhibition, to which my parents took me in September 1972. The exhibition lasted for seven months and attracted 1,694,117 visitors – which remains a British Museum all-comers' record – but it seemed as if most of those visitors were filling the streets of Bloomsbury on the day we went. Even now I can remember that queue vividly, yet I can remember scarcely anything about the actual exhibition, which is no doubt the exact opposite of whatever impact my mother and father hoped the visit would have on me. Of the family next to us in the Tutankhamun queue I have almost total recall, including the fact that they had come all the way from Rotterdam in Holland and had a son of about my age called Leo, with the rosiest cheeks I had ever seen. Of the Boy King's death mask, zilch.

At Wimbledon, Danny and I eventually got in, and the pleasure of finally being inside the All-England Club was immediately compounded by the exciting spectacle of Reggie Bosanquet, the ITN newsreader, ambling or more likely – given his reported fondness for a tipple – staggering by. Celebrity sightings in Southport at the time were restricted to the occasional Everton or Liverpool footballer, Bill Tidy the cartoonist, and Tom O'Connor, the comedian. Reggie Bosanquet seemed like proper glamour.

We took our places on Centre Court. Actually, I can't remember whether we bought tickets to stand there, or whether standing room on Centre Court was available just to those who got there first. Either way, they got rid of it in 1990 and that seems a shame. Maybe it's just because the most exhilarating moments of my formative spectating years came on the terraces at Goodison Park, being swept forward or side-ways in a sweaty mass of humanity, that I so regret the demise of standing room. It certainly heightened the Centre Court experience, which was further heightened by the remarkable prospect of Borg – not only the pre-tournament favourite but generally considered unstoppable in pursuit of his third con-secutive singles title – being defeated in the first round. With the champion down by two sets to one and three games to one, and facing break point on his second serve to trail 1-4, it looked as though my Wimbledon debut would coincide with the biggest upset for years. But then I saw what Borg was made of, and perhaps something of what so appealed to Philip's older sister. There was fire beneath the ice. He caught Amaya unawares with a huge second serve down the middle of the court, and the Puerto Rican then began to fall apart, a victim less of Borg's game than his extraordinary willpower.

Borg won the fourth set 6-3, and the fifth set by the same comfortable margin. A fortnight later, by now back at home in Southport, I watched him annihilate Jimmy Connors 6-2 6-2 6-3, to become the first player since Britain's Fred Perry four decades earlier to win three Wimbledons in a row.

The competitive thrills, that year, came in the women's singles final, in which Martina Navratilova eventually prevailed over Chrissie Evert, 2-6 6-4 7-5. Evert was contesting her fourth final, having won the thing twice before, beating Olga Morozova in 1974 and, distressingly, the former Miss Goolagong in 1976. For Navratilova it was her first Wimbledon final. In 1975 she had reached the finals of both the French Open (losing to Evert) and the Australian Open (losing to Miss Goolagong shortly before she became 'the former'), so it is surprising that it took so relatively long for finals day at Wimbledon, of which she was to become such a staple ingredient, to be graced by her presence.

Not that the Centre Court crowd warmed to her right away, or even for some years to come. As so often with great champions, it was not until the enormous talent began to ebb, until she became fallible, that she acquired real popularity. It was the same with Pete Sampras. Steve Davis experienced it in snooker. It will doubtless be the same with Tiger Woods, whose victories tend to be received respectfully rather than rapturously. Plus, it was Navratilova's misfortune, if only as far as the Wimbledon crowd was concerned, to be muscular, tempestuous and a lesbian, when her rival was feminine, unflappable and sleeping with Britain's very own John Lloyd. Rather like the handshakes game in which you derive pleasure by proxy, shaking hands with someone who has shaken hands with someone, British tennis fans managed to extract some patriotic pride from the fact that Chris Evert, who had been engaged to Jimmy Connors, now preferred one of our boys to one of her own. Remote as the chance was of a British man getting his hands on a Wimbledon singles title, at least there was one who'd got his hands on a woman who'd had her hands on one, if you get my drift.

It was Evert's burgeoning love for Lloyd, indeed, that she cited as the main reason for her defeat in 1978. 'In the last four games, all I could think about was going out with John,' she said later. 'Something fresh and wonderful was happening to me. I should have beaten Martina. If I had been hungry, the match was mine.'

Navratilova and Evert were friends, and remain so, but Navratilova chuckled when she heard that Evert was laying the blame at Cupid's chubby feet. 'When I started falling in love I always played my best tennis because it gave me such freedom,' she said. 'You know, there were very few times when Chris came out and actually said I beat her. There was always something that happened, some other reason for it.'

I had friends like that, too. A headache, a verruca, a cold; glandular fever, hay fever, yellow fever: just about all of them were blamed at one time or another for losing to me at tennis, perhaps to diminish the indignity of being beaten by a boy who was less like Jimmy Connors in his speed around the court, and still more like Jimmy Osmond. But I found that I wasn't bad at tennis. I started playing when I was eleven and there was one summer when my parents even shelled out for me to have coaching once a week, so before too long I could hit the ball with something approaching authority.

My problem was that my friends in Lynton Road, the Sykes brothers and John Hepworth, were all fellow members of Hillside Tennis Club, and all better players than me. Kids in Southport, or certainly those I knocked around with, all seemed to be gifted in at least one sport, and usually in several. There must have been something in the local water supply. At any rate, it took a long time, now that I think about it, before I started playing sport with people who were less proficient than I was. Until then I dragged an inferiority complex on to most tennis courts, golf courses, cricket pitches and football fields. And when I was selected to play for the Hillside Tennis Club junior team the summer after my dad died, I couldn't help wondering whether I had been picked on merit, or out of sympathy.

Still, there was fierce competition between the local clubs, and selection meetings were taken roughly as seriously as meetings of the Nobel Peace Prize committee, so I like to think that sympathetic feelings would have been brushed aside in the ruthless quest for bragging rights. Besides,.I did OK in the team, at least until I myself succumbed to glandular fever when I was fifteen.

One compensation for losing my place on the Hillside team was that glandular fever was widely known as the kissing disease, supposedly transmitted among teenagers by indiscriminate tonsular exploration, and this I found rather pleasing. The sad truth was that at fifteen I hadn't French-kissed anything except my cuddly toy panda, named Panda, on whom I practised regularly so that I might have a degree of expertise when the big moment finally arrived. What I hadn't allowed for was that the recipient of my first proper snog with a fellow human being, which I remember with rather alarming clarity, would not be as conveniently inert as Panda was. Her name was Rebecca and she was unlike Panda in most other respects, too. She didn't have buttons for eyes, or a wisp of stuffing emerging from a hole behind her right ear, for example, although that didn't worry me unduly. When her tongue started wrestling with mine, however, finally forcing it into a kind of half-Nelson on the floor of my mouth, I was downright panic-stricken. It was all I could do to stop lashing out in terror, like a man drowning.

The tryst with Rebecca took place at her friend Joanna's house in Dunster Road. My friend Andy Boothman fancied Joanna, and Joanna fancied him, so Rebecca and I went along to lend each of them moral support. But when they disappeared into Joanna's bedroom and shut the door, Rebecca and I were left in the lounge with nothing much to do except snog. We were far too awkward with each other to talk.

A few years later a remarkably similar situation arose in somewhat different circumstances. In the summer of 1983 I went to America for the first time, staying with people Mark Sutcliffe and I had met on our inter-railing trip round Europe the summer before. They included Robyn, the frisky Californian, although the pair of us failed to recapture the closeness we had enjoyed on the Ghost Train at Blackpool Pleasure Beach – perhaps because I still couldn't quite forgive her apathy towards the thrilling cricket match I had taken her to at Southport & Birkdale CC, or more likely because she now had a muscle-bound boyfriend called Vince.

Before I visited Robyn, however, I went to Kalamazoo, Michigan, to hook up with a cheerful nutcase called Zig whom Mark and I had befriended on a train journey from Innsbruck (where, to our barely containable delight, we stumbled upon a sporting goods shop named Robert Wanker) to Rome. Zig was as attentive a host as he could be given that he and his new girlfriend Paula couldn't keep their hands off one another for more than forty-five seconds at a time. This made driving rather awkward for him, but one night, with Paula in the passenger seat of his rickety old Buick, he managed to keep at least one hand on the steering-wheel and, intent on offering me an all-American experience, drove us up the interstate to a beautifully preserved and fully operational 1950s-style drive-in cinema.

With me in the back of the car was a friend of Paula's, a

nurse, whose name I have sadly forgotten, although the name of the town we went to is for ever etched in my memory. I can't remember what was showing that night at the drive-in cinema just outside Climax, Michigan, but I do remember that with Zig and Paula necking furiously in the front seat, the nurse and I were left with no option but to neck furiously in the back. Actually, I suppose there was the option of watching the big screen, but as it was a porn film, snogging each other, rather than sitting in silence in a place called Climax watching a woman performing fellatio in thirty-five-foot high Technicolour, was definitely the lesser of the two embarrassments.

I realise that I have strayed rather a long way over the baseline, so to speak, in terms of this chapter's principal subject matter. But sex is relevant, because no sport was more inextricably entwined with my gradual sexual awakening than tennis, indeed it became kind of a leitmotif in my sex life, such as it was, as I progressed through my teens and twenties.

When I was twenty-eight, for example, I split up with my girlfriend of six years, much to the surprise of most of our friends, who had expected the relationship to go the full five sets. My married friends Paddy and Sarah then took it upon themselves to fix me up with single female friends of theirs, which was most considerate of them, and tennis was always the principal tool in these match-making endeavours.

Paddy had been a contemporary of mine at St Andrews, one of the many public schoolboys I had got to know well, having previously never even set eyes on the species. My schoolfriends more or less all came from the same kind of lower middle-class background as me, but my mates at university included old Etonians, Harrovians and Wykehamists, as well as the sons of milkmen and dockers from Glasgow, Belfast and Liverpool, and I really can't think of anything that a four-year university education gave me – including and possibly above all a Master of Arts degree in modern history – that was more useful than that lesson in mixing with all kinds of people.

Of course, what threw different classes, creeds and colours together more effectively than anything was sport. How else but through the university football club would I have got to know Araz Ali, the Iranian biochemistry postgraduate who once referred to a friendly football match as 'a lovely'? And how else but through cricket and rugby would I ever have befriended proper thoroughbred toffs, some of them genuine aristocrats?

Paddy and Sarah were not aristocracy but they seemed awfully posh, and kept inviting me down to various country piles with tennis courts to play mixed doubles with women whose real names I was rarely privy to: they mostly preferred to be known by slightly silly nicknames. So although they might have been called something like Charlotte or Camilla or Lucinda or Louisa, they were introduced to me as something like Bingo or Snorky or Fleegle or Drooper, which for a chap who had spent a large part of the early 1970s glued to Hanna-Barbera's monumentally fine television show, *The Banana Splits*, was slightly disconcerting. I had grown up knowing Bingo as a bongo-playing gorilla, Fleegle as a guitar-strumming, lisping basset-hound, and neither as a willowy Home Counties blonde in an Alice band.

Still, it was nice that my suitability as a tennis partner was considered a useful first step on the stairs to a west wing bedroom, because in my early, and indeed mid-, and possibly even late teens, tennis had always seemed to represent my terminal gaucheness as far as the opposite sex was concerned. Hillside Tennis Club discos were tempests of unreciprocated longing, and I stood awkwardly in the shadows, avoiding the dance floor as if it were a seething pit of vipers.

Later, of course, I would learn that I was far from being the only one to emerge from the teen years with traumatic disco recollections. My own dear wife, Jane, tells a heartrending tale of a disco at Elsecar Village Hall near Barnsley, in 1977 when she was fourteen. She was wearing a long, floral gypsy skirt, bought especially for the occasion, which swished with what she fancied was considerable chic (or whatever word they used instead of 'chic' in South Yorkshire in 1977) as she walked back across the room from the loo, to where her friend Melanie was sitting. It was left to Melanie to inform her quietly that she had completed the entire journey with the hem of her skirt tucked into her knickers. She was so mortified that if they'd been serving arsenic behind the bar, rather than just warm, slightly flat Dandelion & Burdock (which I went through most of my childhood thinking was called Dandy, Lime & Burdock, a great name for a firm of private investigators but an odd one for a fizzy drink), she would have downed a pint in one.

None of which was any consolation to me at the same time, maybe even on the same evening, on the other side of the Pennines. Perhaps if I'd been a better player, capable of reaching the final of the hallowed Bingham Trophy, I might have stood a better chance of copping off, as we used to call it. After all, sporting talent has been an aphrodisiac since time immemorial, at all levels. Otherwise, there would have been no chance of Nick, a guy I knew in Southport with a complexion like a cheese-and-tomato pizza and a personality to match, but who happened to be a county rugby player, going out with a goddess I worshipped called Mandy. Similarly, but on a different scale, had John McEnroe been only an averagely decent tennis player, he would never have successfully wooed a Hollywood star, Tatum O'Neal.

I always thought it a missed opportunity, by the way, that O'Neal, following her divorce from McEnroe, did not take up with a much less bellicose sportsman, Sandy Lyle, and become Tatum Lyle. That's a flight of fancy I enjoy almost as much as I do the idea that the former footballer Imre Varadi – who played for Everton among about twenty-seven other league clubs – might be married to a woman called Olive.

I interviewed Frank Skinner once and told him my Olive Varadi gag. After the split second it took to sink in, he laughed long and hard. Making a comedian laugh is a rare pleasure, I suppose like nutmegging a professional footballer. But the comedian, doubtless like the footballer, never lets you get away with thinking you might be top dog. Skinner had just been appearing in the play *Art*, which had been brought to the West End by Sean Connery's wife Micheline. 'Wouldn't it have been funny,' he said, 'if she had married the novelist Thomas Mann. Wouldn't that have been one of the greatest names ever?' And while I was laughing he scored on the rebound. 'What about Whoopi Goldberg, don't you think she should have married Peter Cushing?'

For all the discomfort I suffered at Hillside Tennis Club disco nights, they were at least an indication of a thriving junior section, and it continued to thrive despite the malignant efforts of a man I'll call Mr Bottomley, whose attitude towards children made *Chitty Chitty Bang Bang*'s Baroness Bomburst look and sound like *The Sound of Music*'s Maria von Trapp. Indeed, my membership of Hillside Tennis Club gave me a useful early education in all the character types with which every suburban sports club is endowed. For example, there is always the Miserable Old Git like Mr Bottomley, who believes that under-eighteens should not be allowed to play during the hours of daylight, and only on a very restricted basis during the hours of darkness. The former British number one Jeremy Bates tells a disturbing story about Queen's Club, where he practised as a junior. One afternoon, apparently, he was ordered to leave an indoor court by a woman on an adjacent court because she was distracted by the noise his shoes were making on the artificial surface. It's no wonder he never came close to winning Wimbledon.

The woman at Queen's was Mr Bottomley's spiritual cousin, and there are thousands of them, alas, all utterly incapable of making a connection between their attitude to juniors and their vehement complaint that Britain produces hardly any world-class tennis players. In Britain in one recent calendar year, only 5000 under-eighteens played tennis more than twelve times, as opposed to 250,000 youngsters in France. And whereas that can't be blamed entirely on the Miserable Old Git, he – and she – is a highly significant factor.

However, while still abundant, the MOG is a diminishing breed. Things have changed since I was an under-eighteen being scowled at by Mr Bottomley. Now in the ascendant is another suburban character type, the Good Egg. The Good Egg understands that every sports club should cherish and encourage its juniors, ensuring that they are taught both to play well and to behave properly, which means exposing them as little as possible to the pernicious influence of two further types exclusive to tennis clubs, the Racquet Chucker and the Wasp Swatter.

The Wasp Swatter is the man or woman – although it is usually a man – whose outlandish service action suggests someone histrionically trying to kill a wasp that has ventured too close. Every tennis club has one. The Racquet Chucker, obviously, is the man or woman – it, too, is usually a man – whose temper on the court is like an enraged, runaway pit bull terrier. Again, most tennis clubs have one. In fact, when I lived in London I was a member of a club at which the Racquet Chucker was a fairly eminent journalist, who would also habitually swear at the top of his voice when he missed an easy shot. Even to be in the same profession as him felt shaming. I used to say animal vivisectionist when anyone there asked me what I did for a living. It was less embarrassing.

At Hillside Tennis Club in the 1970s there were quite a lot of Racquet Chuckers, most of whom were juniors. I suppose it was grist to Mr Bottomley's mill that there were some brattish antics the like of which even the emerging John McEnroe might have baulked at; at the end of most juniors' events, there was usually at least one wooden-framed tennis racquet in splinters, and I fear that I might even have launched the odd Slazenger myself.

Paradoxically, it was McEnroe who turned me into a paragon of self-control on the tennis court. At Wimbledon in 1977, as an unknown, 18-year-old qualifier, he reached a men's singles semi-final. But it was his quarter-final match that made more of an impact on me. He played the number 13 seed Phil Dent, and lost the second set to a tie-break, having won the first set 6-4. That was the point at which a British audience got its first glimpse of the behaviour that would soon earn him the sobriquet 'Superbrat'. Furious with himself, McEnroe first tried to break his racquet under his shoe, then disgustedly kicked it along the grass as he walked back to his chair. The Court One crowd was horrified, and McEnroe recalls the episode in his 2002 autobiography, *Serious*.

> The English were quite upset with me, but I have to tell you, at that moment I felt mostly amused. As impressed as I may have been with Wimbledon and its tremendous history – and unlike a lot of young players then (and almost all young players now), I really did have respect for tennis history – I found England to be strange and stodgy and quaint.
>
> When I saw those dozing linesmen, I thought, 'This isn't what Wimbledon should look like.' The club and the

tournament were beautiful, but the whole atmosphere was totally set in its ways and self-important beyond belief. I couldn't help resenting how badly the organisers treated the lesser players and how they genuflected to the stars. I was incredulous at all that bowing and curtsying to royalty and lesser royalty. It felt like the class system at its worst. I was a kid from Queens, a subway-rider. How could anybody expect me to take all this strawberries-and-cream malarkey seriously?

In the third set, convinced that he was on the receiving end of some bad line calls, McEnroe started moaning to the umpire, who was decidedly unsympathetic. McEnroe moaned louder. And then the crowd actually started booing him, as he recalled in *Serious*. 'Callow kid that I was, I found the crowd's extreme investment in the match and its decorum strange and rather comical.'

Watching at home, I was firmly on the side of the crowd. I had seen Nastase misbehave on court, and in truth he could be pretty boorish, but more often than not there did at least seem to be an undercurrent of humour. McEnroe was different. Moreover, he was a teenager like me, and if this was what teenage petulance on the tennis court looked like – as discordant and ugly as this – then I resolved to put my racquet-wanging habits behind me. At the same time, I was enraptured by his ability to play tennis, and years later I was able to rationalise his outbursts – and now that he is part of the establishment he once scorned, it is hard to remember just how repugnant they were – as being indivisible from his talent. It is what I call my Nick Faldo theory. Faldo is rather a jolly chap these days, but in the early 1990s his aloofness on the golf course, and his apparent fondness for his own company off it, provided arch-critics such as Mark James with cruel gags like the one about Faldo's idea of a night out being dinner for one on his hotel balcony.

However, this anti-social streak was merely the flip side of the same temperament that won six major championships. Thus, those who took pleasure in Faldo's achievements while lambasting his personality were, at best, being naive. It was the same with Paul Gascoigne. The Gazza who could do exquisite things with a football was the Gazza who belched into microphones and once told the whole of Norway to fuck off. Belching into microphones, wearing plastic breasts, that's why he could do amazing things on a football pitch. Similarly, the only way to curb Wayne Rooney's expressive language on the field is to curb his expressive feet. It's regrettable, but it's the way it is. We can't choose which part of the package we take. And thus it was with McEnroe's tantrums, a theory I got to put to the great man himself shortly before Wimbledon 2005.

'Well, usually the first thing that came into my mind was to say something funny, to defuse a situation with a joke,' he told me. 'But I was also brought up to play best when I kept up a level of intensity. I could scream, then go back and hit an ace. If I said something funny, I would lose it a little bit. Connors was different. He'd mutter "motherfucker" to himself, then put his arm round someone in the crowd and say "It's tough out here, isn't it?" And he'd have people eating out of his hand. It used to drive me crazy.'

'You know,' he continued, 'when I was young I felt like I was going to break down barriers. Here was this upper-class, cissy sport, and I believed 100 per cent that I was going to change it. I played every match as if it were my last. I wanted to be accepted like a baseball player or a footballer, and the irony is that in those sports guys get pictured screaming at the umpire, and they're not saying "Hey, how you doin?" But they are never criticised for it. When you look at the horrible things

that happen in other sports, me yelling at those umpires was
not all that bad. But I remember a poll in a Miami paper to
find the worst people of all time. Charles Manson was one,
Attila the Hun was two, I was three and Jack the Ripper was
four. It was funny in a way, except that was me they were talking about.'

I found myself sharing his wonderment at the absence of
proportion; how could people have been so thumpingly pious
about those strops of his? But when I got home I flicked
through some of Clive James's old *Observer* columns, always
my first reference point when considering tennis in the 1970s
and early 1980s, and was usefully reminded that McEnroe,
whether it was unavoidable behaviour or not, really was not
entitled to sympathy, either at the time or retrospectively.

'Thus Borg progressed majestically into the closing rounds,
continually pulling out that little bit extra,' James wrote.

When McEnroe pulled out his little bit extra, you rather
wished that he would tuck it back in. For a long time he did
his best to contain his awful personality, tying his shoelaces
between games instead of during and merely scowling at
the linesmen instead of swearing. When sulking he kicked
the ground but raised no divots, nor did his service take
more than a quarter of an hour each time. You have to
realise that McEnroe is serving around the corner of an
imaginary building, and that his wind-up must perforce be
extra careful. He has a sniper's caution. Finally the rain got
to him. By Thursday he was behaving as badly as ever,
thereby confirming the rule that Wimbledon, like alcohol,
brings out the essential character.

These days, of course, McEnroe is a hero even to those who
once watched his hissy fits with slack-jawed incredulity. When

Wimbledon comes around, he is rightly feted as one of the
BBC's principal assets; insightful, authoritative and never, ever
dull. I yield to nobody in my admiration of him as a television
pundit, but at the same time it tickles me to hear people talk
about him as though he has undergone some kind of personality transplant. The truth of the matter is that, while a good
deal less uncouth than he used to be, he is still the same guy
Clive James wrote about, still the same guy who made Dan
Maskell wince. He can be spectacularly charmless. I have met
him twice now and on neither occasion has he looked as
though a single corpuscle of his being was pleased to make my
acquaintance. Most interviewees at least essay some pretence.

Actually, I wasn't there to interview him the first time I met
him; I was there to play tennis with him. For a few years, the
organisers of the Honda Challenge, an annual seniors tournament at the Royal Albert Hall, used to hire the indoor courts
at Queen's, and invited representatives of several favoured
media organisations to spend the morning before the tournament playing doubles with the pros. I went along to three or
four of these events and had the privilege of sharing a court
with Boris Becker, Pat Cash, Peter Fleming, John Lloyd and
Henri Leconte, among others. I don't suppose that a morning
playing tennis with various out-of-condition journalists was
exactly their idea of a fun time, but they were contractually
obliged to show up, and did so with unfailing good grace,
offering advice and encouragement even to one portly Sunday
newspaper columnist whose tennis was not rusty so much as
condemned.

The way it worked was that the hacks – tracksuited or even,
in one or two frightening instances, wearing tennis shorts
revealing acres of mottled flesh – would be assigned in threes
to a particular player. The trick was not to look too thrilled if
you got assigned to Boris Becker as opposed to, say, Chris

Wilkinson, nor too disappointed if you got Wilkinson instead of Becker. Sports writers are not supposed to radiate anything other than world-weary cynicism, and actual excitement is a no-no. I learnt this the hard way in the press box on Centre Court, the first year I covered Wimbledon.

I was reporting on a match involving Andre Agassi, who at one stage not only managed to retrieve a near-perfect lob, but from well behind the baseline, and practically off his toes, whipped a fantastic cross-court winner. The crowd erupted into thunderous applause and I erupted with them, before realising that not a single other occupant of the press box was even smiling, let alone clapping, and that one or two of them were shooting me disdainful sidelong glances, like grizzled old cowboys in a saloon noticing that a fresh-faced youngster at the other end of the bar has just puked up his whisky. I felt like I'd stepped into a Bateman cartoon: 'The Journalist Who Clapped In The Press Box At Wimbledon'. I stopped clapping immediately and wondered whether, if I could get my tongue lolling and my eyes rolling up into the back of my head, I might at least convey the impression that I had suffered some kind of fit, rather than, more embarrassingly, a lapse in professionalism. To my shame, of course, I am now one of those who shoot the disdainful sidelong glance when a press-box newcomer commits the unpardonable sin of applauding.

Anyway, in December 2001 when I arrived at Queen's for this enjoyable annual curtain-raiser to the Honda Challenge, we were told that McEnroe, for the first time, would be among the pros. Thrillingly, I was then assigned to play with him, and did my professional damnedest to suppress my excitement. It wasn't easy, although I was at least able to pick up some tips from the way he suppressed his excitement at playing with me. A wonderful photograph was later published alongside my column, with me serving in the background, my face contorted with effort, my every sinew practically popping with determination, while McEnroe stands at the net in the foreground, gazing with palpable boredom into the middle-distance. The caption, written by a heartless sub-editor, read: 'Brian Viner shows his doubles partner, the slightly bored John McEnroe, just how unorthodox a serve can be.'

McEnroe and I played against the BBC presenter John Inverdale and the ITV motor-racing commentator James Allen, a match notable for the fact that Inverdale, a highly competent club player, would have needed cardiac treatment if he had tried any harder. Even with a semi-detached McEnroe, however, we still won easily. Not that he seemed to care two hoots. All the other old pros feigned a degree of satisfaction upon winning, but my partner had no time for nonsense like that. In my column I wrote: 'I did not high-five him as I did Cash in the following match against the man from the *Daily Telegraph* and his partner. Even when he is smiling there is something about McEnroe that discourages intimacy. But he is a god, all the same. Maybe that's it. You can't get too fraternal with gods.'

Back in 1977 he was still some way from achieving godlike status, indeed in many ways McEnroe is synonymous more with the 1980s, the decade in which he won all but one of his seven Grand Slam titles, and contested two unforgettable Wimbledon finals with Borg. But the seventies spawned him, and it is entirely apt that it was 1977, Silver Jubilee year, when he first burst like a big angry zit into the consciousness of the British public, because his rebelliousness and rudeness were so stridently at odds with the joyful but respectful mood of a bunting-bedecked monarchy.

That mood is hard to remember now, as Andrew Collins explains in *Where Did It All Go Right?*, his delightful account of 'growing up normal' in the seventies. In his 1977 chapter, Collins describes a photograph of his family taken on the Silver Jubilee Bank Holiday, 7 June.

> Mum, Simon and I are wearing identical red, white and blue 'Jeans' T-shirts with Union Jacks on the sleeves, and Jubilee-styled party hats. Melissa is waving a flag. Not a trace of irony here, but it's difficult to convey to people how royal the nation was in 1977. I have decorated my diary by writing each letter in alternate red and blue Tempo [yet] as I write it is the Queen's Golden Jubilee year and I feel I am in good company not giving a fuck.

This is perhaps a slightly crude analysis of Britain's diminishing esteem for the royal family, but Collins was right to recall our heartfelt collective genuflection to the monarchy in 1977, and when Virginia Wade won Wimbledon that summer, soon to be followed by Geoff Boycott scoring his hundredth hundred, it certainly seemed as though God was a cravat-wearing Englishman, taking time off from tending his herbaceous border in Esher to watch over his mortal flock.

It is no wonder that McEnroe thought us stodgy and quaint, nor any wonder that we thought him insolent and despicable. To this day he is like a one-man counterblast to traditional British virtues, only now we admire him for it. And, of course, those virtues have been diluted even at Wimbledon, where the umpires, who used mostly to be English, now come from pretty much everywhere. This, I have to say, is a shame. I treasure the memory of an English umpire a few years ago becoming increasingly exasperated with a restless Centre Court crowd. 'Please!' he said, into his microphone, in an attempt to shut them up. And then he said 'Please!' again, slightly louder. Still there was a hubbub of noise. 'Thank you!' he said, sharply. And then 'Please!' one more time, louder and more sharply still. Please! Please! Thank you! Please! Only in England could that amount to a rebuke.

The strange thing is that the English tradition of respectful gentility, and the American tradition of brash irreverence, are completely transposed when it comes to the activities of the press. This was rammed home to me in the media centre at Wimbledon in 2005, where I sat polishing my golden prose alongside my *Independent* colleague Richard Edmondson. For that morning's paper, Edmo had written a report on an over-thirty-fives women's doubles match in which Tracy Austin and Jana Novotna hammered Carling Bassett-Seguso and Mima Jausovec 6-0 6-1.

'Two words described the difference in this match and they were "Jana Novotna",' Edmo wrote. 'The Czech, who won the women's singles in 1998, is, at 36, a newcomer to this category and took full advantage. Austin, a squeaky presence on the BBC analysts' couch this fortnight, delivered a service that would not crack an egg, but that did not matter with Jana patrolling the net.'

I had read his report, smiled, and thought nothing more of it. But suddenly I was aware of a squeaky presence behind us. 'Pardon me, which of you is Richard Edmondson?' said Tracy Austin. Edmo owned up. 'I've read your article,' she said. 'I'm trying really hard, you know. It's not fair of you to say that I can't play.' There was a brief, awkward silence. 'Erm, I didn't write that you can't play,' Edmo said. 'I wrote that your service couldn't, erm, crack an egg.'

There was another awkward silence, during which Austin, astonishingly, started to cry. It was funny and appalling at the same time, and I later reflected that an American journalist would never have written that her serve couldn't crack an egg, because actually her serve, unthreatening though it may have been, probably could crack an egg. 'Have you ever seen her serve with an egg?' would come the query from some professional pedant, a sub-editor or fact-checker, terrified of an expensive libel action. 'If you did, and it failed to crack, then that's fine. Otherwise, it's horseshit and we can't print it!'

Whatever, as a stricken Tracy Austin left the media centre, I couldn't help feeling a most unhacklike twinge of sympathy. After all, she loomed large in my memories of the 1970s, because she was among the first competitors of roughly my own age, male or female, to make an impact on international sport, becoming front-page news as she reached the third round of the women's singles – and took two games off the defending champion, Chris Evert – as a fourteen-year-old in 1977 . I wouldn't go so far as to say that I felt an affinity with her because of it, and I certainly couldn't fancy a girl who had more metal in her mouth than Richard Kiel's character Jaws, in the latest Bond film *The Spy Who Loved Me*, but, nonetheless, here was a fourteen-year-old competing with the very best in the world. A certain amount of respect was due.

8

Olga Korbut's Pigtails

Tracy Austin was not quite the first contemporary of mine to arrive in the spotlight on the global sporting stage. In July 1976, almost twelve months before Austin became the youngest competitor at Wimbledon for seventy years, Nadia Comaneci, born less than three weeks after me on 12 November 1961, took the Olympic Games by storm. I felt, in an entirely vicarious way, as if I had come of age. Here was a fellow fourteen-year-old setting the world alight, and although I could scarcely perform a forward-roll on an Axminster carpet, let alone a backward walkover on a four-inch beam, I felt somehow empowered, at least twenty years before anyone even used the word.

Comaneci – a small, dark-eyed sprite of a child – was a revelation, the more so because she seemed to spring, almost literally, so completely from the blue. Obviously people in gymnastics knew something of this Romanian prodigy, but the rest of us had no idea that Olympic history was about to be rewritten. About a year earlier, however, she had served notice of what might unfold. On the beam at the pre-Olympic gymnastics tournament in Montreal in the summer of 1975, Comaneci scored a perfect 10 from a judge who had never given one before, a Hungarian woman called Grete Treiber.

'Philosophically, I was opposed to giving a 10,' Treiber told David Walsh of the *Sunday Times* years later. 'It is perfection and perfection exists only in nature, or so I thought.' This was nicely expressed, although, in fact, the presumption of perfection was how gymnastic disciplines were judged. All competitors started with a 10 and then had marks deducted as they made mistakes. It is perhaps not entirely coincidental that some religions reckon the same is true of God: that in the eyes of the Almighty we all start out with an unblemished record, and then start blotting our copybook by lusting after Evonne Goolagong and even more sinful excesses. That must be why some gymnastics judges down the years have had God complexes.

Anyway, Grete Treiber watched in growing astonishment as Comaneci performed on the beam that day.

She had such continuity of movement, such fluency, control, dynamism, daring, and so beautiful to watch. As it was happening, I could see my problem, and I began to hope she would make a mistake so that I wouldn't have to give her a 10. But there wasn't the slightest error. When it was over I looked at my notepad: the page was completely blank and I felt such a fool. 'Have you been out to lunch while this was happening?' I crushed my own belief and flashed the first 10 in my whole life.

The following year, back in Montreal for the Games themselves, the same thing happened again. But this was different, this was the Olympic Games. And no Olympic gymnast – not even Olga Korbut, the darling of the Munich Olympics four years earlier – had ever scored so much as a single 10. Comaneci scored seven. Her first routine, on the asymmetric bars, lasted only nineteen seconds. The four judges passed their scores to the chief judge, whose job it was to eliminate the highest and the lowest marks, and find the average of the two remaining. Even someone as hopeless at maths as me could have worked out the average – and I was truly hopeless, needing intensive after-school tutoring from a retired schoolmaster called Mr Smith even to scrape a C at O-level. The highest score was 10, so was the lowest, and so were the two remaining. But the electronic scoreboard flashed not 10.00 but 1.00; it had been programmed only to show three digits. 'That is actually a 10, a perfect 10,' explained the official announcer. The crowd, aware that they had witnessed something momentous, something even beyond the compass of the electronic scoreboard, went wild. Comaneci, having scarcely reached puberty, left Montreal with three gold medals.

Several thousand miles to the east, I, too, had scarcely reached puberty, and had three merit cards in French. This was not on quite the same scale of achievement as three Olympic golds, but it was still no mean feat, and secured a rare visit to the headmaster's office to receive his personal congratulations. Incidentally, someone once said that people who claim to have enjoyed their schooldays are either liars now, or were bullies then. All I can say to that is that I look back at my schooldays with nothing but affection, although there is no doubt that my affection is boosted by the knowledge that I won't ever again have to sit on the number 15 bus frantically trying to learn Ovid's 'Pyramus and Thisbe' in time for a Latin test, nor will ever again have a board rubber hurled at me by a furious teacher, nor will my testicles ever again drop in the company of dozens of other testicles in various stages of pubescence.

At KGV, as with everything else in an all-boys' school, there was an element of competition about puberty. There were some boys who at twelve had voices as deep as Paul Robeson singing 'Ol' Man River', and other boys who at fifteen still spoke in a shrill treble. Then there was the in-between part, when the voice soared on one word and plunged on the next, to the uncontained amusement of Mr Clough, who succeeded Blod as my Latin master. 'Right, Viner,' he would say. 'In your finest basso profundo, please give me an example of an ablative absolute.'

As well as ablative absolutes, there was body hair to worry about. But I was far more worried about not getting it than getting it. In fact, I was so envious of the wisps of underarm hair that seemed to be proliferating before my very eyes in the changing room before Mr Stichbury's PE lessons that I decided to do something about it even before I was biologically ready. In my bedroom one morning – and this has been a closely kept personal secret until now – I carefully cut some hair from my head and stuck it, with the help of a tube of Bostik, under both arms.

What kind of early teenage neurosis propelled me towards this drastic adhesive measure, I cannot now imagine. By some miracle I wasn't rumbled, even though I for one was decidedly conscious of a strong smell of glue emanating from under both arms as soon as I removed my shirt, which hadn't stuck fast to my armpits, thank God. Anyone in my class who was into glue-sniffing – and I suspect there were one or two – had only to stand next to me while changing for PE to get his fix for the week.

Moreover, it wasn't as if there was the slightest authenticity to my sudden thatch of underarm hair, which was weirdly and randomly matted to the skin's surface. I can only give thanks that one of my classmates didn't spot it, and have a quiet word with Mr Stichbury ('Sir, Viner seems to have stuck some hair under his arms!') who already, in the time-honoured tradition of PE teachers everywhere, had a sadistic streak. His idea of a worthwhile lesson was to line us all up against the wall of the gym and belt a volleyball at us. Those it hit had to go and stand by the wall bars, very often in a certain amount of pain having just copped a volleyball in the bollocks, so that eventually there was only one survivor. These days, it could almost be the premise for a reality television show. In those days, to be fair to 'Stich', it was a game most of us actually enjoyed. Our other weekly PE lesson was with his senior colleague Eric 'Windy' Gale, who did immensely useful and worthy things like teaching us the principles of artificial respiration, but given the choice most of us would have preferred to dodge Stich's volleyball.

Whatever, I don't hold one little bit with the notion that only bullies and liars enjoyed their schooldays, although I can appreciate that the memory is highly selective. The pleasures of school – games of football at dinner time; snowball fights; gales of hysterical laughter; throwing soggies; burgeoning friendships that are now more than thirty years old – remain vivid in my mind. The horrors, by contrast, have mostly been suppressed. But occasionally one horror or another comes floating to the surface, unshackled either by a dream (in times of anxiety I always dream that I am about to sit my French Literature A-level paper, having done no revision whatever), or by circumstance. In some shape or form this happens to almost everyone I know. When my wife Jane took our daughter Eleanor to see her prospective new secondary school, she was shown into the chemistry labs, and despite the fact that she had been rubbish at chemistry she at first felt a not-unpleasant wave of nostalgia as she clocked the racks of test tubes and Bunsen burners. When her eye fell upon the huge, laminated Periodic Table fastened to the wall, however, she felt an overwhelming need to retch. She related this sorry tale to me later that evening, and I could sympathise entirely.

Jane – whom you have so far met as a fourteen-year-old returning from the toilet at Elsecar Village Hall disco with the hem of her dress caught in her knickers, and as a 41-year-old mother retching in a secondary-school chemistry lab – now enters this story for solid sporting reasons. She turned ten just before the 1972 Olympic Games and whereas the entire world was charmed by Olga Korbut, the Russian waif who won gold medals for her scintillating performances on the beam and the floor, Jane, transfixed in front of the television in South Yorkshire, was shaken to the very core of her being.

Not even a growing passion for David Cassidy – who a week or so after the Olympics registered his first British number one with 'How Can I Be Sure' – could distract her from her principal ambition in life, which was, effectively, to become Olga Korbut. The fact that she was seven years younger than Olga was not an insurmountable problem; the 17-year-old Russian's body shape was far closer to that of an average ten-year-old. And, happily, Jane had mousey brown hair like Olga's, which she started wearing in Olga-style pig-tails. Even more felicitously, she had some gymnastic talent. Obviously, it was not ever going to take her to the Olympic Games, but it did take her to Huddersfield, where she took part, alas unsuccessfully, in the all-England under-thirteens trials.

Of course, the idea that there might be English girls of ten, eleven or twelve whose gymnastic ability was as yet undiscovered, would have tickled the Russians no end, causing them to splutter vodka over each other in uncontrollable attacks of mirth. Olga Korbut's talent had been spotted practically before she could walk. If they'd had ultrasound equipment in her home town of Grodno then her ability to perform a flick-flack might have been identified in the womb. It was not by accident that the USSR had won women's team gold at every Olympics since 1952; behind the Iron Curtain during the Cold War, Olympic success was deemed a political imperative.

Cold War, Iron Curtain, USSR; it is amazing how these terms, such a fact of life during my childhood, have now acquired a thick layer of dust. If my children get to know them at all, it will only be from history lessons. Which can only be a good thing, I suppose, although in many other respects I think that it was better to be a child in the 1970s, when the world was an altogether more naive, impressionable place. For example, I don't suppose anyone in 1972 gave the remotest thought to the sexual needs of the athletes, whereas before the 2002 Commonwealth Games in Manchester I was handed a fact sheet containing the frankly astounding information that, along with 3119 flags, 1011 computers, 70,000 litres of milk, 11,600 kilos of mushrooms and 3.5 million paper napkins, 150,000 condoms had been stockpiled for the competitors' use.

Around 5000 athletes descended on Manchester that summer, so to get through the contraceptive mountain by the end of the Games, every single one of them would have to have had safe sex thirty times. Even allowing for an over-zealous purchasing strategy, the organisers were clearly anticipating an awful lot of friskiness, which begged all kinds of questions. I wondered, for instance, whether the Commonwealth Games might be a bit like Crufts, where, although sexual activity between contestants of different breeds is frowned upon, same-breed sex is not merely encouraged but actively engineered. Thus, in the same way that a pair of pedigree shitzus might be brought together for a quickie in the hope of producing a top-class litter, might a national coach with a long-term development strategy steer his cute female pole-vaulter towards another team's handsome male pole-vaulter, suggesting that they go somewhere quiet without availing themselves of the copious supply of condoms?

Whatever, I'd never previously given much thought to the carnal activity that goes on between athletes at big international meetings, but I realised it made sense that all those young men and women, at such a peak of physical fitness and virility, might have had eyes not only on a gold medal, but also on each other. In that respect, things were probably no different at Munich in 1972. Of course, no matter what the levels of lust were in Munich's Olympic Village, it can't be called an age of innocence, not with the corpses of eleven Israeli athletes to be repatriated. But the world was undoubtedly more naive and impressionable than it is now, which in turn made the Olympics more thrilling. It is impossible to picture an Olga Korbut today, emerging from nowhere to enthral a global television audience and to change the entire perception of a sport. Nadia Comaneci was better, Nelli Kim was prettier, Ludmila Tourischeva was more elegant, and yet gymnastics can reasonably be divided into two periods: before Olga, and after Olga.

A whole year after the Munich Olympics, Jane's Olga fixation had not abated. If anything it had intensified, the more so as Kirk Balk Comprehensive in Hoyland, near Barnsley, which she joined in the very week that I started at KGV, had a gym team. In no time at all she was its star performer, or at least vying for star status with a girl called Fran Gooder, the Tourischeva to her Korbut. It was a gym display for pupils, staff and parents at the end of the Christmas term that elevated Jane to top dog. Her mum and dad had an LP of ragtime music, and she worked out a tumbling routine to Scott Joplin's 'The Entertainer', which went down an absolute storm. After that, she was known to every other pupil as 'Little Olga', in which regard she was certainly not unique in Britain as a whole. While I was writing this book Jane logged on to eBay for the first time, and had to provide a password. But intriguingly, the one she chose – Little Olga – had already been snapped up, almost certainly by some other ex-schoolgirl gymnast now in her early forties.

At Kirk Balk, however, Jane was the only Little Olga. This probably pissed off Fran Gooder mightily. It certainly pissed off Jane's elder sister – now my dear sister-in-law Jackie – who had already spent two years at the school and suddenly had to suffer kids coming up to her saying, 'Hey, are you Little Olga's big sister?'

That the Kirk Balk gym team continued to thrive, Jane remembers as being principally the achievement of an extraordinarily dedicated teacher called Miss Schumacher, a pleasingly exotic name for the Barnsley area in the 1970s, although Miss Schumacher then did an Evonne Goolagong and went and married a Mr Hodgetts. I'm sorry to say that I know Jane's old school stories almost as well as I know my own, which is either the sign of an extremely vibrant marriage or one in need of professional help. Either way, I'm also inordinately fond of her tale of Mrs French the German teacher, or it may have been Mrs German the French teacher, who announced one day that she would be leaving at the end of that term 'to try for a baby'. Apparently, nobody batted an eyelid. Trying for a baby was a quintessential 1970s reason for a married woman to leave her job, and I don't suppose anyone was heartless enough to suggest that it might have been just about possible to hold down a nine-to-four job and try for a baby during out-of-school hours. Was Mr French, or Mr German, expected to mount his wife around the clock? It probably never occurred to anyone to ask.

Nor, of course, did the thought occur to Little Olga that her future husband might be a chubby lad, Big Brian, living on the other side of the Pennines. If she was going to marry anyone from outside Yorkshire then it could only be David Cassidy. But, had a fortune-teller actually broken the bad news, at least she would have drawn comfort from the fact that I, too, had been entranced by Olga Korbut's performance in the 1972 Olympics, albeit for the diametrically opposite reason that here was a girl who could do things that I could never do in a million years.

I had been too young to take much notice of the 1968 Olympic Games in Mexico City (what cosmic forces, by the way, had conspired to give Mexico the Olympics and the World Cup just two years apart?), but by 1972 I loved the idea that an entire fortnight of BBC television – in an era of only three channels, don't forget – should be devoted to sport. In those days, moreover, the BBC could do no wrong. In its relationship with television anchormen, Britain was still gripped by the spirit of the 1950s. I looked upon Frank Bough, as I did the cricket presenter Peter West, like a favourite uncle, not that any favourite uncle of mine was later revealed to spend his leisure time snorting cocaine at orgies, more's the pity.

With Bough leading the way, the partisanship of the BBC – invisible to most people brought up in Britain, who considered the BBC to be the very definition of noble non-partisanship – greatly exercised Clive James in the *Observer*. 'Heights of lunacy were scaled,' he wrote, 'when a British hope called Brinkley set off on the first lap of a butterfly event. "And there's Brinkley, quite content to let Mark Spitz set the pace." What was actually happening, of course, was that Brinkley, like all the other competitors, was already contenting himself as best he could with being totally destroyed.'

It is perfectly common these days to find newspaper

columnists criticising the British bias of BBC sports commentators. I did it myself when Paula Radcliffe pulled out of the 2004 Olympic marathon, causing Brendan Foster almost to commit ritual suicide on air, while only the most fleeting, grudging attention was granted to the doughty Japanese woman who actually won the thing in that searing heat. Moreover, most newspapers now employ not just TV critics, but even sport-on-TV critics. All of which makes it easy to forget that James was a pioneer: most people writing about telly in the seventies were above writing about sports coverage, but he knew a productive seam when he saw one. He was also the first to recognise a tendency which continues to dog televised sport more than thirty years on: the assumption on the part of most commentators that words speak louder than pictures.

'The brute fact so far has been that the swimming commentaries have added nothing to the pictures except file-card titbits about little Lodja Gdnsk of Poland being born in Pfft and just missing out on a medal at the pan-European dry-pool Games at Flart,' James wrote. 'But the voices-over on the swimming are a *Principia Mathematica* of condensed argument compared to the vocal gas enshrouding the visuals from the diving pool. "Here she comes, into the back position," says our irrepressible voice as the diver walks to the end of the board and turns around, "and look at those toes working at the end of the board: and there she goes, round into the twist, and round and down and . . . in." Television for the blind.' Nothing much has changed.

As you will have gathered by now, I remain a huge fan of Clive James the TV critic, but there is one thing about his column of 10 September 1972 that mystifies me: every word is devoted to the Olympic Games, yet not a word refers to the massacre of the Israeli athletes. That tragedy unfolded on

5 September, only five days earlier, so it seems strange that James should not give it even a passing mention.

On the other hand, this tallies entirely with my own memories of the Munich Olympics. I'm ashamed to say that the appalling terrorist outrage chronicled so vividly in Stephen Spielberg's 2006 film, *Munich*, at the time made nothing like as much impact on me as the achievements of Mark Spitz in the swimming pool. This at least gives me something in common with Sir Steve Redgrave. He and I are about the same age, and he told me once that one of his most vivid childhood memories was being sent to buy the *Daily Mirror* during the 1972 Olympics. He walked back to his house staring at the banner headline 'Spitz For Six', and thinking how much fun it would be to win an Olympic gold medal. It is nice to know that we both, aged ten, found the achievements of Mark Spitz inspiring, one notable difference being that Redgrave was inspired to become Britain's greatest Olympian, and I wasn't.

The other thing that appealed to me about Spitz – who ended up with an astonishing tally of seven golds – was his peculiar name. I have always had an affection for wacky American names, and still derive a good deal of puerile fun from them, indeed when my friend Davey and I have had one or two over the eight, we can cheerfully fill an hour or so just by reciting the names of American golfers at one another. As a source of hilarity it's not exactly Wildean, but it never fails to tickle us. I give him Fred Funk, he trumps me with Howard Twitty, and so it continues. There is a limitless supply of such names, and what particularly amuses us is that Americans don't recognise them as daft at all. When I lived over there in the mid-1980s, I opened a bank account with the First National Bank of Atlanta. They asked me to write my name, address and other details on a form, and a few days later I went to collect my first chequebook. Unfortunately, someone had misread my form and so the name on my chequebook, and the name by which the bank knew me thereafter, was Briad Unier. Nobody questioned it for a second.

To get back to Mark Spitz, another reason I so admired his extraordinary prowess in the pool was that, like Olga Korbut, he excelled in something at which I was utterly crap. I didn't learn to swim until I was eleven, although it was not for want of my parents doing all they could to get my feet off the bottom.

At Southport's Victoria Baths I had lessons with a woman called Mrs Lee, whom I remember as having the easy-going charm and child-friendly demeanour of the Wicked Witch of the West, while I'm sure she remembers me as being as lovable as Damian, the satanic child in *The Omen*. Let's just say we didn't hit it off, and as a result my swimming went backwards, if not downwards. To compound my dislike of swimming lessons, I was not, let me be frank, very good at drying myself. It wasn't that I couldn't grasp the mechanics of applying a towel to my wet bits, more that I couldn't be bothered. I have a vivid memory of going for swimming lessons with the Taylor sisters, girls of around my age who lived in Clovelly Drive, and sitting on the back seat between Kay and Alison Taylor as their mum drove us home, with Alison complaining that I didn't seem notably drier than I'd been in the pool. To be perfectly candid, I'm not much better even to this day. There is something about swimming-pool changing rooms that makes me want to get out of there as rapidly as possible, dry or not.

I didn't tell any of this to the mandarins of the Amateur Swimming Association, my hosts at an event called the Olympic Gold Ball, a posh black-tie do which took place at the Savoy Hotel in London in September 2002. It is a perk of my job as a newspaper columnist to be invited to occasional fancy dinners, although there are times when it feels more of a pain than a perk, and thus it was, at least to begin with, that evening at the Savoy

I had been invited by the ASA chief executive David Sparkes, and his director of communications Dee McIntosh, but didn't have a clue what either of them looked like. So I spent most of the pre-dinner reception on my own, ostentatiously trying to avoid looking like Billy No-Mates by employing the time-honoured technique of wandering around the room pretending to be looking for close friends. I knew I didn't have any close friends there, but thought I might spot at least a few acquaintances. A few other journalists, perhaps. Yet the only faces I recognised belonged to famous Olympians, some of whom I'd met before but all of whom seemed to be in the middle of sparkling conversations.

When you're on your own at a function, I have noticed, everyone around you seems to be having the most enjoyable conversation of their entire lives, and if they glance at you at all, it is only a glance of pity, a fleeting expression of sympathy that you are unfortunate enough to be excluded from the most fun they have ever had with their clothes on. Whatever, by the time I had completed seven circuits of the room, I had convinced myself that my fellow guests had me pegged, correctly, as a sad git with imaginary friends. Other strategies had to be adopted. So I started to loiter on the fringes of other people's social intercourse, in the hope that they might gather me into the fold. I didn't dive in, not even in honour of the Amateur Swimming Association. I'm no shrinking violet, but there are times when it is acceptable to butt into a conversational twosome and times when it's not, and when both conversationalists are roaring with laughter, and one of them is the Princess Royal, it's probably not.

Let me take another short diversion here to tell you my

Princess Royal story. In the early 1990s I was invited to play in the Princess Royal charity golf tournament at a golf club in Surrey, and very much to my surprise, my three partners and I won the thing. The distinguished patron of the event duly arrived to dish out our cut-glass decanters. But before she did so, an officious royal flunkey sidled up and asked whether I had ever met royalty before. I hadn't. So he explained the form, that Her Royal Highness would, on being introduced to me, extend her hand, which I would take and at the same time slightly incline my head, addressing her throughout as 'Ma'am'.

This was fine by me. I was by no means an ardent monarchist, but nor did I believe that they should all have their heads chopped off, or even be pensioned off to live a quiet, upper-class life in Gloucestershire: I was broadly, although not passionately, in favour of the Royal Family, and rather looking forward to meeting HRH, without feeling notably apprehensive about it.

When eventually she swept in and stopped to engage me briefly in conversation, I did exactly as I had been told, inclining my head slightly and taking her proffered hand. Later, when I reported the day's events to Jane, I said that I'd been struck by how regal the Princess had seemed, but that I had been composed and frankly rather debonair in her formidable presence. Anyway, a few weeks later the organisers of the tournament kindly sent me a photograph which had been taken at the precise moment of this introduction, and when I looked at it I could scarcely believe my eyes. The photographic evidence made it clear that, far from having slightly inclined my head, I had in fact swept into a low bow, like Sir Walter Ralegh before Queen Elizabeth I, while looking up at her with a sickly, ingratiating smile. More Edmund Blackadder, perhaps, than Sir Walter Ralegh. I still shudder when I think about it.

Back at the Savoy Hotel, having decided not to butt in on

the Princess Royal and ask if she perhaps remembered me –
'Oh yes, aren't you the fellow who performed that ridiculous
bow?' – I eventually contented myself with standing back and
enjoying the spectacle of athletes in dinner dress. It is rare to
see an athlete, present or past, who looks entirely comfortable
in formal dress, and at the Savoy that night only the admirable
Mary Peters looked entirely at ease. Having grown into features that were always a little on the matronly side, she looked
every inch the Dame that she had become.

The men, heavyweight boxer Audley Harrison in particular, reminded me of the birds of prey you see in zoos, stuck in
an unnatural habitat, unable to swoop and soar. A man born to
wear Lycra just doesn't look right in a wing collar. In fact it
occurred to me that formal dinners are probably the only occasions when florid-faced sports administrators – not only born
to wear velvet bow ties and cummerbunds but very possibly
born wearing them – look looser-limbed than the athletes they
administer.

These thoughts were clattering around inside my head
when dinner was announced by a red-jacketed toastmaster,
and my evening promptly took a considerable turn for the
better when I found myself seated next to David Wilkie, 200
metre breast-stroke champion at the 1976 Olympic Games
and a very fine fellow indeed, with whom I felt I had bonded
even before we had finished the plum tomato carpaccio with
goat's cheese timbale. By then he had confided that, while
commentating on the 1988 Olympics for ITV, he was taken
completely unawares when Anthony Nesty, a rank outsider
from Surinam, won the 100 metre butterfly. So off the top of
his head (an area which had become slightly shinier since he
stooped to receive his gold medal in 1976), Wilkie started
inventing all sorts of facts about the guy, for example that
Nesty's father was a general in the Surinamese army.

Now, I've spun some yarns myself down the years, but to do so in the television commentary box during the Olympic Games was, as they say nowadays, different class. Indeed, Wilkie's story made me wonder how often we have the wool pulled over our eyes by television commentators either to amuse themselves or because they've been caught on the hop. Quite a bit, I should think.

Wilkie's own tale, however, needs no embroidering. He knocked a staggering 3.1 seconds off the world record in winning his gold medal, and only cynics such as – surprise, surprise – Clive James pointed out that such an exceptional performance did not enjoy an entirely British provenance.

'For the Beeb's harassed commentators it was hard to know how to follow that climactic moment at the swimming pool when David Wilkie won a gold medal and Alan Weeks had an orgasm,' James wrote in the *Observer*, on 1 August 1976.

So loud was the shouting from the commentary box that it was sometimes difficult to sort out who was screaming what. Hamilton Bland, Alan's new technical assistant, is not very quiet even when he is talking normally. 'But tonight the Union Jack is raised and is being waved very proudly indeed!' 'A proud Scot!' 'And so the big moment has arrived!' 'The Flying Scotsman!' 'We have a certain gold medallist!' All these were among the things yelled, but the loudest bellow of all was unmistakably Alan's: 'David Wilkie is absolutely superb!' And so he was. It was a proud moment for England. Well, Britain. All right, Scotland. What? Oh yes, and the University of Miami.

Still, the commentary-box orgasms, and the partisanship of Uncle Frank Bough in the studio, were understandable. Britain, to say the least, did not enjoy the best of Olympic success during the 1970s. It was a notable decade for the Olympics – with the mighty deeds of Lasse Viren, Franz Klammer and Shane Gould joining those of Spitz, Korbut and Comaneci in the annals – but for Britain's Olympians there was very little to cheer, which is why that very little was cheered very loudly indeed.

Mary Peters, of course, won the pentathlon at Munich, and Richard Meade won a three-day eventing gold, and John Curry did us proud at the 1976 Winter Olympics in Innsbruck (I like to think that while he was in town he dropped in on my old friend Robert Wanker, the sporting goods merchant). There were also a couple of sailing golds in categories that I can't quite recall by men whose names escape me. But for gold medals, apart from Wilkie's breast-stroke heroics over 200 metres, that was it. Indeed, the British track-and-field team returned from Montreal in 1976 with a solitary bronze medal, won by Brendan Foster in the 10,000 metres. Now, I have met Foster, who's a jolly nice chap, and I certainly wouldn't want to diminish his achievement – especially as in six years at KGV I never once managed to complete the school cross-country course, except on one notable occasion by bus – but it has to be said that his bronze medal in 1976 imbued him with an enduring celebrity slightly out of proportion with his record.

Coincidentally, Jane recalls being on holiday on the Isle of Wight one summer in the 1970s with her mum, dad and sister Jackie, and them all assembling in the TV lounge of the Keats Green Hotel in Shanklin to watch Foster run in some big international race or other that he was considered to have a decent chance of winning. In Jane's family, athletics was taken deadly seriously on account of the fact that her Auntie Jose's dearest friend, practically a member of the family, was Dorothy Hyman, who'd won a silver medal at the Rome

Olympics in 1960, finishing just 0.03 seconds behind the great American sprinter Wilma Rudolph. Dorothy had been BBC Sports Personality of the Year in 1963, as indeed had Foster in 1974, partly because of his athletic achievements, but also because he had the pleasing features of a contented chipmunk. Anyway, it gradually became clear that day, with Jane's family gathered expectantly around the telly, that not only was Foster not going to win, he was going to finish a good deal nearer the back of the field than the front.

Anne, Jane's mum, let out a huge, exasperated sigh. 'Well, Brendan, you're rubbish,' she muttered. Even aged fifteen, or however old she was at the time, Jane was struck by how dreadfully unfair this was. Poor old Brendan had run his guts out, yet the verdict from the TV lounge of the Keats Green Hotel in Shanklin was: you're rubbish.

Actually, the truly remarkable thing about Britain's miserable haul of athletics medals in 1976, looking back now, was that the Olympic Games in Moscow four years later yielded a veritable cargo of them, with Sebastian Coe, Steve Ovett, Daley Thompson and Allan Wells all winning gold. This was not unconnected with the fact that the United States of America boycotted the Games that year, although in Coe, Ovett and Thompson at least, Britain manifestly had athletes to match the best of the Yanks.

For me, though, these medals came too late. By 1980, my impressionable teen years were over, and the only athlete who had really made an impact on me during the 1970s was my bandy-legged chemistry teacher, 'Bog' Marsh.

I can't remember a teachers' 100 metre race being an annual tradition at KGV, but I do remember one being organised for the morning of sports day, I think in the summer of 1977. We had another chemistry teacher, 'Tog' Allen, so nicknamed because the registration plate on his car read TOG, whereas

Mr Marsh was Bog because of the venerable rule in every English school which decrees that all teachers called Marsh are nicknamed Bog, Boggy or Bogger. It's practically the law. Tog took the teachers' 100 metres extremely seriously, training for it and even equipping himself with spikes. But when the big moment arrived, with hundreds of baying schoolboys looking on, he set off like a jack rabbit and almost immediately sprawled flat on his face.

He was a nice man and, uncharacteristically for a 15-year-old schoolboy, I couldn't help feeling sorry for him; the jeers are probably ringing in his ears even now. Meanwhile, Bog, without spikes, scorched to the finishing line in what seemed like nine seconds flat. It was magnificent, the more so as none of us knew that he was a fellow of even vague athletic prowess. The only time anyone had seen the slightest turn of pace from him was when he raced to put out a small fire involving a Bunsen burner and somebody's exercise book.

Had there been a single dominant male British athlete in the 1970s, Bog Marsh's memorable sprint notwithstanding, I might have been inspired to add running to my own modest sporting repertoire. After all, I tried tirelessly to hit a golf ball like Jack Nicklaus and a tennis ball like Ilie Nastase, and a cricket ball like Derek Randall, and a football like Duncan McKenzie, yet athletics did not seem to offer a comparable role model. This changed, oddly enough, in a cinema near the Arc de Triomphe in Paris, one night in 1981. I had left school the previous December, having stayed on for an extra term after my A-levels to try to get into Oxford. By the time Jesus College very sensibly rejected me, St Andrews University had offered me a place the following autumn, which left me with the best part of a year to fill.

This was before 'gap year' became a phrase as familar to A-level students as 'UCCA form' and 'revision timetable'. I was great at putting together revision timetables, incidentally. If revision timetables had been marked, I would have been among the top 1 per cent of A-level students in the country. Mine was a work of art, with different colours representing different subjects, and a pleasing tabular construction. But I spent so long perfecting my revision timetable that I left scant time for revision, and in those circumstances the A, two Bs and a C with which I ended up, while a result that would be considered catastrophically humiliating by any self-respecting pupil now (I know someone recently who got nine starred As and an A in her GCSEs, and was so disappointed with the unstarred A that she asked for that paper to be re-marked), was a wholly unexpected triumph.

As for the notion of taking a year out, at KGV almost everyone going to university or polytechnic went straight from school. So with only my schoolfriends as a point of comparison, by the time I did turn up at St Andrews, having spent ten months or so working in a Parisian hotel and living on my own in a grotty attic room up seven flights of stairs on the rue de Courcelles in the 17th arrondissement, I considered myself to be an adventurer with Sir Francis Chichester's zest for travel and Sir Edmund Hillary's head for heights. This self-image was shattered within about ten minutes of arriving in my university hall of residence.

'Did you take a year out?' asked a fellow first-year, unpacking his bags.

'Yes,' I said. 'I worked in Paris. What about you?'

'Oh, I trekked from Khartoum to Nairobi through a couple of slightly hairy war zones,' he said casually. 'But that was nothing like as interesting as what Graham over there did.'

'What did you do, Graham?' I said weakly.

'I spent six months working for Mother Teresa in Calcutta,' he said. 'Then I did a sponsored unicycle ride along the Great

Wall of China. And then I went hot-air ballooning in Indonesia. What about you?'

'Erm, I was a concierge in a hotel in Paris,' I said.

'Wow,' said Graham, kindly.

Still, going to Paris, having resolved to find myself a home and a job, and not to return to Britain at least until I could speak decent French, was by my own and most of my school-friends' standards singularly intrepid. Although a sociable kind of guy, I was compelled to spend entire weekends exclusively in my own company, and there is no doubt that for this and one or two other reasons my time in Paris made a man of me.

Like plenty of lonely people in big cities all over the world, I spent a lot of time going to see films on my own, and it was in a cinema on the avenue Wagram one Sunday afternoon that I sat, enthralled, in front of the newly-released *Chariots of Fire*. Now, I know there are some people who think *Chariots of Fire* a pile of chauvinistic plop; the *Time Out Film Guide*, for example, rather mean-spiritedly assesses it thus: 'Gosh, aren't the British remarkable? They win Olympic races despite running in slow motion, they castigate old conservatives while revelling in patriotic claptrap, they win Oscars galore while making crappy films. OK, so some of the acting's all right, but really this is an overblown piece of self-congratulatory emotional manipulation perfectly suited for Thatcherite liberals. Pap.'

Well, for overblown, self-congratulatory film critics maybe that's so, but as a homesick, sports-mad nineteen-year-old in Paris, where of course much of the action takes place (even though I later found that it was shot at Bebington on the Wirral, the City of Light's rather improbable double), I was welded to my seat all the way through the closing credits.

At some of the cinemas I went to, I would find myself

welded to my seat less figuratively, wondering exactly what the person there before me had been doing during that afternoon's screening of *Emmanuelle in Tokyo*. But this was different. I emerged into the fading light of that Parisian afternoon positively bursting with exhilaration, having to suppress the impulse to hug and kiss passers-by. And for weeks afterwards I spent my leisure time running all the way to the Bois de Boulogne and then much of the way through it, a fad which eventually wore off when I realised that I was getting to know the transvestite prostitutes, who hung out there in more ways than one, practically by name. By this time, however, I was no longer the podge I had been through most of my teens. The *Chariots of Fire* effect, combined with the daily haul up and down the seven flights of stairs to my attic room, had turned me, if not exactly into a hunk with a washboard stomach, then certainly into a considerably slimmer version of my former self.

The homesickness never wholly wore off, though, and whenever it receded it soon reared up again with the awareness that extraordinary things were happening across the English Channel. Traipsing to and from my miserable garret on the rue de Courcelles, I missed one of the great FA Cup finals goals, by Tottenham's Ricky Villa against Manchester City, and one of the great Wimbledon finals, John McEnroe finally bringing the curtain down on the age of Borg in four sets, 4-6, 7-6, 7-6, 6-4. Worst of all, I missed the Ashes, and in particular England's miraculous, Botham-inspired comeback at Headingley.

Later, I would wear out not one but two videos of *Botham's Ashes*, and at the time I read every inch of newsprint I could find on the subject, even though the cost of English newspapers in Paris ate considerably into my concierge's wages, dispensed weekly in a small brown envelope by Mademoiselle

Casado, the formidable manageress at the Hotel de Castile. In fact, now that I think about it, and even in the knowledge that my children will one day read this book, I fear that I may have purloined the odd copy of *The Times* or the *Daily Telegraph* from those admirable Parisian newsstands, preferring to keep my money for a *sandwich de jambon*. On further reflection, I fear I may have purloined the odd *sandwich de jambon* as well. I was certainly pretty adept at hurdling the turnstile in the Metro, especially after watching Nigel Havers in *Chariots of Fire*.

Quite apart from the remarkable summer of sport, the race riots that were erupting in English inner cities, and the wedding of Charles and Diana, intensified the feeling that I was altogether a long way from the action. Only once did I feel as if I was in exactly the right place at the right time, and that was on 27 May, when Liverpool fans poured into Paris for the European Cup final against Real Madrid. I didn't have a ticket, but it was a pleasure, even for an Evertonian, to hear thick Scouse accents up and down the Champs-Elysées.

'Hey, Joey, we've gorra pair o' tickets!'

'Yer jammy fucking get! How d'yer get' em?'

'We rolled a couple of fucking Spaniards!'

Bless their donkey jackets and Doc Martens; hearing their sweet exchanges made my heart yearn for Merseyside. It was such a pleasure to be surrounded by Liverpudlian vowels again that I found myself tagging along all the way to the Parc des Princes, where I meandered around for a couple of hours before kick-off, just soaking up the atmosphere outside the stadium. I ended up watching the match, and Alan Kennedy's eighty-first minute deciding goal, on the flickering black-and-white television of a French family who had kindly neglected to draw the curtains of their ground-floor apartment. And afterwards, as everyone piled away from the stadium, I stood on a street corner hoping to see the one man I felt sure would have been in the crowd, my dad's old business partner Jack Fry.

I had never known Jack Fry as anything other than Mr Fry, and had never seen him on anything like a social basis, except at my dad's funeral five years earlier. He was a character of the kind Liverpool specialised in: as tough as old boots and as sentimental as an old Hollywood weepy. He was also a passionate fan of Liverpool FC, and had been at the European Cup finals of 1977 and 1978, so I was certain he must be among the happy Liverpool fans pouring out of the Parc des Princes. I searched every face of the passing throng, and was just about to give up and head back to my attic, when remarkably I spotted him walking towards me. 'Mr Fry,' I called. He looked at me and did a double take. 'Brian!' he exclaimed. 'Brian Viner! Bloody hell!'

He insisted that I join him and his friends in a bar opposite the fleapit of a hotel that some Liverpool travel agent had booked them into, miles from the stadium. It was almost midnight by the time we got there, and one by one his friends peeled off, leaving only Mr Fry and myself sitting in an almost deserted bar at 3 a.m., utterly inebriated and clinking glasses of cognac for the seventeenth time. It was the experience I had never had with my dad: sitting in a bar late at night, setting the world to rights. But this was as close as I was ever going to get, well and truly arseholed with the man who'd known him best. I think I may even have pointed this out. I certainly recall tears being shed. For me it was a powerful rite of passage, and I remember thinking how odd it was that I should wind up, as an Everton fan, having one of the more enjoyable evenings of my 19-year-old life at least partly in celebration of Liverpool's third European Cup victory.

I also remember that we were not entirely alone in the bar.

There was one other customer, a raddled old hooker who told us that she had learned one or two English expressions from British soldiers she had 'met' following the liberation of Paris in 1944. Then, when Mr Fry and I finally lurched into the night, she gave us a beam that was almost entirely toothless and, dredging up from her memory banks what those Second World War tommies had doubtless said to her as they left her company, called fondly after us.

'Goodbye,' she croaked happily, 'and good riddance!'

9

Red Rum's Hooves

For some of the reasons that I had so enjoyed getting drunk with Jack Fry in Paris in May 1981, I looked forward to meeting Pat Eddery in his Buckinghamshire farmhouse in July 2003. Having never known my father on man-to-man terms, I could at least contrive some kind of connection beyond the grave by forming an enthusiasm for some of the performers he had most admired, such as Eddery, Lester Piggott, Terry Biddlecombe, Peter O'Sullevan, and for that matter Duke Ellington, Count Basie and Shirley Bassey.

It was my dad, too, that I had in mind when I went to interview John Cleese one day while I was working for the *Mail on Sunday*. For some reason it had been arranged that I would interview Cleese over lunch at a Greek taverna in Camden Town, north London, and I wondered whether to tell him that the fondest and most vivid memory I had of my late father was of him howling with laughter at *Fawlty Towers*?

It was true enough. The first series of *Fawlty Towers* began on BBC2 on 19 September 1975, the Germans episode was transmitted on 24 October, and my dad died on 4 February the following year. Had there been a couple of months less between Basil saying to his German guests, 'I'll just get your hors d'oeuvres . . . hors d'oeuvres vich must be obeyed at all times without question . . .' and my dad's demise, then it would have been perfectly reasonable to speculate that he died of laughter. He sat in his armchair that evening of 24 October (ten years practically to the minute before the birth of one Wayne Rooney, for those of you interested in dates) doubled up almost as if in pain, laughing so hard that it was noiseless. And in later years, when I reflected on the things that he had missed by so very inconveniently dropping dead, things that he would have loved to have seen, the second series of *Fawlty Towers* featured high up on the list, not far behind the grandchildren that he never knew, and Lester Piggott winning a ninth Derby at the age of forty-seven. Whether the spectacle of his grandchildren would have pipped that of Piggott winning the Derby is another matter altogether.

Whatever, at the taverna, Cleese and I had scarcely ordered our starters and started to talk than I found myself thanking him for providing me with such a wonderful image of my dad. Written down, it comes over as a rather saccharin impulse on my part, as if I were desperately trying to win his favour. But I don't think I was being maudlin or manipulative; I just wanted to express my genuine gratitude before we moved on to other things. I hadn't reckoned on Cleese being particularly moved by what I said. If anything, I supposed that after so many years he would be rather fed up with people telling him how much they admired *Fawlty Towers* and why. But instead, Cleese's eyes filled instantly with tears. To my horror he rose to his feet, bumping his head on the low taverna ceiling, and reached across the table towards me. I wasn't at all sure whether he wanted to hug me or shake my hand, so we ended up doing rather awkward high fives, and I got a blob of taramasalata on my elbow.

I was thinking of this exchange as I sat down at Pat Eddery's kitchen table, and decided to spill my emotions again, telling him that the 1975 Derby, which Eddery won on Grundy, was the last my old man had ever seen. But this time there were no high fives, awkward or otherwise. Nor, even if he had stood up, was Eddery in the slightest danger of bumping his head on the ceiling. Nor were there any bowls of taramasalata to worry about. In fact, there was no food in evidence at all. This came as no great surprise. I'd talked to people who knew Eddery well who said they had never even seen him finish a sandwich. Meanwhile, I told him how heartwarming it was for me to be able to back his rides just as my late father had all those years ago. He looked at me with bright blue, unmoist eyes. 'Right,' he said. Here was a sportsman, it was fair to say, whose deeds spoke more eloquently than his words.

It is a common enough trait among jockeys, indeed the greatest of them, Lester Piggott, long ago turned reticence practically into an art form. The venerable thriller writer and former jockey Dick Francis tells a marvellous story about sitting down with Piggott shortly after he had been commissioned to write the great man's authorised biography, and, wanting to get things moving, asked what Piggott had thought of Sir Ivor, the most precious of his nine winning Derby mounts. There was a long, long silence while Piggott contemplated the question, and eventually he said: 'Good 'orse.'

I cherish the image of Francis sitting there with his tape recorder, thinking 'Mmm, this project could take some time.' And I cherish, too, the celebrated story about the Old Etonian trainer Jeremy Tree, who supposedly once said to Piggott: 'I've been asked to speak at my old school, Lester. They want me to give a speech about everything I know about racing. What do you think I should tell them?' Again, there was a long silence, and then the mumbled, nasal reply, 'Tell 'em you've got the fucking flu.'

Eddery was not in Piggott's class, either in reticence or in deed. But what deeds they were, all the same. I was there to talk to him because at the age of fifty-one he had just announced his impending retirement as a jockey, lowering the curtain on one of flat racing's most remarkable and yet relatively unfeted careers. Piggott, Willie Carson, Frankie Dettori, all were much more renowned. Yet Eddery had ridden more winners than any of them, an astounding 4632, second only in the all-time list to Sir Gordon Richards. Moreover, Eddery had had more century seasons than anyone, riding more than 100 winners every year from 1973 to 2001, with the exception of 1982. And that didn't matter because 1982 was the year he won the Derby on Golden Fleece. 'The best horse I ever rode,' he told me, once I'd moved on from all that sentimental nonsense about my dad. 'He was a freak, seventeen hands, a great big, highly strung horse. He had so much bean, yet he stayed a mile and a half. He wasn't easy to ride, though. Used to pull very hard.'

As I listened to this genial little Irishman, I had to stop myself from falling into a nostalgic reverie. In 1974, my first full year at KGV and the year in which Eddery became the youngest champion jockey for more than half a century, I had started a betting scam in which he, unwittingly, played a part. I used to draw up lists of seven or eight horses, with invented names but real jockeys, and give each horse a starting price. I still have a history exercise book with one such list in the back of it. The favourite was Royal Blue, ridden by Lester Piggott, priced 2/1, and the rank outsider was Sky High, ridden by Terry Biddlecombe, at 5/1. I didn't give very generous odds, and I didn't make any distinction between jump jockeys and flat jockeys. They all took part and every race was a steeple-chase. Pat Eddery rode Hurricane Hal, a 3/1 shot.

At lunchtime, or in breaks between lessons, I would read out the names of these horses and the accompanying odds. My assistant Mike Mahoney would collect bets, and I would then commentate on a fictitious race. I knew all the jargon – short heads, blinkers, sheepskin nosebands, three furlongs from home, and so on – because my dad watched the racing on telly every Saturday afternoon, except those Saturdays when he actually went to the races, and when he did I frequently went with him. So I could do passably authentic Peter O'Sullevan-style commentaries, the idea being that I didn't know who had backed what, although Mahoney (always Mahoney, never Mike) and I had a sly arrangement whereby he would tip me the wink during the race. So if Royal Blue was leading by six lengths with only one fence to jump, and I got a sign that Royal Blue had been heavily backed, then poor old Royal Blue came crashing down disastrously at the final fence, and Hurricane Hal, carrying only a 2p bet from Stefan Walker, would burst from nowhere to win.

Mahoney and I weren't exactly Robert Redford and Paul Newman in *The Sting*, and there was a strict betting limit of 3p per person per race, but we still managed to subsidise our daily visit to the sweet shop. Unfortunately, word of this nefarious business somehow reached the deputy headmaster, George Wakefield, and in afternoon registration one day I got the dreaded summons to Room 27, where Mr Wakefield – irreverently and unimaginatively known as Pegleg on account of the prosthetic limb with which we were told he had been equipped after losing the original in battle during the Second World War – used to mete out punishment for all sorts of schoolboy transgressions.

Pegleg later took me for English and made Shakespeare's

Julius Caesar come alive, for which I am for ever indebted to him. It can't have been easy to make Shakespeare thrilling for a class of 15-year-old boys – most of them more interested in how to get served at The Shakespeare – but he pulled it off, and although he's long dead, I salute him now. In my first year, however, I knew him only as a terrifyingly strict figure, Lord High Executioner to the headmaster's Mikado. The walk to Room 27, which forbiddingly was at the end of one of the long parquet corridors, was KGV's equivalent of the walk to the electric chair. I only did it twice, but even now I can remember that terrible feeling in the pit of my stomach as I knocked on his door. For some reason he had an arrangement of lights outside his office which flashed red for 'wait' and green for 'come in'. I hoped forlornly that I might be made to wait for ever, but eventually, to my horror, the red light went off, and the green light came on. I'm quite surprised I haven't developed a Pavlovian reaction to traffic lights, wetting myself slightly every time they turn green.

Pegleg was predictably wrathful about the horse-racing thing. I was given a detention and a fierce bollocking, and I think I was forced to repay every single losing bet, which, of course, was practically all of them. Nor were the winners asked to repay me, so my short career as a bookie, after a promising start, ended up being no more successful than my dad's had been.

Dad opened his betting shop in Moorfields, Liverpool, in 1966 and it wouldn't surprise me at all to learn that the first bet he took was a double on Everton to beat Sheffield Wednesday in the FA Cup final (which, glory be, they did 3-2) and England to win the World Cup. Actually, the betting-shop licence wasn't in his name but that of his faithful secretary in the import-export business, Christine Elliott. The magistrates' court hearing, at which the licence was applied for, had inconveniently coincided with the Cheltenham Festival. So my dad took himself off to the races to see the great Arkle winning the Cheltenham Gold Cup for the third year in succession, leaving Christine, who was only in her early twenties, to face the Liverpool magistrates.

'He gave me one hundred pounds for the licence and bought me a pillbox hat to wear in court,' she told me, when, in pursuit of a little more detail on my father's bookmaking years, I tracked her down in July 2005. I hadn't seen Christine since I was a small child, but dimly remembered her as being long-haired and glamorous. She explained to me that in the mid-1960s she used to be told that she looked like Catwoman, in the ITV series *Batman*. So one day when my dad took me to his office, above the Midland Bank on Leece Street, she tried to ingratiate herself with the boss's 6-year-old son by saying, 'Do you think I look like Catwoman?' And almost forty years later she could recall the withering contempt in my voice. 'You looked me up and down and said "Not in the slightest."' All I could do was make a belated apology.

I spent an hour laughing and crying with Christine, who was still long-haired and glamorous, and moreover had that unique Liverpudlian skill with a story, reminiscent of my father himself. I had phoned her out of the blue scarcely ten minutes before I arrived on her doorstep, wanting to hear dusty anecdotes about her life four decades earlier, and she had them all ready by the time I arrived, polished and sparkling. She recalled that in 1966 there had been three objections to the application for a bookie's licence for the premises on Moorfields, two from other bookmakers and one from a phi-latelist who ran the shop next door.

'One of the magistrates was an old guy, who kept nodding off, like a little dormouse, while I was being cross-examined. I was asked whether anyone had said to me that there should be another betting shop on Moorfields, and I said, "Well, nobody's going to stop me and say "Excuse me, Mrs Elliott, there should be another betting shop round here." At which the little old guy woke up and said, "Hear, hear." Afterwards, our barrister said, "Very well done, my dear, almost a professional witness."'

I like to think that my father had correctly calculated that Christine would have more success with the magistrates than he would have had, although I don't doubt for a second that he really, really wanted to go to Cheltenham as well. Whatever, she duly became the first woman in Liverpool with a bookie's licence, and the shop opened, with her as manageress and a small elderly man called Jackie, doubtless some old Liverpool acquaintance of my dad's, marking the fluctuating prices on a blackboard.

My dad had hundreds of old Liverpool acquaintances. Once, he was driving my mother along the Dock Road through Bootle on their way home from some dinner or other, when a drunken tramp lurched out of a pub into the road directly in front of them. My dad swerved and narrowly avoided ramming a lamppost. He leapt out of the car in his finery and started yelling at the tramp that he'd nearly killed all three of them, only for the guy to stagger towards him with an outstretched hand, mumbling, 'Allen Viner, s'bloody marvellous to see you again!' And two minutes later the pair of them were sitting on the bonnet reminiscing about the good old days while my mum sat there wondering whether she was hallucinating.

I love Liverpool pub stories. Some of them are simply jokes – like the one about the guy who realises that even the local scallies have taken on board the significance of the city being voted European Capital of Culture 2008 when he comes out of a pub to find his car, all four wheels nicked, propped up on four encyclopedias. But some of them are true, and of the true ones my friend Alan Bleasdale – already honoured in these pages for having gone out with a girl purely because she looked like Ian St John – has one of the best.

It happened on the Sunday afternoon after John Lennon died in December 1980, when a hastily organised memorial rock concert took place on the steps of St George's Hall. Over 25,000 people turned up, and the concert ended in the most poignant way possible, with everyone singing 'Imagine' together. As the concert-goers, many of them genuinely distraught, drifted away, a nearby pub – called The Queen's, in Williamson Square – was opening for the evening. A friend of Alan's went in with his wife to drown their sorrows, and couldn't help noticing that a man of about sixty, sitting on his own at the far end of the bar nursing a pint of Guinness, kept looking up in bewilderment every time the doors burst open and more people came in crying. Eventually he leant over to Alan's friend's wife and said, 'Er, what's going on, girl?'

She said: 'We've all just been to a memorial concert for John Lennon.'

The man looked blank.

'He's dead,' she explained. 'John's dead.'

'Oh,' said the man, and returned to his Guinness, just as another group of grieving Lennon fans walked in, wailing, 'John is gone!'

'Fucking hell,' said the man, almost to himself. 'Just imagine the scene when Ken Dodd goes.'

To return to Christine's betting-shop tales, she told me that Jackie, the diminutive board-marker, had no more hair on his head than Yul Brynner. 'He was as bald as a coot,' she recalled. 'But one day I was walking along Duke Street when I saw him walking towards me with a Beatles haircut. I couldn't believe my eyes, but I stopped and had a conversation with him, and had to pretend I hadn't noticed, otherwise I might have started laughing. Eventually Jackie said, "Haven't you noticed anything different about me?" I said "No, what?" He said, "I'm wearing a wig." I took a step back and said, "Gosh, so you are."'

The shop, meanwhile, was as profitable as Jackie was hirsute. 'You have to lay off your bets,' said Christine, 'and one betting shop's no good for doing that; to spread your risk you need a string of shops. Also, your dad lived a little dangerously. I remember one year that there was a double-page spread in one of the Sunday papers a week before the Grand National, about a guy who claimed that he dreamt the winners beforehand. He dreamt that this 150-1 shot was going to win, and all week little old ladies kept coming in and betting on it. Your dad told me to take as much as we could get. He said, "If that horse wins I'll show my bum in Bold Street." Well, it led for a whole circuit, before it eventually fell.'

Had the horse won, I suppose the operation would have collapsed even sooner than it did. My dad closed the shop in 1970, for reasons of health as well as business, because by then he had contracted a rare kind of septicaemia, and had become haemophilic. It is wondrous, looking back, that he made it as far as 1976. I certainly remember the seemingly interminable journeys by train and bus from Southport, to visit him in Walton Hospital in Liverpool, where he spent weeks at a time in the late 1960s and early 1970s. My mum visited every day, and every afternoon at around the same time, he used to suggest gently that it might be a good idea for her to leave. She put this down to tiredness on his part; in fact, it was time for his fellow-patients to arrive for the daily poker school at his bedside.

With my mum spending most of her days travelling to and from the hospital while also trying to keep the import-export company afloat, Mrs Carter, a splendid and redoubtable woman who came to our house most mornings to do some gentle dusting and Hoovering, moved in to look after me. I think it was Mrs Carter's baking that was largely responsible for my expanding girth. I was skinny until I was about ten, but gradually my body began to take on the wobbly consistency of Mrs Carter's bread-and-butter pudding.

Although my dad was a big man, I was not genetically programmed to take after him for the simple reason that I'd been adopted. I was adopted as a fortnight-old baby, a fairly significant piece of news that my mother delivered to me – outside Hillside Post Office for some odd reason – when I was nine. She also told me that for my first couple of weeks on the planet I'd been called Robin, which made me feel a bit funny, especially as there was a boy called Robin in my class at Farnborough Road Junior School, who cried a lot and had a habit of wetting his pants in moments of stress, like when he was asked to hand out the triangular morning-milk cartons. My mum and dad couldn't – or wouldn't – give me more details than that of the circumstances of my birth. But it didn't matter. I felt completely secure both about my own identity and theirs, and was never keen to find out anything about my so-called natural parents, not when my dad died, nor even when I became a parent myself, which is the point at which many adopted children feel a need to piece together the genetic jigsaw.

The information, however, came my way most unexpectedly one morning in 1997, when I received a letter from an organisation called the Post-Adoption Society. It told me that a woman called Doris had given birth to me on 25 October 1961, and that she had been trying for some years to find me. She would very much like to meet me, but would respect my wishes if I didn't want to meet her. I remember my knees giving way slightly and having to sit down. I had never expected this moment to arrive, and had never wanted it to, but now that it had, it clearly would have been perverse of me not to follow it through, especially when it transpired that Doris lived barely three miles from where we lived at the time in north London.

So we met, in a restaurant, and liked one another. As a habitual eavesdropper myself in public places, I recall thinking that it would have been a hell of a conversation to overhear. Her efforts to find me had been repeatedly thwarted, she said, but she had finally discovered my name, shared by only a handful of men in the United Kingdom, and then it became a matter of eliminating the wrong Brian Viners to find the right one.

The moment of revelation came when she saw my picture in the *Mail on Sunday*. She was a *Guardian* reader, but fortuitously I had won one of that year's *What the Papers Say* journalism awards, which was reported one Saturday by the *Guardian*. So she excitedly bought the following day's *Mail on Sunday* – not a natural impulse on the part of a *Guardian* reader – and duly found a photograph of me receiving my award from Tony Blair. Rarely can Mr Blair have been so superfluous in a photograph. Doris caught a train from London to Manchester that Sunday morning, and spent the entire journey gazing at my beetling brow and Roman nose. Apparently, I looked notably like her old boyfriend: Robin.

She filled me in on the circumstances of her unwanted 1961 pregnancy and my adoption, all of which was fine by me; I'd had a much more stable upbringing than I would have done had she kept me. Best of all, she told me that she had gone on to have two more sons. Moreover, she said that she was still in touch with Robin, and that he had later fathered a son and two daughters. So suddenly I had three half-brothers and two half-sisters, all of whom I subsequently met, forging close and loving relationships with several of them. As for Robin, it turned out that he had been, for several consecutive years, the squash champion of Suffolk. And while Suffolk is not the most densely populated of counties, nor too tightly packed with squash courts, this was definitely lineage to be proud of.

An even greater source of pride, however, was the revelation that I had a blood connection with a minor sporting scandal. In 1986, while England's cricketers were in Australia winning the Ashes, there were some high jinks one evening at a beachside restaurant in Sydney, during which several players, including the team's captain, Mike Gatting, high-spiritedly threw a pretty waitress into the ocean. She thought this no less hilarious than they did, and was photographed emerging from the water wearing a broad grin on top of a very wet black pinny, yet these larks were considered 'unbecoming' and Gatting was given a rap over the knuckles by the mandarins of English cricket, whoever they were at the time. In 2004, when I played against Gatting's Ashes XI for the Lord's Taverners, I asked him if he remembered the episode. He did, so I told him that the pretty waitress given a soaking was none other than my sister Samantha, and I'm pleased to report that he actually said, 'Well I never!' It is a rather neglected expression, I often think, so much more wholesome than 'Fuck me!'

Now, one reason for going into all that is to show that nurture is much stronger than nature when it comes to sporting enthusiasms: by the age of ten or so I had no interest in squash and could read horse-racing form, and had accompanied my dad to at least a dozen racecourses all over England, where I was usually handed a shilling (another word my children will encounter only through history books) to bet with.

At home I even had playthings connected with horse racing,

notably a fabulous game called Escalado. This consisted of four lead horses and a plastic track which was clamped to a table. Attached to this was a handle which, when turned, made the track judder and the horses jiggle forward. Across the track were little plastic studs which represented fences, and when the horses hit them they pinged backwards. I can hardly describe how much fun this was, especially with someone performing an enthusiastic commentary. The Sykes brothers four doors up had a Scalextric set which I coveted with all my heart, but I don't think I would ever have countenanced a swap with Escalado.

Besides, Scalextric never lived up to expectations. I would be almost sick with excitement when I was handed the controls, and then my car would either get stuck on a bit of fluff, or cartwheel off the track on reaching the first bend. In truth, it didn't even cartwheel. A cartwheel would have been dramatic. It just ground to a halt on the carpet. And yet I would always go back for more, stubbornly refusing to lose faith in a racing-car that couldn't take bends and was vulnerable to fluff.

Moreover, the Sykes's Scalextric set acquired even more glamour in 1976, the year that James Hunt won the Formula One World Championship. I was never particularly sold on Formula One, and I'm still not, but for a while Hunt's charisma sucked me in. And I have to admit that the motor-racing people I've subsequently interviewed – among them Stirling Moss, Eddie Jordan, Nikki Lauda, Bernie Ecclestone and dear old Murray Walker – have been as charismatic a bunch as any sporting folk I've come across. I should also admit to being very fond of the question: which four Formula One drivers share or shared their first names or surnames with places in Scotland, the answer of course being Stirling Moss, Johnny Dumfries, Eddie Irvine and Ayr Town Centre.

But it was real horsepower, not the mechanical sort, that

always interested me more, and I suppose that was down to my dad. A Saturday trip to the races with him was the biggest treat within the entire compass of my boyhood experience, rivalled only by the trip to the tearoom in Liverpool, the name of which I forget, where they served sumptuous chocolate eclairs in the shape of swans.

He seemed to know everyone, that was what I loved most. He was even on nodding terms with Peter O'Sullevan, and in the grandstand at Haydock Park one Saturday afternoon in 1974 or 1975, he introduced me. O'Sullevan shook my hand avuncularly and signed my programme 'Peter O'Sullevan and Attivo', the latter his much-loved and highly successful horse, winner of the Triumph Hurdle, Chester Cup and Northumberland Plate. At home I carefully cut out the autograph and stuck it in my autograph book, next to Terry Biddlecombe and the man who played Widow Twanky in the production of Aladdin I'd so enjoyed. It was an encounter I was able to tell O'Sullevan about when I met him some twenty years later, when he became – lucky chap – the subject of my weekly column in the *Mail on Sunday*'s *Night & Day* magazine, 'Brian Viner's Telly People'.

I took him for lunch at the Churchill Hotel in Portman Square, just across the road from the Jockey Club, and we had an extremely convivial time, so convivial that I felt able to ask him to record a message for my telephone answering machine. In the hope that he might do so, I had presumptuously written a snatch of commentary which went: 'And The Evertonian comes to the last, Brian Viner's given him a most wonderful ride . . . and he's over, Brian Viner on The Evertonian has surely got this year's Grand National wrapped up now . . . he's just three furlongs from home [pause] . . . and when he gets home he'll call you back, so at the tone please leave a message.'

O'Sullevan cheerfully agreed to this, read through the

script, made one or two slight amendments, and then leant over my tape recorder delivering it exactly as if he were commentating on the closing stages of the Grand National. Bless his heart. And bless, too, the hearts – whether still ticking or not – of John Motson, Barry Davies, Des Lynam, Richie Benaud, Peter Alliss, Bill McLaren and Brian Johnston, all of whom did the same for me at one time or other.

It all began with Johnners, whom I took to lunch at the Savoy in 1990, when I was working on the *Hampstead & Highgate Express*. As features editor, I had started a series called 'Out to Lunch'; not a particularly original idea, but at least one which yielded a meal and even an accompanying bottle of wine on expenses. This was a pretty rare perk for journalists on local newspapers, even one as august as the *Ham & High*, as it was generally known (which led to an interesting misunderstanding with my friend Geoff, who thought for three years that I was working on a publication for the meat trade).

The idea was that some local celebrity would choose his or her favourite place for lunch, and would duly be interviewed there. These places were meant to be in north London, the cheaper the better, and were definitely not meant to include the Savoy, so when Johnners identified it as his favourite I had to beg the editor's permission, omitting to mention that I would gladly have stumped up out of my own pocket to have lunch with the leading light of *Test Match Special*.

In truth, though, Johnners wasn't my favourite cricket commentator, even on the radio. For anyone who listened to cricket coverage in the 1970s and before, John Arlott was peerless, and Russell Davies phrased it perfectly in his 1994 *Sunday Telegraph* obituary of Johnners, writing: 'In Arlott's day the radio team had a centre of gravity; in the age of Johnston a centre of levity.' It was a marvellous line and absolutely right;

the most memorable Johnners quotes were the witting or unwitting bloopers – 'the bowler's Holding, the batsman's Willey', . . . 'Neil Harvey's at slip, with his legs wide apart, waiting for a tickle' – while of course his most cherished piece of radio commentary is the famous giggling outburst with Jonathan Agnew after Ian Botham hadn't quite managed to get his leg over – 'Oh do stop it, Aggers' – which I, like many cricket fans, would include among my desert island discs. It's simply impossible to listen to it without feeling better than you did a moment or two earlier.

But Arlott's most memorable quotes are different, each of them radiating his extraordinary wit and fleetness of thought. David Rayvern Allen, in his majestic biography of Arlott, lists some of my favourites, such as the description of Ernie Toshack's batting as being 'like an old lady poking with an umbrella at a wasps' nest'. With Arlott to supply images like that, there really was no need for pictures. And he had the keenest of eyes and ears for some of cricket's more absurd complexities, once turning to Bill Frindall during an Ashes series in the 1970s, and growling: 'What I really want to know, Bill, is if England bowl their overs at the same rate as Australia did, and Brearley and Boycott survive the opening spell, and that the number of no-balls is limited to ten in the innings, and assuming my car does 33.8 miles per gallon and my home is 67.3 miles from the ground, what time does my wife have to put the casserole on?'

It is an enduring regret that I never met Arlott, but a source of considerable pleasure that I not only met Johnners, but over the course of three or four interviews towards the end of his life got to know him slightly, and that he ended up calling me 'Viners'. Besides, Arlott could by all accounts be a bit prickly and might not have been quite so obliging had I asked him to record a bit of already-written commentary for my answering machine, whereas, following a bibulous lunch at the Savoy, Johnners agreed readily. He took the task jolly seriously, too, recording it three times until he was satisfied that those fabulously plummy Old Etonian vowels carried an appropriately fervent note.

'And Brian Viner on his Test match debut,' said Johnners into my tape recorder, 'ninety-nine not out here at Lord's, and it really has been the most extraordinary innings. Alderman now . . . comes in from the Nursery End, with that lovely smooth action of his . . . he bowls, it's short-pitched, Viner hooks [escalating excitement], is it six, will he reach his century with a six? . . . Border's dashing round from deep square, and oh, it's a most marvellous catch! Viner is out! It's very sad for England but Brian Viner is out! [pause] So please leave a message after the tone and he'll call you back as soon as he possibly can.'

These days, of course, novelty answer-machine messages are hardly novelties any more, in fact they are deeply annoying, but in 1990 my Johnners message was considered a hoot, so much so that friends of friends, and even friends of friends of friends, started phoning me just to listen to it. However, there was always the danger that I might actually be in. One day I answered the phone to hear someone saying 'shit', followed by a click as they hung up. I realised then that the Johnners commentary had come to the end of its own innings. Also, my girlfriend's mother was getting heartily sick of having to sit through Brian Viner holing out to Border on the boundary for the umpteenth time, just to say, wearily, 'Jane, it's me, can you call me back.'

After that, I added bits of bespoke commentary to my collection, without actually using them as messages for more than a day or two, but they were no less valued for that. I've stopped asking now on the basis that it seems – what can I say? – a little bit childish. Not quite appropriate for a chap on the senior side of his forty-fourth birthday, anyway. But every now and then I have a listen to them, and the one that pleases me most is O'Sullevan calling me over the last fence in the Grand National. My dad would have loved that.

In March 2005 I met O'Sullevan again. I needed an interview for Grand National week, and my first choice, Carrie Ford – considered to have a pretty good chance, on Forest Gunner, of becoming the first female jockey to win the great race – was being a bit elusive. So I suggested to Matt Tench, the *Independent*'s sports editor, that 87-year-old Sir Peter O'Sullevan might fit the bill. It wasn't as though he was going to Aintree as anything other than a punter, but hell, he had listened to his first Grand National in 1927, and graced the event in person every year, except when it was cancelled during wartime, since 1938. Nobody on earth had a pedigree remotely like that, and best of all, I still had his home phone number. 'Of course, dear boy,' he said, when I called to beg an hour of his time. 'Absolutely delighted.'

It was a decade since I had lunched with him at the Churchill, yet he claimed to remember me. Whether as the prat who had asked him to record some mock-commentary, he was, of course, far too courteous to say. This time I went to his flat in Chelsea, where he greeted me at the door looking almost indecently spry for a man only a couple of lengths, as it were, short of ninety. I had once asked Richie Benaud, himself a popular choice as the greatest of all commentators, and whom I had met several times since our exciting first encounter at the Augusta National, to name his own favourite commentator. Without hesitation he chose O'Sullevan. It wasn't just the skill of calling the horses, explained Benaud, it was also that marvellous voice. Well, the voice seemed completely unimpaired by age, and so, too, the rest of him.

He led me past walls festooned with paintings of racehorses through to a sitting room where I sat listening to his enthralling recollections of the Grand National, and when I wrote up the interview the following day I began with a line about him possibly about to become the only man in history to pick the winners of the National seventy-seven years apart. All he had to do was pick the 2005 winner, having, as a ten-year-old in 1928, astutely wagered sixpence each way on the 100-1 shot Tipperary Tim, which sounded beguilingly like one of the names I had made up in my betting scam at KGV.

Since the legalisation of betting shops was then more than three decades away, he told me, he had placed his sixpence bet with the local butcher. 'I remember it clearly,' he said. 'The shop with its sawdust floor and the butcher with his straw hat. I was brought up by my grandparents near Reigate in Surrey because my mother and father had discovered early in their marriage that they were incompatible, so I became a refugee from Ireland when I was about five or six. My grandmother hunted, and her groom, the chauffeur and other members of staff would all have their bets. I was the runner. I would hand the butcher the slips, which he would look at and say, discreetly, "The order will be taken care of, young man."'

I asked O'Sullevan which Grand National winners, apart from Tipperary Tim, he remembered most fondly. He said it had given him great pleasure to call home Merryman II in the first televised National in 1960, not least because he'd backed it heavily (although, as ever, even in the case of his beloved Attivo, he kept his partiality to himself). And Bob Champion's victory on Aldaniti had been easily the most emotional. But he had never, he said, seen anything quite like Red Rum's three wins.

I was pleased to hear this because Red Rum had loomed large in my childhood; in fact, he had clip-clopped past my house most mornings along with Glenkiln and other horses in Ginger McCain's stables a mile or so away. On the day of the 1973 Grand National, Red Rum was 9/1 joint-favourite with Crisp. As usual my dad went to Aintree, but without me. It was the one race meeting he wouldn't take me to, which was ironic, because Aintree was comfortably the nearest racecourse to our house. But he didn't think children belonged in big crowds; it was for the same reason that I wasn't allowed to go to Goodison Park.

I asked him before he left whether he'd be backing Red Rum, and he laughed and said the horse hadn't a hope. Just about everyone else in our town had backed him, and that alone was a good enough reason for my dad not to, combined with the fact that he thought very little of McCain, a Southport man – indeed an alumnus of my primary school, Farnborough Road – who kept a few horses behind his second-hand car dealership on Upper Aughton Road. McCain, in my dad's considered opinion, was a scoundrel and a chancer, who had about as much chance of training a Grand National winner as a woman had of becoming Prime Minister before the decade was out. He took more or less the same view a year later; while the rest of Southport backed Red Rum to win his second successive Grand National, my dad, with the superior air of the true aficionado, stuck his money elsewhere. In some ways it was as well that he had already expired by the time Red Rum won the thing for the third time in 1977. That might have finished him off.

Still, it was a sensible enough decision not to back Red Rum to win the 1973 Grand National. He was not yet the legend he became, and the mighty Australian horse Crisp, though given a punitive twelve stone handicap, was manifestly better in all departments. My dad had duly backed Crisp, and probably not lightly, either.

I recalled all this one spring day in 2003 as I turned off the M5 into Frankley service station, where I was due to meet the jockey-turned-broadcaster Richard Pitman. The Grand National was a week away and I wanted to interview someone associated with Red Rum's epic victory thirty years earlier. Ginger McCain had declined once he had established that I wasn't offering to pay him anything (I fancied I heard a distant snort emanating from a cemetery in Southport), so I turned to Pitman, who had ridden Crisp in the 1973 National. He agreed to meet me at Frankley services on his way to a speaking engagement in Wolverhampton.

I bought him a cup of tea and asked him to tell me the story of the 1973 race. Obviously, he'd told it thousands of times before, but he can never have done so more stirringly. He even delivered sound effects – horses snorting, hooves thundering – very much to the amusement of two lorry drivers sitting at the next table, although somewhat to the detriment of their sausage, beans and chips.

Pitman told me that he and Fred Winter, Crisp's trainer (and the man credited with that marvellous line about there being three racecourses beginning with F, namely Fontwell, Folkestone, and effing Plumpton), had discussed their tactics over and over. 'Fred told me not to go tearing off like a madman. He said: "Set off in front, and because you're a senior jockey riding for a good stable, people will respect you." The idea was to slow the race down from the front. Lester Piggott used to do it on the flat. You can sometimes kid the other jockeys, who think, "He knows what he's doing." You slow it down to suit yourself.'

On the morning of the race, Pitman and Winter walked the course. Winter always wanted his Grand National runners to keep to the inside, where the drops are steeper, the turns sharper. They both knew that would suit Crisp, but as soon as the race began, Pitman realised that the other part of the plan, to keep him in front but restrained, was not going to work. Crisp set off like a dervish. 'There's a long, long run to the first fence, and when he spotted it he couldn't get there quick enough,' said Pitman. 'Before he touched the ground he could see the next one. He was almost galloping in mid-air, it was just magic.'

But Crisp and Pitman were not alone. On the outside was Bill Shoemark on Grey Sombrero, a winner of the Whitbread Gold Cup. Not that Pitman was remotely perturbed by their presence, as Crisp flew towards Becher's Brook.

'The drop at Becher's was ten feet from the top – it's not as big now – and you had to let the reins slip through your fingers, and sit back in the saddle to act as ballast and keep the horse's backside down, because once his tail comes past your eyeline, you're in trouble. On landing, a lot of horses' noses touch the ground. But Crisp jumped it so cleanly, I never even felt the jolt of the drop.

'The next one is the Foinavon fence which caused the debacle [in 1967, when the rank outsider Foinavon emerged from the mayhem to win], and that's another trap, because it's the tiniest fence. At Becher's you're expecting the ground to be there and it's not; at the next you're expecting the ground not to be there but it meets you quicker than you think. The whole place is a series of tricks.'

Crisp arrived at the right-angled Canal Turn several lengths clear of Grey Sombrero. 'Even on the first circuit,' said Pitman, 'you can win or lose a Grand National at the Canal Turn, because any length you can gain in the air is more economical than having to gallop it. And as you turn you can see the grandstand, which is always exciting. We were steadily going clearer and clearer, and we flew the Chair, and then I heard on the commentary that Grey Sombrero had fallen at the Chair; in fact, he broke his shoulder and was killed. It was so sad.' Grey Sombrero had been ten lengths back; Crisp now led the rest of the field by twenty-five lengths.

'This was the most amazing of Nationals,' Pitman continued, 'because I could hear the drmmm drmmm of my horse's feet on the fast ground. It was eerie. Normally you hear crashing and banging and jockeys cursing, but there was nothing, except drmmm drmmm and the commentary, and Crisp was showing no signs of weakening. He was saying, "Let me at it! I want to eat the fences, not jump them."'

'At Becher's second time round I saw David Nicholson sitting on his horse. I remember it vividly, because he had his arms folded and the horse was picking grass, like an Indian chief at the top of a mountain. He shouted: "Richard, you're thirty-three lengths clear. Kick on and you'll win."'

At the same time, Pitman could hear the unmistakable voice, through the course loudspeakers, of Michael O'Hehir. 'And Red Rum is coming out of the pack, but Brian Fletcher is kicking him hard,' cried the excitable Irishman, now, sadly, watching with my still-disbelieving father through the celestial binoculars. 'I thought, "That'll do me",' recalled Pitman, 'but I wasn't cocky, I knew we had to conserve energy. We flew Becher's as if it didn't exist, cut across the Canal Turn and saved three lengths there, and everything was going to plan, then up over Valentine's and the next few, the stands coming nearer all the time. I had a look over my shoulder and could see Red Rum, but he was very distant.

'From there we had three to jump. We jumped the third-last fine, and then, between the third-last and second-last, the whole picture changed. It was like petrol going out of a car. Suddenly his legs started going sideways. He had these floppy ears, which he kept sort of half-cocked, and the strength even went out of his ears. He had gone to the bottom of his barrel.

'He jumped the second-last out of instinct, and went to the last, and now I can hear Red Rum coming. Now, Red Rum was different from most horses, because as he exhaled his nostrils flapped, and made a noise. They went pwwwrrr, pwwwrrr, and I can still hear this drumming, drmmm drmmm, but now there's a pwwwrrr, pwwwrrr, and it was then that I made a mistake that will haunt me for the rest of my life.'

I was agog, and so, by now, were the lorry drivers at the next table. 'I thought, "I've got to wake the old boy up, get him out of his reverie." And I made a mistake that a boy starting out shouldn't make, let alone a senior jockey. I picked the stick up in my right hand to give him a whack, but I had to go right-handed to get round the Elbow. The instant I lifted my hand, he fell away left-handed. So I quickly put the stick down, gathered the reins, and pulled him back.

'But I had to change his stride pattern, and he lost momentum. I got him to the Elbow, which is half-way up the four hundred and ninety-four-yard run-in, and I've got the rail to lean on now, because a horse's instinct is to race a rail. I could hear very loudly drmmm, drmmm, pwwwrrr, pwwwrrr, and he could sense Red Rum coming. Even in his almost drunken state of exhaustion he tried to quicken, but he'd given his all. Two strides from the post that pwwwrrr, pwwwrrr became reality.'

Even in defeat, Crisp had broken, by fully twenty seconds, a track record that had stood for forty years. By the time the horse was being led in by his distraught stable lad Chippy Chape – 'who looked as though someone had shoved a red-hot poker up his backside' – Pitman was aglow with a strange kind of euphoria. 'I knew,' he told me, 'that it had been the ride of my life.'

In Southport, meanwhile, we only had eyes for the winner.

Red Rum received a heroic welcome home from everyone except my father, and by the time he had completed his astonishing five-year cycle of first, first, second, second, first, he was by some distance the town's biggest sporting celebrity, well ahead of Jimmy Rimmer.

It being the 1970s, however, efforts to cash in on Red Rum's fame and success were exquisitely cack-handed. Someone on the town council proposed that a statue be built, and most others on the council agreed that this was a splendid idea, but when they found out how much a life-size bronze would cost, it was decided to erect a scaled-down version. This is the reason why a foreigner visiting Southport even now might reasonably wonder what an Alsatian named Red Rum did to deserve immortality in bronze.

Still, it seems a shame to conclude the Red Rum story on such a downbeat note, so let me instead finish with the inimitable, and yet strangely much imitated, Peter O'Sullevan. This is a piece of commentary which deserves a place in the annals alongside Cliff Morgan's, recorded just two months and four days earlier in that same remarkable year of 1973, with one of the most memorable of FA Cup finals – Leeds United 0 Sunderland 1 – yet to come.

At the second last . . . Crisp is over and clear of Red Rum who's jumping it a long way back. In third place is Spanish Steps and then Hurricane Rock and Rouge Autumn and L'Escargot. But coming to the final fence in the National now . . . and it's Crisp still going in great style with twelve stone on his back. He jumps it well. Red Rum is about fifteen lengths behind him as he jumps it. Dick Pitman coming to the Elbow now in the National. He's got two hundred and fifty yards to run. But Crisp is wandering off the true line now. He's beginning to lose concentration! He's been out there on his own for so long! And Red Rum is making ground on him! Still, as they come to the line, it's a furlong to run now, two hundred yards for Crisp, and Red Rum is still closing on him, and Crisp is getting very tired, and Red Rum is pounding after him, and Red Rum is the one who finishes the strongest! He's going to get up! Red Rum is going to win the National! At the line Red Rum has just snatched it from Crisp! And Red Rum is the winner . . . and Crisp is second and L'Escargot is just coming up to be third.

Unforgettable.

10

Kevin Keegan's Back

For my money, a decade in which Red Rum won the Grand National three times and Kevin Keegan fell off his bike on *Superstars* (actually it was *The Superstars*, but time seems to have erased the definite article) is without compare in the sporting history books.

Nevertheless, there is a good case for saying that it wasn't, in fact, the greatest sporting decade of them all. After all, there was unprecedented violence, in the form of murderous terrorism at the Munich Olympics and, less egregiously but more damagingly, escalating football hooliganism. There was tragedy: sixty-six people died in the Ibrox disaster in January 1971. And there are solid sporting reasons for rejecting the 1970s, at least as far as the English are concerned, principally the failure of the national football team to reach the 1974 and 1978 World Cups.

Then there are the strong competing claims of other decades: the 1950s had a famous Ashes win and Roger Bannister's four-minute mile, as well as the Busby Babes, Rocky Marciano, Sugar Ray Robinson and the 'Matthews'

Cup final of 1953; in the 1960s, England won the World Cup, Celtic and Manchester United won European Cups, Arkle won three Gold Cups and Tony Jacklin won the Open Championship; the 1980s had Borg v. McEnroe, Coe and Ovett, Torvill and Dean, Europe winning the Ryder Cup, Shergar, Desert Orchid and 'Botham's' Ashes. I could go on, but this time I won't.

Moreover, some of those whose feats illuminated the 1970s were either on their way down the mountain having reached the summit of their powers in the 1960s, such as Muhammad Ali, or were scaling the mountain and would not reach the summit until the 1980s, such as John McEnroe. I use the examples of Ali and McEnroe because I believe that the greatest sporting decade cannot be judged parochially, simply by the standards of British achievement. On the other hand, what could be more parochial than my own firm belief that Andy King's goal against Liverpool helped to elevate the 1970s above all other decades?

In the final analysis, I have made up my own rules, and according to those rules, the decade of Gordon Banks saving from Pelé, of George Wood saving from Alan Hudson, of Lillee and Thomson and Derek Randall, of Gareth Edwards and J. P. R. Williams, of Björn Borg and Evonne Goolagong, of Red Rum and the Duel in the Sun and the Rumble in the Jungle, stands supreme. However much I love sport now, I will never be so hopelessly in thrall to it as I was then, even though there are things I take for granted these days for which I would once cheerfully have given my right arm.

A few years ago, for example, I got to know the Everton owner Bill Kenwright, and on several occasions he has generously provided me with tickets, enabling me to watch Everton from the front row of the directors' box, where on chilly days they actually give you a blanket to pull over your knees. A couple of times I have taken along my university friend Chris Barry, the man who once substituted a broken Subbuteo player with a metal Grenadier Guard. Like me, Chris spent every other Saturday of his teen years standing on Everton's Gwladys Street terraces. Like me, he never even imagined sitting down at Goodison Park, let alone in the directors' box.

One Saturday, Chris came with me to watch Everton v. Derby County. It was miserably goalless until late in the second half, when Everton finally broke the deadlock. Chris and I both leapt to our feet, embraced, and then sat down again. 'I never thought I'd say,' he mused on the way back to Lime Street station, 'that I was so excited by an Everton goal that my blanket slipped off.' I couldn't have put it better myself.

Chris, incidentally, is a teacher, and a bloody good one, I should think. I have quite a few friends who are teachers or doctors, and in reflective moments I sometimes envy them for doing so much for a society which prefers to reward self-centred sportsmen and women. There was hell to pay on Merseyside when the Liverpool players who lifted the 2005 European Cup did not get MBEs in the next New Years' Honour's List, and Downing Street later admitted that it had been an embarrassing oversight, yet these are men already rewarded with six-figure salaries and the adulation of millions. What about the men and women who have spent entire careers inspiring kids at down-at-heel Liverpool schools? Where were their MBEs? That was surely a far more embarrassing oversight.

Still, those reflective moments of mine never last long. On the whole I'm glad that ours is a society which worships sport; which worships even those who make a living describing sporting performance. Mind you, while my admiration for the likes of Sir Peter O'Sullevan and Richie Benaud knows no limits, I can see that it is rather odd how, in Britain, certain sports broadcasters are lionised as much as, and in some cases more than, the performers whose deeds they describe. I once found myself in a bar in the company of John Motson and a couple of extremely famous ex-footballers, and it was Motty's presence that generated the glances and nudges, not theirs. Quite extraordinary, as David Coleman used to say, if only on *Spitting Image*.

I have a friend who is scathing about the cult of the sports broadcaster. He doesn't object to the popularity of Gary Lineker, Alan Hansen, Richie Benaud and others who distinguished themselves in the arena before climbing the ladder to the TV studio. What he objects to is the iconic status conferred by sports fans on the anchorman or commentator whose greatest sporting feat is puffing his way through the Great North Run, or playing eighteen holes at Sunningdale three shots below his fifteen-handicap.

I understand, but I disagree. In fact, I take almost the opposite point of view: great batsmen, while not exactly ten a penny, have been fairly plentiful down the years. But nobody ever described their deeds as captivatingly as John Arlott, who was as singular in his profession as Don Bradman was in his. Similarly, there have been many nailbiting football occasions, but nobody ever introduced them as perfectly as Desmond Lynam, who with scarcely more than a twitch of an eyebrow managed to convey the notion that it was only a game while at the same time encouraging the feeling that it mattered more than anything.

It's also worth remembering that Bill McLaren did not play international rugby union; shortly after the war, just as he was entering the thoughts of the Scotland selectors, he was struck down with tuberculosis and carted off to a sanatorium. For the rest of us that counts as a result; he could hardly have left a greater legacy as a player than he did as a commentator. Yet I once asked him if he would have swapped his entire broadcasting career for just one full Scottish cap, and after considering the matter for a moment or so, he said, wistfully, 'Aye. Aye, I would.'

My point is that great broadcasters play at least as much of a part in the nation's enjoyment of sport as the performers themselves, and this was never more so than in the 1970s, when each sport had a Voice – be it Bill McLaren or Peter O'Sullevan or David Coleman or Eddie Waring or Dan Maskell – if only because sport, compared with today, had such limited air time.

For this and other reasons, such as the novelty of colour, it was, for those watching on television, unarguably the greatest of sporting decades. The relative scarcity of sport on television meant that every sports programme – *Match of the Day, Sportsnight, Grandstand, World of Sport,* even *Indoor League* – was an event. And if you were a sports lover, you watched regardless of what was featured. If David Coleman introduced showjumping from Wembley Arena on *Sportsnight,* then showjumping was what you watched. There was no alternative.

In any case, for a few years in the 1970s showjumping was almost racy: Harvey Smith's two-fingered salute to the Hickstead judges in 1971 – which caused an eruption of Establishment outrage not unlike that unleashed by Eric Cantona's assault on a Crystal Palace fan at Selhurst Park a quarter of a century later – was precisely what was required by a sport that was given voice by Dorian Williams and Raymond Brooks-Ward, both so posh that they seemed interchangeable. That's the thing about plummy English accents: they suppress individuality. Mind you, I don't think I would ever have jumped to the conclusion reached by the prostitute Divine

Brown, as recalled by the late Harry Thompson in his book *Penguins Stopped Play*. She said she knew it was an actor she was pleasuring on Sunset Boulevard, moments after Hugh Grant had notoriously invited her into his car, because she recognised his voice as being unmistakably that of Captain Peacock in *Are You Being Served?*

To return to Harvey Smith's controversial gesture, it was almost as if a public relations company – its brief to dilute the elitist image of show-jumping, which after all was the sport of Princess Anne and Captain Mark Phillips – had put dear old Harvey up to it. But that can't have been the case. Public relations was so much in its infancy then that it was still surviving on Farley's rusks soaked in milk, but corporate sponsorship was beginning to burgeon, and actually showjumping was well ahead of the game. How else would Harvey Smith come to ride a horse that was called Sanyo Music Centre? Even nowadays that would strike people as commercial endorsement gone mad.

But by the end of the 1970s, big business had woken up to the fact that every nook and cranny of every televised sport was ripe for sponsorship. The problem was that there wasn't yet enough televised sport to sponsor, not that it seemed so to my mother, who thought that sport on television was utterly relentless just because I watched *Indoor League* on Sunday lunchtimes, followed by *The Big Match* presented by Elton Welsby. I don't know what happened to Elton Welsby, by the way, but in the late 1970s, among football fans in the north of England, he was no less famous than Pelé. As for *Indoor League*, I'll come back to it because it still occupies a small part of my heart, but first I should consider the growth of corporate sponsorship, which was spearheaded – of all genteel, middle-class sports – by tennis.

In 1971, a fine American writer called John McPhee wrote

a brilliant article in *Playboy* about how the ogre of commerce had even Wimbledon in its uncompromising grasp. To read extracts from it now is highly enlightening, because it is commonly thought that the degree of sponsorship McPhee describes is a much more modern development.

'Rosewall wears on his shirt the monogram BP,' McPhee wrote.

What is this for? Has he changed his name? Not precisely. Here in this most august of all the milieus of tennis, here in what was once the bastion of all that was noblest and most amateur in sport, Rosewall is representing British Petroleum. Rosewall represents the oil company so thoroughly, in fact, that on the buff blazer he wears to the grounds each day, the breast pocket is also monogrammed BP. There is nothing unusual in this respect about Rosewall. All the tennis players are walking billboards. They are extensions of the outdoor-advertising industry. Almost everything they drink, wear and carry is an ad for some company . . .

All things together, Ashe makes about $125,000 a year through such deals. He gets $50,000 for using the Head Competition, the racquet that looks like a rug beater. He gets $25,000 from Coca-Cola for personal appearances arranged by the company and for drinking Coke in public as frequently as he can, particularly when photographers happen to be shooting him. Lutz and Smith are under contract to consume Pepsi-Cola – in like volume but for less pay. Ask Pasarell if he likes Adidas shoes. 'I do, in Europe,' he enthuses. He is paid to wear Adidas in Europe, but in the United States he has a different deal, the same one Lutz, Graebner, Smith and King have, with Uniroyal Pro Keds.

Players endorse nets, gut, artificial court surfaces, and

every item from the jock[strap] out. Some players have lately begun to drink – under contract – a mysterious brown fluid called Biostrath Elixir. Made in a Swiss laboratory, it comes in small vials and contains honey, malt, orange juice, and the essence to 90 kinds of medicinal herbs. Others have signed contracts to wear copper bracelets that are said to counteract voodoo, rheumatism and arthritis.

And so it went on, McPhee making no attempt to contain his disapproval. The 1970s showed that sport could be bought by big business, the 1980s that it could become a big business in its own right. Another dimension to this was World Series Cricket, the circus ringmastered by the Australian media tycoon Kerry Packer. This sent shockwaves through cricket the like of which had not been felt since the Bodyline series of 1932/3, except that the Packer case was more serious.

When the Australian Cricket Board refused to let Packer's Channel 9 television company buy exclusive rights to cover Test matches, he decided that he would set up in opposition to established Test cricket, luring the best players with his chequebook. Richie Benaud, no less, aided him in this endeavour. And on 9 May 1977, it was announced that Packer had successfully lured thirty-five players – including the England captain Tony Greig, as well as Alan Knott, John Snow and Derek Underwood. The horror-struck executive of the International Cricket Council then declared that the so-called rebels would no longer be eligible to play Test cricket, although in the High Court – this time with Mr Justice Slade as the umpire, rather than the arbiter of the George Davis case, Mr Justice Blofeld – this was subsequently ruled illegal restraint of trade.

The row nevertheless rumbled on, with Tony Greig as Packer's recruiting sergeant and Geoff Boycott probably the highest-profile player to defy him. My hero Derek Randall, to my great relief, was another of those who turned down the Packer dollar, and I don't suppose he gave the matter a second thought. But if you think it was all water under the bridge long ago then you didn't see Boycott and Greig in the Channel 4 studio during the 2005 Ashes series, the air positively crackling with mutual loathing.

For good as well as ill, the 1970s established the way in which sport would develop. For example, by the end of a decade that had begun with Clyde Best as the country's only high-profile black player, football had started to become multiracial and was demonstrably the better for it. Even Subbuteo kept pace, painting three players in every team brown. They must have had West Bromwich Albion in mind. Despite the strides that had been made by 1979, of the twenty-two First Division teams only West Brom regularly fielded three or more non-white players.

On Boxing Day 1978, while staying at my grandmother's house in north London, I took myself off to Highbury to watch Arsenal play West Brom. It was the first time I had been on my own to a First Division football match, as well as the first time I had gone without supporting either team, and to my surprise it was an exhilarating experience. I found it thrillingly liberating to sit there not caring which side won or lost, the more so as everyone around me cared so deeply. I had already come of age as an Everton fan, but to feel a frisson of excited anticipation whether it was Liam Brady with the ball on the edge of West Brom's penalty area, or Lawrie Cunningham on the edge of Arsenal's, in a way represented my coming of age as a football fan.

For the record, West Brom won 2-1 that Boxing Day afternoon, part of a five-game winning streak which included three successive away victories, at Wolves, Man United and

Highbury. At Old Trafford they were drawing 3-3 at half-time, and won 5-3, a thrilling victory overseen by Ron Atkinson, the most successful of a string of managers whose most noteworthy collective legacy was a remarkable sequence of names: between 1973 and 1988, West Brom were managed by Don, Johnny, Ronnie, Ron, Ronnie, Ron, Johnny, Ron and Ron. It was a sequence rudely interrupted, I'm proud to say, by the arrival of a Brian. Brian Talbot followed Don Howe, Johnny Giles, Ronnie Allen, Ron Atkinson, Ronnie Allen again, Ron Wylie, Johnny Giles again, Ron Saunders, and Ron Atkinson again.

Under Atkinson the first time round the Baggies were a terrific, free-scoring side, who had also put seven past Midlands rivals Coventry City in that 1978/9 season, and would finish in third place, a point behind the previous season's champions, Nottingham Forest. It was so nearly second, and they might even have pushed Liverpool all the way to the wire had they been able to continue the form of March and early April, when they registered a further six successive wins. Everton and Chelsea were among those unable to contain Cunningham and Cyrille Regis, who with Brendon Batson formed, as the joke went in those unenlightened times, The Three Degrees.

All of which brings me to a snowy day in February 2003, when I turned up at the home of Ron Atkinson in a Fooballers' Wives-belt of suburbia south of Birmingham. I drove up very much hoping to find electronic wrought-iron gates that might glide open after some form of communication through an entryphone, and I was not disappointed. The interior of the house matched my expectations, too. Even the swags and tails had swags and tails, and the predominant shade – of floors, walls, soft furnishings and human-beings – was tan. When a tanned Mrs Big Ron brought us tan-coloured coffee in tan-coloured mugs, it occurred to me that if the

Atkinsons ever chased each other naked through the house, they would be virtually impossible to spot.

After an hour or so of convivial chat, we started discussing the West Brom team of the 1970s, and I asked Big Ron whether he thought of himself as a pioneer of racial equality. This, don't forget, was a year or so before his notorious, career-rupturing comments about Marcel Desailly. He roared with laughter, and said: 'Hey, I'm not taking the stick for those asylum-seekers. No, it was a great time, that. Actually, I think there's more racial prejudice now than there was then, though we used to make them sit at the back of the bus going to away games. We all used to laugh and joke about it. Cyrille would say, "If you don't stop giving me stick I'm going to buy a house next door to you."'

Big Ron roared with laughter again, and although his light-heartedness on the matter made me feel uneasy, I certainly didn't have him pegged as a racist. But then he used the noxious words 'fucking lazy thick nigger' in reference to Desailly, and when it transpired that he'd unknowingly been on air and the media storm broke, his earlier comments to me about making Cyrille Regis and the other black players sit at the back of the bus were picked up by several other newspapers. It seemed a little bit unfair to use the stuff about Regis to reinforce the case against him, because it was affectionately meant, but then for a while it was open season on Big Ron. It even became morally dubious to call him Big Ron, as if somehow that implied empathy and support. Whatever, it was a sad, unseemly business, but it tickled me that, as a measure of how Britain had evolved as a society since the 1970s, it was now quite rightly deemed shocking and unacceptable to utter the word 'nigger' on television, but perfectly reasonable to say 'fucking'. In the 1970s it had been precisely the other way around.

In that respect, as in so many others, television has changed almost beyond recognition over the past thirty-odd years. Obviously it is a huge step forward that offensive references to a person's race or skin colour are no longer tolerated. Even on *Coronation Street* in the mid-1970s, Billy Walker and Ray Langton would crack jokes about 'Pakis', and much as Warren Mitchell likes to insist that the joke was on rather than with his monstrous character Alf Garnett, the actress Meera Syal once told me that the casual racism in her school near Wolverhampton was always notably nastier on the morning after *'Til Death Us Do Part* had been transmitted.

But the march of progress often tramples on things that were once deeply cherished. And that applies to sport as much as to anything else. Sky, by offering us unprecedented sporting riches, paradoxically devalues them. If we're not enjoying one European football match, we can always find another. If not much is happening in the US Tour golf, we can always take a look at the snooker from Preston. Bored with indoor tennis from Toronto? Then see how Sri Lanka's cricketers are getting on in the second Test against the West Indies.

In many ways, this is a wonderful state of affairs. It's great that there's so much live football on the telly, and since that which is not live is recorded, the cameras never miss a single goal, in any of Europe's top divisions. But there is a price to pay. When George Best died in November 2005, the same clips of his footballing genius were shown over and over again, and it was sobering – if that can ever be the right word to use in connection with the great man – to think that many of his goals, and so much of his sublime skill, had not been televised, that they lived on only in people's memories. I felt that although he was rightly mourned by all decent football supporters, only Manchester United supporters aged about fifty or over were truly entitled to grieve. Because they alone had watched him week in, week out. These days, the constant accessibility of sport on television has diluted the purity of that relationship between players and fans. It also means that my children will never know the breathless wait for *Match of the Day*, which in the 1970s started pretty much as soon as *Football Focus* had finished. And that, I think, is sad.

Nor will my kids ever know what it is to watch Fred Trueman, with a pint pot in one hand and a pipe in t'other, introducing bar billiards on *Indoor League*. Maybe that's not quite so sad. Besides, as a reminder that each generation thinks itself more blessed than the next, I have no doubt that the fathers of the 1970s went around hurrumphing that their children knew Trueman only as the geezer who said 'Ah'll si thi' at the end of *Indoor League*, and not as Fiery Fred, the quick bowler who had taken over 300 Test wickets in the 1950s and 1960s. Similarly, it disappoints me that my kids know Gary Lineker only as a TV presenter and crisp enthusiast.

I loved *Indoor League*. It ran for four years between 1972 and 1976, and made television sports out of bar billiards, shove ha'penny, arm-wrestling, skittles and darts, which took some doing. Of these, only darts really caught the public imagination, with *Indoor League*'s producer, a charismatic and eccentric Geordie named Sid Waddell, going on to become its Peter O'Sullevan, Bill McLaren and Dan Maskell rolled into one.

As a commentator Waddell would later acquire a cult following (actually, I've never been too certain what distinguishes a cult following from a following, but this is no place to get bogged down in semantics), who adored his markedly surreal line in imagery. I have met darts fans who can quote Waddell one-liners all night and, sadly, quite frequently do. 'This game of darts is twisting like a rattlesnake with a hernia.' 'Steve Beaton, he's not Adonis, he's THE donis.' 'That lad could throw one hundred and eighty standing one-legged in a ham-mock.' 'When Alexander of Macedonia was thirty-three he cried salt tears because there were no worlds left to conquer. Bristow's only twenty-seven.'

But it was *Indoor League* in 1972 that first brought his inter-esting turn of phrase to the attention of a television audience, because Waddell used to write Fred Trueman's autocue. Not that the plain-speaking Yorkshireman was exactly adept with the autocue, and Waddell's circumlocution made it even harder for him to master. Waddell once wrote the line 'the Narcissus of the knotted knuckle', referring to an arm-wrestler called Sinclair-Scott, who dressed in leather and came from Chelsea. This was turned by a bemused Trueman into 'the Nancy Boy with natty knuckles'.

While *Indoor League* was paving the way for a televised world championship in darts, *Pot Black* was doing the same for snooker. Television historians would probably not choose *Pot Black* as the most significant new programme to hit Britain's screens in 1969, the year in which we first set eyes on *Monty Python's Flying Circus*, not to mention other iconic cultural landmarks such as *Up Pompeii*, *Wacky Races*, *The Clangers*, *Mr and Mrs* and *The Wombles*. In 1969, moreover, only a minority of British televisions were receiving programmes in colour. But by 1977, when snooker's world championship was staged for the first time in the Crucible Theatre, Sheffield, *Pot Black* had shown that the marriage of colour telly and snooker could be a blissful one, and not just for half an hour on a Friday night. When the BBC introduced snooker to its day-time schedule, it found an unexpected audience in the form of the nation's pensioners.

For me, however, there was nothing unexpected about it. Whenever my mum and I went to stay at my grandma's house in London, I always found myself watching *Pot Black* in the company of my great-uncle Lew, my grandma's brother-in-law, who lived with her. I knew just how appealing snooker could be to the over-sixty-fives because hardly anything in life gave Uncle Lew more pleasure than declaring the score just before the referee had announced it. Thus, if John Spencer pocketed a red in his match against Doug Mountjoy, Uncle Lew would say 'one'. A second or two later the referee said 'one'. Then Spencer might follow his red with a pink.

'Seven,' said Uncle Lew.

'Seven,' said the referee.

This was followed by another red.

'Eight,' said Uncle Lew.

'Eight,' said the referee.

And then the black.

'Fifteen,' said Uncle Lew.

'Fifteen,' said the referee.

And so on, and on, and on. Uncle Lew was a gentle man – and I hope he is resting in peace, preferably with his feet up watching Fred Davis complete a century break – but he introduced an element of Chinese water torture to the Friday-night *Pot Black* viewing experience. I desperately wanted to find an outlet for my rising frustration, perhaps by screaming 'For fuck's sake, we all know how many points the balls are worth!' But, of course, I never did, and looking back I can be more generous than I felt at the time. For the elderly, televised snooker offered reassuring certainties in an increasingly bewildering world. It still does. Indeed, if I am lucky enough to live as long as Uncle Lew did, I very much hope that I will get to annoy the hell out of a teenage relative by watching snooker and uttering the score just before the referee. It's practically an ambition.

In the meantime, to return to pioneering sports programmes of the 1970s, my favourite, and the favourite of all my friends, was *Superstars*. It began in 1973, and was pioneering in a variety of ways. It was a neat idea to invite stars from different sports to compete against each other in a whole range of disciplines, and a neat idea eventually to make it pan-European, even if there was always a sense that the table-tennis player from Sweden was only there to make up the numbers.

It was pioneering, too, in the way in which competitors were relentlessly interviewed by David Vine and Ron Pickering while they were still gasping for breath after performing sixty squat thrusts in sixty seconds. Before *Superstars*, sportsmen were afforded time to sweat in private. But Vine and Pickering changed all that. Their microphones knew no restraint, even if it was somebody not only gasping for breath, not only sweating buckets, but also scarcely able to speak English. 'Then in a finish I go, go, go, and then the same,' was how the panting Olympic downhill skiing champion Franz Klammer once analysed his strategy in the gym exercises, to a gravely nodding Pickering.

This, of course, shows the danger of opening the door to foreigners. A few years later, Henry Kelly hosted a pan-European television quiz show called *Going for Gold*. It was an admirable concept, but I remember watching the grand final one year and thinking that it inadvertently highlighted the insurmountable obstacles that a federal Europe would present. The final brought together a woman from Ireland and a man from Norway, and by the end they both had the same number of points, so Kelly had to ask a tie-break question.

'Name one American state beginning with the letter V,' he said.

'Visconsin,' said the Norwegian, and lost.

The European edition of *Superstars* that will be remembered when all others are forgotten was recorded in 1976 at

Bracknell sports centre, the one in which Kevin Keegan came a terrible cropper on the cycling track, his front wheel clipping the back wheel of the bike ridden by the Belgian footballer Gilbert Van Binst . . . and if you want a tricky 1970s trivia question, there it is: with whose bike did Kevin Keegan's bike collide disastrously on *Superstars*? Keegan slid spectacularly across the cinder track, losing half the skin from his back in the process. David Vine, needless to say, was there within seconds. 'You had a tremendous wobble on coming up the strait,' said Vine. 'Yes,' said Keegan, nobly trying to disguise the fact that he needed a doctor more than he needed David Vine.

Still, following some emergency medical treatment and another couple of interviews, he gamely got back on his bike and even qualified for the final. He then won the steeplechase and with it the overall prize, a princely $5000, pipping the Ajax captain Rudi Krol. Whatever anyone tells you, there was no more Herculean sporting feat in the 1970s than Kevin Keegan winning the edition of *Superstars* on which he fell off his bike. Muhammad Ali beating Joe Frazier was child's play by comparison.

It was doubtless to boost audience figures that there was such a preponderance of footballers on *Superstars*, not that all footballers performed quite so impressively as Keegan and Krol. Indeed, it was a footballer, Stan Bowles, who in the programme aired on 10 November 1976 recorded the lowest-ever score, registering just seven points out of a possible 80. This was no great surprise. Their performances on *Superstars* reflected their personalities perfectly. Bowles and Keegan were almost exact opposites: one, a footballer blessed with only modest natural talent, who had turned himself into one of Europe's best footballers by sheer force of will; the other, abundantly gifted, who really couldn't be arsed.

In his edition of *Superstars*, Bowles, managed by his

Queen's Park Rangers team-mate Don Shanks, had to compete against J. P. R. Williams, Malcolm Macdonald and David Hemery among others, all of whom took the occasion more seriously than him to the power of about 100. Shanks entered him for the swimming race even though he could barely swim, and Bowles was lapped doing the doggy paddle. JPR, a former junior Wimbledon champion, slaughtered him 6-0 6-0 in the tennis. And Bowles was so hungover in the pistol-shooting event, that his first shot hit the table in front of him, and his second and third missed not only the target, but also the protective wall behind it. Even the army shooting instructor – memorably described in Bowles's entertaining 1996 autobiography as being 'as hard as nails, he could kill a bloke from two hundred paces just by gobbing on him' – beat a hasty retreat.

It's a quintessential 1970s story; one of the reasons, perhaps, why Bowles remains an iconic 1970s figure. In October 2005 I met him in a shabby pub in Spitalfields, in the East End of London, and omitted to mention that the last time I had seen him, in the late seventies at Goodison Park shortly after Mrs Bowles had reportedly walked out on him, I had been among the 20,000 or so Everton fans chanting 'Stanley, Stanley, where's your wife?'

Remembering that chant, and waiting for him long after the time of our planned rendezvous, it occurred to me that nostalgia is fundamentally delusional. That might seem like a curious assertion near the end of a book inspired by nostalgia, but there it is. England's footballers had just qualified for the 2006 World Cup, and here I was waiting to meet a man who, more than most, symbolised a decade in which England failed to reach successive World Cups, who walked out on his national team over a perceived slight, who openly consorted with gangsters (Manchester's Quality Street gang, so named not because of their soft centres), who once accepted a bribe to throw a game (QPR against Leyton Orient in the final of the national five-a-side tournament), who made some of the most poorly behaved players in modern football look like paragons of virtue, yet to most football lovers of my generation, me included, the name Stan Bowles evoked a golden age. Odd.

He could play, that was the thing. I told him that Alan Hudson, as an example of how England had overlooked players with flair down the years, had told me that Bowles, Frank Worthington and himself between them had won fewer caps than Carlton Palmer. 'Yeah,' said Bowles. 'I even had less than Ralph Coates. I played with him at Orient, when I went there after Forest. And I thought "How the fuck did you get any caps?."' In his book he was more vulgar; Coates, he rudely wrote, was as useful as 'a parrot's fart'.

But if he didn't care about playing for England himself, why should it bother him who did? Maybe, in his own way, he cared too much. When caretaker manager Joe Mercer took him off just after half-time in the home international against Northern Ireland on 15 May 1974, he decided he'd had enough of the England set-up. 'I left the hotel the next day, before the game against Scotland. Mick Channon was my room-mate, and he said, "You can't do this to England." I said, "Watch me. You see that car outside, that's the one I'm jumping in." I went to White City dogs that night, and there were a load of reporters following me round. Unfortunately one of them, a *Daily Mirror* reporter, got knocked out by one of my . . . associates. He fell down the stairs and hit his head on the concrete. The next day it looked as if about eight people had beaten him up, but it wasn't like that.'

Whether it was like that or not, such behaviour is unimaginable now, as is the notion of a modern-day Premiership footballer making ends meet in retirement by doing a bit of repping for a Brentford-based tile company. That was how

Bowles was earning a living when we met, supplemented by occasional Q&A sessions in pubs. At 56, he was still as lean as I remembered him, and his blue eyes as keen as ever, but the dirty-blond locks had turned snow white, and that's the only way that Snow White and Stan Bowles are ever likely to feature in the same sentence. He held his cigarettes, I noticed, between thumb and forefinger with the glowing tip almost brushing his palm, reminiscent of someone in a Glasgow bus queue, circa 1955. I can't claim to have dredged up that Glasgow bus queue all on my own, alas. It was a line used by the *Guardian*'s Martin Kelner about someone else entirely, but I can find no more evocative image.

Bowles seemed cheerful enough, but it was hard not to feel a little gloomy in the company of a man holding on for dear life to the vestiges of fame. I felt the same way about another icon of the greatest decade, Charlie George, whom I met shortly before the 2005 FA Cup final. Not that the passing decades will ever erode his claim to fame. After all, those readers of this book who need reminding that the 2005 Cup final was contested by Arsenal and Manchester United, will require none at all to remember that the 1971 final, between Arsenal and Liverpool, was won in the second period of extra time by a Charlie George pile-driver, and that it clinched the League and Cup double for the Gunners in the days when doubles really meant something special.

Since the start of the Premier League, alas, the League and FA Cup double has become downright commonplace, but in 1971 it still represented English football's Holy Grail, in which case Charlie George was Arsenal's Sir Lancelot. Not that Sir Lancelot ever celebrated anything by lying flat on his back with his head lifted, apparently gazing respectfully at his codpiece. For years George did little to dampen speculation that the goal had made him instantly aroused, and he was simply admiring the result. But the more mundane truth is that it was a time-wasting tactic. 'I used to think ahead of other people, and I knew it would take quite a while to pick me up off the floor,' he told me. I didn't even try to conceal my disappointment.

As in the case of Bowles, as in the case of Hudson, thirty-odd years of living dangerously had stripped away all the glamour and turned George into little more than a cracked and faded repository of all that youthful promise. There was even a finger missing on his right hand to compound the feeling that here was a man with a past that was both colourful and murky. 'Caught it in a lawnmower, years ago,' he explained, cheerfully, but I couldn't help wondering whether there was perhaps a less wholesome explanation.

In many ways Charlie George was the prototype 1970s footballer; frittered the money, got the divorce, ran the pub. Losing the finger was just an optional extra. And before it went, he had, like Bowles, pulled the plug on his own England career, in his case by telling manager Don Revie to 'go fuck yourself' after being substituted at half-time against the Republic of Ireland, in September 1976. It was his only international appearance. Which brings me to Kevin Beattie, who at least managed nine, although that was an even greater travesty.

I mention Beattie because Sir Bobby Robson once told me that his centre half at Ipswich Town in the 1970s was the finest player he'd ever played with or managed, a remarkable compliment when you consider the competition: Duncan Edwards, Bobby Charlton, Romario, Figo and Paul Gascoigne, among others. 'He was a colossus,' Robson recalled. 'Like Duncan Edwards, he was made for football. Built like a battleship. Thighs like Allan Wells. Remember him, the sprinter? That's where Kevin got the power. Those bloody thighs, those bloody hamstrings. That's what gave him the elevation. He could jump nine feet, above the bar heading down.'

I was pleased to hear this because in October 2001 I took my 6-year-old son Joseph to his first Premiership football match, Ipswich Town v. Everton, a memorable occasion for all sorts of reasons, not least of which was that we met Kevin Beattie. We were guests of a pal of mine, Neil Farrar, whose company had a box at Portman Road, and before the game, Beattie, who was one of the club's match-day hosts and also a friend of Neil's, popped in to say hello. I tried to impress upon Joe that this middle-aged bloke in a suit had been one of the greatest defenders of his generation. That was a tricky concept for a 6-year-old to grasp, although he was thrilled to bits when Beattie gave him a copy of his autobiography, *The Beat*.

I leafed through it, and was reminded of the magnitude of Ipswich's achievements in the glory years under Robson. In the 1973–4 Uefa Cup, for example, having knocked out Real Madrid in the previous round, Ipswich hammered Lazio 4-0 at Portman Road – and all four goals were scored by Trevor Whymark. I asked Beattie if he knew what had become of Whymark, and he said he did, that Whymark now drove lorries for a Suffolk chicken factory. This, significantly, was in a week when £40,000-a-week Premiership footballers were discussing strike action because they wanted the PFA to get a bigger share of a new broadcasting deal. Afterwards, Neil told me that Beattie himself lived in an Ipswich council house, caring for a wife crippled with multiple sclerosis, and barely getting by. I didn't try to explain all that to Joseph. I didn't really understand it myself.

But that's the danger of scrutinising a sporting decade from long ago, if not the danger of sport itself: even and sometimes especially those with the greatest talent are destined to live the rest of their lives being unfavourably compared with their former selves. Some cope, some don't. Either way, it is unbearably poignant to consider how many glittering stars of the 1970s ended up with more than just their talent ebbing away. To think of only three people mentioned in this book: Muhammad Ali lost his health; Lester Piggott, his liberty; James Hunt, prey to a massive heart attack in his sleep at the age of forty-five, his life.

We are inevitably reminded of our own mortality when icons of our childhood die. If you're my age then you'll know the sort of people I mean: legends such as Elvis Presley, Keith Moon, Freddie Mercury, Leslie Crowther. But as always, sport intensifies this effect. In early 2004 two great football men of the 1970s actually departed the earthly touchline on the same day, which really got my nostalgic juices flowing. One was Bob Stokoe, the other Ally MacLeod, both of whom, in their different ways, encapsulated football in the 1970s every bit as much as, if not even more than, Bob Hazell's hairdo.

Moreover, Stokoe's joyful adventure with Sunderland in 1973 had an impact, as did MacLeod's less happy adventure five years later with Scotland, which transcended football. Sunderland's Cup run by all accounts had a significant effect on productivity in local factories and shipyards. You'd have thought that absenteeism might have increased with all those hangovers, but in fact it diminished. Everyone wanted to go to work on Monday mornings, albeit mainly to talk about the footie. It was a classic example of how football then seeped into people's daily lives, and Scotland's World Cup campaign of 1978 provided another classic example, though in a negative rather than positive way.

The obituaries of MacLeod, in the English newspapers at least, rather glossed over the wider implications of Scotland's humiliation in Argentina, a humiliation which was greatly compounded by the manager's premature triumphalism. He even gave his name to an entirely new 'ism'. Somehow or other the term MacLeodism was in Scotland coined to mean a kind of circumspection, the very opposite of how the man himself operated, as if his name alone should be warning enough not to get carried away. And unlikely as it might seem for a football manager to inspire an -ism, I know some Scots who are quite certain that the devolution vote of 1979 was influenced by what had happened in Cordoba the summer before. Their argument goes that the boot of Teofilo Cubillas, the principal weapon in Scotland's devastating 3-1 defeat by Peru, so damaged Scottish pride, which was further eroded by the 1-1 draw with Iran and the Willie Johnston drugs affair, that the pro-devolution movement lost crucial momentum and the referendum was lost.

Whatever, I remember being astonished, at the age of forty-two, to realise from Stokoe's obituary that on the magical day when Second Division Sunderland beat First Division Leeds United, and a trilby-hatted Stokoe scampered across the Wembley turf, surprisingly nimbly for an old guy, to embrace his heroic goalkeeper Jim Montgomery, the manager was himself only forty-two.

I wonder whose faces will be seared into the memory of my own three children when they get to forty-two and think about football around the turn of the twenty-first century, and whether it will startle them to realise that they have reached the age their sad old dad was when he wandered round the house for a week muttering, 'Bloody hell, I'm the age Bob Stokoe was when Sunderland won the Cup'?

Acknowledgements

Writing about my formative years as a sports nut was a labour of love, but it was still a labour, and would have been a sight more arduous without the assistance of quite a number of people.

I am grateful to some old friends from Southport for indulging my nostalgia-fest, notably Jonny Cook, Chris Taylor, Mike King, Pete Venables, Steve Ridley, Steve Mallinder and John Hepworth. Chris Taylor's mum also helped, even though she still thinks (wrongly) that I failed to return her guitar case in 1982. It was a particular pleasure to have an excuse to re-kindle a 40-year-old friendship with Chris and Jez Sykes. Not everyone would agree that they did me a favour by turning me into a committed Evertonian, but I know better.

I must thank a number of colleagues at the *Independent*, among them Phil Shaw, Paul Newman, Ken Jones, Glenn Moore, Angus Fraser, Jamie Corrigan, Matt Tench, David Edwards, John Roberts, Chris Maume, Matt Denver, Vicky Henson, Nicole Wilmshurst and James Lawton. In the West End of London one evening in February 2006 I had the considerable pleasure, even for a Blue, of painting the town a modest shade of red in the marvellous company of Jim Lawton and Hugh McIlvanney, two distinguished veterans of the sports-writing game whose memories I have shamelessly plundered in this book. They taught me a thing or two that night, and how to make a drinking session last until 6 a.m. was the very least of them.

I should also mention my old friend Graham Spiers, whose elegant prose graces the back pages of the *Herald* in Glasgow, and he'll know what I mean when I say that he must soon be due his biennial Scottish Sportswriter of the Year award.

Heartfelt thanks, too, to Fran Gibson who helped with research, to Helen Vasey at *Radio Times*, and especially to Christine Elliott, my father's loyal secretary getting on – she won't thank me for saying so – for half a century ago. My mother provided further memories of my dad, gently encouraged with his customary kindness by my stepfather. I am further beholden to my friends Dominic Walsh, Chris Barry and Alan Bleasdale for sharing their anecdotes with me, and to the evergreen Hunter Davies for writing *The Glory Game*.

At Simon & Schuster, Edwina Barstow did a fine job of desk-editing, and my editor Andrew Gordon was cool-headed, sure-footed and always there in support, the Carlos Alberto of publishing. My agent Camilla Hornby weighed in with good advice and strong encouragement when they were needed most.

Finally, I must acknowledge the help I received closer to home. My children encouraged me to get this project finished on time so that I could start the next one, in the sense that to be able to feed and clothe them and ferry them constantly around the county to netball, hockey, football and cricket matches, I need the money. Meanwhile, my wife, Jane, was the Angelo Dundee to my Muhammad Ali: always in my corner, offering helpful suggestions, the occasional bollocking, and, when required, applying a cold compress to my sweaty brow.

Brian Viner, Spring 2006

Index

Abrahams, Harold, 189
AC Milan, 21
Adolph, Peter, 24
Agassi, Andre, 205
Agnew, Jonathan, 253
Alberto, Carlos, 21, 143
Aldeburgh Golf Club
  (Suffolk), 92–4
Ali, Muhammad, 156,
  162–3, 176–7, 178,
  181, 266, 287; v.
  Foreman (1974), 1,
  153, 154, 168–9,
  170–1, 172, 176;
  v. Frazier (1974), 162,
  163, 166–7; v. Frazier
  (1975), 1, 154, 178;
  v. Shavers (1977),
  178, 180
All Blacks: v. Barbarians
  (1973), 2, 121–3,
  142–3
Allen, David Rayvern,
  253
Allen, James, 206
Alliss, Peter, 95, 113,
  119, 121, 252
Almond, Marc, 9, 133
Amateur Swimming
  Association, 223
Amaya, Victor, 188, 190
Amin, Idi, 31
Amiss, Dennis, 73
Apollo 11 moon
  landing, 166
Ardiles, Osvaldo, 58
Argentina, 15

Arlott, John, 62, 252,
  253, 268
Arsenal FC, 50, 52, 273,
  284
Ashdown, David, 108
Ashe, Arthur, 271
Asher, Jane, 65–6
Ashes, 77–8, 154, 233,
  265; (1968), 38–9;
  (1972), 79, 80; (1975),
  69–70, 71, 72, 75–6;
  (1977), 67–8, 77;
  (1979), 78; (2005), 74,
  77, 79, 88
Association of Tennis
  Professionals (ATP),
  185
Atkinson, Ron, 274,
  274–5
Austin, Tracy, 208–9
Australia: Test matches
  against England see
  Ashes
Azinger, Paul, 100

Baddiel, David, 50
Ball, Alan, 20
Ballesteros, Seve, 15,
  99–102, 108, 110
Banks, Gordon, 12, 43,
  266
Bannister, Roger, 265
Barbarians: v. All
  Blacks(1973), 2,
  121–3, 142–4
Barker, Sue, 177
Barry, Chris, 21, 267

Bates, Jeremy, 198–9
Batson, Brendan, 274
BBC: partisanship of,
  220–1
*BBC Sports Personality
  of the Year*, 66, 72
Beatles, 65
Beattie, Kevin, 285–6
Becker, Boris, 204
Beckham, David, 33
Bedser, Alec, 73, 76
Benaud, Richie, 68, 89,
  90, 252, 255, 267,
  268, 272
Bennett, Phil, 123, 136,
  143
Best, Clyde, 273
Best, George, 13, 18,
  276–7
Biddlecombe, Terry, 237
Blanco, Serge, 148
Bleasdale, Alan, 26, 245
Blofeld, Henry, 66–7
Blofeld, John, 76
Boat Race, 2
Bodyline cricket tour
  (1932/3), 153, 272
Bond, Jack, 81
Boothman, Andy, 83–4,
  194
Borg, Björn, 1, 154,
  187–8, 190–1, 203,
  206, 233, 266
Bosanquet, Reggie, 190
Botham, Ian, 15, 61–4,
  66, 66–8, 76, 233
Botham, Liam, 63

291

Index

Index

Ali, Pelé, Lillee and Me